EMOTIONS IN MOTION

MASTERING LIFE'S BUILT-IN NAVIGATION SYSTEM

ILENE L. DILLON, M.S.W.

WITH
ARLENE GALE

EMOTIONS IN MOTION

MASTERING LIFE'S BUILT-IN NAVIGATION SYSTEM

ILENE L. DILLON, M.S.W.

WITH
ARLENE GALE

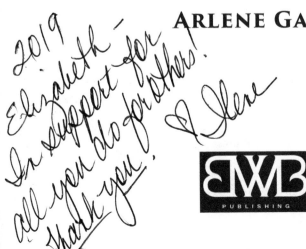

2019 – Elizabeth –
In support for
all you do for others!
Thank you! Ilene

BWB PUBLISHING

Printed in the United States of America

Published by:

BWB Publishing
Ft. Worth, TX 76108
BWBPublishing.com

Book Writing Coach and Editor:
Arlene Gale, BookWritingBusiness.com

Cover Design:
LimitlessGraphicDesign.com

ISBN Number: 978-0-9991363-1-7

DEDICATION

I dedicate this book to my husband,

Neurosurgeon Robert A. Fink, M.D. (1938-2016)

The most dedicated learner and teacher I've ever encountered

Who was always supportive and proud of me and the
work I do.

Thanks for everything, Sire Bobbles!

ACKNOWLEDGMENTS

Every single person who touches my life—ever has or ever will—offers me the opportunity to learn and grow. Thank you.

There are some who have supported me and my work over the years, deserving special mention. My earliest teachers, my parents, assisted with the set-up of the learning tasks of my later life. While I wasn't always grateful for these, as I realized that I chose the lessons and wanted to complete them, my gratitude has grown exponentially.

My children have provided feedback and helped me work out what did (and didn't) work. My son is unsurpassed in his support, concept discussion, and helping me to keep a spiritual focus. My stepchildren were supportive and especially helped illuminate my experiences as a step-child. Starting at age 19, my husbands were my steadfast learning partners. Kay Hammel, now deceased, taught me how to fit the pieces together, as she consulted with me, especially during my 20 years as a single parent. Sister, Keriac, also deceased, supported my ideas with her suggestions and by using my writings as the basis of some of her performance pieces. My sister, Martie Russell, and brother-in-law, Dennis Lindeman, have provoked my thinking, given support, and named this book. Martie knew I'd need pictures for the back of the book, and took them for me! I am grateful beyond measure.

Longtime friends and colleagues, including Marge Kaiser, Karilee and Rich Shames, Marty and Rich Friesen, Carmen Lynch, "Futon Mary" Hughes, Shirley Luthman, Melinda Henning, John Clopton, Lynette Rivard, Gene Gerlach, Paul and Robin Johnston, Cory Susser, Rosanne Valentine, and my wonderful neighbors Terri Hammet, Deb and Merrill Chandler, Priscilla Leadon and Tony Muir, Reni Aniela and Miguel Zuliani, and so many others, have listened to me, cared for me, and tolerated me as I learned. Thank you for your friendship and support.

Special mention is highly deserved by my friend and colleague, Deki Fox. My friend for 36 years, Deki has accompanied me on business trips, co-hosted three internet radio programs, read reams of my writing, counseled me and members of my family, and made herself available for long talks to help me work things out. Most amazing is that Deki came to stay with Bob and me for two weeks in 2012, and ended up staying for the entire course of my husband's struggle with cancer and his death in 2016. In my wildest dreams, I never would have imagined having a friend who would have my back, and go through with me, such an intense life experience—always loving, kind, objective, and ready to help. Thank you, thank you, thank you!

I also acknowledge and am grateful for the spiritual sources that offered me needed information and learning over the years, including Richard Goodwin, Jon Fox/Hilarion, Lazaris/Concept Synergy, Seth/Jane Roberts, and Simon.

Lastly, in more than 50 years of helping people in psychotherapy, through classes and lectures, I've met a *lot* of people, who were trusting enough to share their deepest concerns, most intimate details, and most fantastic "wins" with me. You have taught me, taught me, and taught me! Sadly, you are too numerous for me to name. You know who you are. Your presence in my life has helped me to grow lightning fast, confirm my learning and discoveries, and feed my heart.

WHAT PEOPLE ARE SAYING ABOUT ILENE DILLON AND *EMOTIONS IN MOTION*

What Ilene Dillon shares in this brilliant book are essential insights and techniques that will absolutely improve your life big time. In studying her universal principles for living, I'm gaining insights to understand and take charge of my emotions, as they affect every part of my being, relationships, and life. Bravo Ilene for giving us the book that every human can benefit from. -- Steve Sisgold, Author: *Whole Body Intelligence*

I am one of Ilene Dillon's biggest fans. She is brilliant and *Emotions in Motion* is a brilliant owner's manual for navigating your inner and outer world. Her superpower is to make emotions simple, understandable, and practical for navigating our inner and outer world. As friends and colleagues, Ilene has taught me that emotions are far from "irrational" and have an important purpose in everyday functioning and achieving fulfillment in our lives. *Emotions in Motion* captures Ilene's wisdom brilliantly and provides a practical owner's manual for embracing emotions as guides to the life and relationships you really want. -- David Steele, MA, MFT, Founder of Relationship Coaching Institute

Are you an empath with a sensitive emotional body? Or maybe you have a hard time feeling your deepest emotions? If you're interested in understanding how the physical and emotional body work together to help you find your way, and how to tap into them, this book is a great tool for your journey! Ilene has woven beautiful examples and complex ideas into a simply organized mindset shift much needed in the world. -- Elizabeth Wood, Quantum Anthropologist and Oracle

THIS is the manual we've all been waiting for. Helping us honor our feelings as guidance from within. Ilene Dillon was born to write this book. She has devoted her life to Emotional Mastery. She spent decades working intimately with clients, helping sort through a lifetime of complex emotions, recognizing the crucial role emotions play in our health. Now, secrets we learned are available to you. May this book help you achieve beyond your wildest dreams and may the power of your emotions help you succeed. -- Karilee Halo Shames PhD, RN, AHN-BC (Retired), Author *Amazing Mentors* and *Thyroid Power*

Ilene Dillon does not try to mystify you with statistics, references, research and hard to understand concepts. She simply tells you in plain English just how important your emotions are, what they are, and how to use them to make yourself a happier person with the ability to radiate love. Is anything more important? -- Jeffrey Masson, PhD, New York Times Best Selling Author, *When Elephants Weep, The Dog Who Loved Too Much,* and more.

A quick testy-moanial: In *Emotions in Motion*, emotional mastery master Ilene Dillon will help you turn your emotions from "tormentor" to "your mentor." E-motions are energy in motion, and they are essential teachers in loving and befriending the one person you are certain to be sharing every moment of your life with: YOU! -- Steve Bhaerman aka Swami Beyondananda, comedian, Author (with Bruce Lipton) of *Spontaneous Evolution: Our Positive Future and a Way To Get There From Here*

Ready to optimize your emotional state so you can use your emotions to fulfill your potential? Ilene Dillon has studied emotions for half a century, looking for the most basic, profound and easy-to-work-with ways of understanding and using emotions. Ilene knows her stuff and she doesn't just know it from a text book: she has walked the journey to understand this topic from deep personal experience, as they say, "from the inside out." To really master one's emotions, the only way is to meet them head on to move through them and out the other side. Ilene shows you how to do this in a simple and effective way. -- Kim Knight, Founder, The Emotional Alchemy Academy

In *Emotions in Motion: Mastering Life's Built-in Navigational System*, Ilene identifies the reason we have emotions, shares how we can manage them, and then decodes the message offered by 12 everyday emotions. Ilene believes that now is the time for all humans to embrace emotions and use them for the purpose for which they are designed--as navigational tools for improving and enjoying our lives. -- Hal Elrod, international bestselling author of *The Miracle Morning* and *The Miracle Equation*

Emotions in Motion is the culmination of Ilene Dillon's lifelong commitment to helping women and men of all ages to understand and befriend the complex inner world of emotions. This is a must read for anyone seeking a healthy relationship with emotions, our human compass and guide. -- Carolyn Hobbs, Licensed Marriage & Family Therapist, Author, *FREE YOURSELF: Ten Life-Changing Powers of Your Wise Heart* and *JOY, No Matter What: Make 3 Simple Choices to Access Inner Joy*

As someone who spent a good part of my life sharing the benefits of humor and positivity, I was apprehensive about a book dealing with emotions. I shouldn't have been. While there isn't much humor here, there is lots of positivity. Particularly in the author's stories from her own life, her in-depth knowledge about emotions, and her assuring me that no matter how difficult things are, we can move past them, neutralize them, and live amazing and happy lives. For those things alone, I am grateful for this insightful life-changing book. -- Allen Klein, Author of *Positive Thoughts for Troubling Times*

Ilene Dillon has studied emotions for half a century, looking for the most profound and easy-to-work-with ways of understanding and using emotions in life. Her amazing new book *Emotions in Motion* identifies the reasons we have emotions and how to best deal with them. If you want to live a happier life, you need to read this book now! -- Debbie Allen, Professional Speaker & Author of *Success is Easy*

Twenty-five years ago, I joined hands with Ilene to create the first emotional literacy book series. Her nine emotional literacy parent guides have helped tens of thousands of children and parents to explore emotions in a new way. Emotions are energy in motion, filled with data and information that can be of immense value. -- Ayman Sawaf, Author, *Executive EQ* and *Sacred Commerce*

Ilene is a captivating and insightful thought leader. Her ability to help guide and develop people to discover within their own insights and actions is unparalleled. I have been blessed to have spent considerable time with her and she has opened doors I never knew existed. I highly recommend *Emotions in Motion* to help you learn to master your navigation system. -- Tyler Hayden, Bestselling Author

I'm blessed to have worked with Ilene on several occasions. From having her supportive content posted to *The Wellness Universe*, and having her as a Wellness Universe Expert, to having Ilene present at the Wellness University spring 2019 SoulTreat retreat. This remarkable woman is an exemplary member of WU and a very dear friend. Ilene's life is dedicated to working through her own transformation and as a therapist passing on her expertise combined with her passion for people to live a better life. She is witty, integrity filled, and authentic. I highly recommend Ilene as a speaker, facilitator, author, contributor to any project you may need input from a reliable source through a heart-filled contribution on emotional well-being. I just love her! -- Anna Pereira, Founder, The Wellness Universe

TABLE OF CONTENTS

SECTION 3: EMOTIONS

SECTION 4: EMOTIONAL PRINCIPLES AND TOOLS

INTRODUCTION

In 1955, my military family returned from a tour of duty in Europe, specifically Germany and France. Initially, we stayed with my grandparents in Georgia and were enrolled in the small country school. The teachers encouraged my sister and me to tell others about our travel experiences. In one class, a boy immediately called out to me: "Speak German!" Though surprised, I was able to sputter out a few phrases.

What if someone commanded of us: "Speak Emotions!" Could we do it?

With a language, such as English, we learn the parts of speech. We know nouns are the names of things, verbs denote action, and prepositions connect words and phrases. Emotions also have parts of "speech," functioning as the "Language of the Universe." For example, many religious traditions teach that LOVE is the principle on which the entire Universe is based. While we know love as an emotion, it's also an essence, a defining principle. Knowing both the essence and the language of love impacts relationships and allows every aspect of our lives to flow better. Our world reflects back the love we carry inside of us; and we, in turn, reflect love back to the world. This is as it is meant to be.

Emotions are part of our lives from the moment of birth. The first seven years of life are designed for learning about emotions as we develop our "emotional landscape," which is the way we see, experience, and deal with emotions. Unless we make conscious changes, whatever relationship we establish with emotions in those early years tends to stay with us for the remainder of our lives, affecting every aspect of our experience.

The way emotions work is ingenious and amazing. Each emotion plays its part by bringing a message.

Love's message is, "Come closer."

Loneliness is, "You've got more energy leaving than coming in."

Fear says, "Watch out! Use caution here!"

As in speaking the English (or any) language, when we experience an emotion, we need to express it clearly and in its proper place, allowing us to know its message and clearly transmit that message as part of our relationships.

That's when we work masterfully with emotions, just as we would communicate masterfully in any language when we know it well. Knowing and working with emotions allows the emotions to stay in motion, as they are designed to do.

Unfortunately, most people have not learned emotions are a language. We don't know the emotions are rising in us to tell us something, to help us make sense of what is happening, and give us direction regarding what to do next. Some people are confounded about how to deal with emotions, often trying to push them away, exorcising them as demons, getting lost in them, regulating where and how to expose the emotion, or working with tremendous effort not to feel the emotion at all. Most of us have not learned to let emotions exist, just to feel and experience them, allowing the message to come forward.

We can't work with something we don't understand. If we don't know how things work, those things continue to be a mystery. If we don't know why we have emotions, where they come from, how they work, how to work with them, what to do with them once they arise, or how to finish with them, emotions are an unruly mystery, a part of life most of us wish we didn't have.

The language of emotion isn't only beautiful, it's practical, ever-available, helpful, and can save lives.

Many people don't realize emotions are vital and speak to us all the time. It's like the sound a young baby makes. Only after several months, and the development of the ability to enunciate, do parents realize the baby has been speaking a specific word. The baby was talking, even if not very clearly. You may have little or no understanding about emotions now, but by the time you finish reading this book, you will be able to "speak emotions."

LIVE WITH PURPOSE

I changed majors five times in college. I couldn't figure out what I was "supposed to do." I had no clear purpose. My parents insisted I become a teacher, which was a "proper job" for young ladies in the early 1960s. I didn't last one semester. The classes offered seemed watered down and uninteresting.

I had lots of abilities, yet none felt like a true purpose. I wanted to do something that helped me feel good about what I was doing every day. I knew at the age of 16 that I intended to write.

My older sister asked me, "What are you going to write about?"

"Life," I said. "But I have to live some of it first!"

My high school writings were published in the school's literary magazine and I became a reporter for the school newspaper. After that, I didn't do any writing for more than 20 years.

In six years of undergraduate education, I never selected my niche. My bachelor's degree was in "General Studies." Today's young people are expected to select a major and course of study before starting college. That would have been impossible for me.

I know now, through the first 20 years of my life I lost contact with my emotions, feelings, desires, and wants. I had no idea that life was about doing what felt right, about filling my wants, and creating my dreams. What I learned growing up was all about what I was "supposed to do." I was supposed to get a college education in case I got dumped from my marriage. Then, once educated, I was supposed to find a man I loved, get married, and have a family. This was what I was told over and over again that I was supposed to do.

How can anyone know where we fit in life—or with whom—if we don't have some life experiences or information about ourselves? If we're cut off from emotions and not taught how living life is really set up, many people either don't identify a real purpose or start to do things one way only to realize how uninspiring that endeavor is.

For example, a woman who worked with me made top grades in a top law school and landed a plum job in one of the best law firms in a large city. It took about two years to realize she hated this job. In therapy, she talked about life unfolding not based on what was important to her, but by following a path other people told her was right. She quit her job. She quit law.

This story may sound familiar. Connecting fully with emotions gives us the opportunity to change directions and work with our inner desires and promptings. This is how life is designed to operate.

SIMPLE THINGS LEAVE US SIMPLY STUCK

Many souls come into this world, a lot born into difficult circumstances. When this happens, it feels impossible to develop according to what we want. Even very attentive and involved parents can fail to help a child develop the ability to identify and fill individual needs and wants. Raising children, helping each one to stay in touch with the love, talents, abilities, and purpose that reside inside when born, is a challenging endeavor. In every experience a young child creates something to learn, a lesson to address in youth or adulthood. And from the very beginning, every experience is paired with an emotion.

These same emotions arise later in life to remind us of the learning and completion still needing to get done. Until we listen to those reminders and complete the learning, life can remain a tangle of unfulfilled wants and desires, and crushing emotions. Thankfully, most of us are stronger by adulthood and can complete the learning. The way things are set up, we are supposed to, and designed to, complete our lessons and learning during our lifetime.

Even if we're not born into difficult emotional or life circumstances, it's likely that the people who helped us grow up knew little about emotions. All people were encouraged for decades to avoid, push down, ignore, and attempt to eradicate emotions. Few people have gotten help or training in how to understand, experience, and work with emotions.

This book offers healthy and successful ways to understand and deal with emotions. It offers a message of hope for ourselves and for humanity.

If we encounter roadblocks, insensitivity, pain, or lack of support at the start of our life on Earth, all is not lost. In fact, these challenges are designed to make us stronger. If we're given over-the-top opportunities and support that isn't right for who we are, those challenges make us stronger, too. Each of us has different lessons.

Queen Elizabeth, queen of England, for example, stepped into her role at the tender age of 25. Leading up to and throughout her long life as Queen, she put the needs of her country and people ahead of her own. Her purpose was expected and she accepted it. She lives in a castle and commands a great fortune, but her life is not her own. Most of us want our life as our own.

In many circles, both personal and psychological, it's believed a person cannot recover and have a good and full life if early childhood was not loving and supportive, or if a child encountered overwhelming obstacles or trauma. Especially if we began our adult life in a business or role selected for us by others, we may feel like it's too late to claim the life we want to live.

In this book we explore how and why permanent scarring due to early-life trauma doesn't have to be true for us. We'll come to understand how it is that children encounter such circumstances, and what we can do to grow and evolve past the places of early wounding, repression, or misdirection. We can, in fact, turn those challenges into powerful, joyful living. From this place we can offer help and support to ourselves, and later, once we feel balanced and whole, to others who may need help, too.

EMOTIONS ARE PART OF EVERYTHING

It's not by accident that all roadblocks, ignorance, insensitivity, and lack of support we may encounter are connected to emotions. Emotions accompany every experience—in fact, every moment—of our lives. Learning is what we have all come here to do. There is no need to be a victim of emotions, at the mercy of out-of-control emotions that cause us to say things we don't mean, hurt people we love, make poor decisions, be addicted, or create havoc in our lives. Instead, we can develop a state of Emotional Mastery, a way of living in which we're in charge of emotions. We experience great benefits when we master emotions and also live by the wisdom of ancient, universal Principles for Living.

Stories enrich the journey, starting with this one. Years ago, a girl was born in war time when her father was halfway around the world. Her mom, who was neglectful, and a sister, 22 months older, were her early family. The girl caught whooping cough at 6 months, her mother leaving her with a sitter "for a few hours," but returning after 3 days. The girl survived; the sitter took her to the doctor. As they grew, the mother often neglected to dress and feed the girls, letting them roam nearby streets, dirty, hungry, and unclothed. Routinely, the girl, age 2, made her own scrambled eggs on a gas stove. One day, climbing onto a cupboard for a glass of water, she didn't see the family dog push a tin can—its jagged metal lid folded up—to where she was. Jumping down barefoot, she landed on this can, severely cutting her right foot near her ankle. She rode alone in an ambulance for care. *The Way Something Starts Off, It Tends to Continue.* This girl was destined for a sad and difficult life. To avoid that fate, she needed to learn how life is set up, and how to heal painful emotion. This book shares her discoveries. This girl was me.

While reading, remember all the knowledge and information in the world is worth nothing unless it's used. Weave the knowledge and wisdom in this book into your life, moving at your own pace. We all deserve to have amazing and wonderful experiences here on Earth. Life is set up for us to be "co-creators," so keep an eye open for what you want, what makes you feel good, how you can release what doesn't feel good, and where you want to go, or really want to do. These emotional "reports" assist our co-creating.

SECTION 1

EMOTIONAL GROUND WORK

1

LIFE IN OUR GIANT SCHOOL

Some people liked going to school growing up; others didn't. Depending on our takeaways about school this statement may be received positively or negatively: All humans are in school because Earth is a "Giant School" to which we've all come in order to learn and grow.

The name of our teacher is: Experience. Every time we have an experience, we're given the opportunity to learn and evolve. It's our choice whether we learn what is offered to us.

Once a lesson is offered to us, it keeps appearing, over and over again, until we learn it. It's important we learn lessons that are presented, because the system is set up so each time the lesson is presented, it's a harsher experience.

Here's an example of what I mean. I once worked with a woman who was very busy. She was the mother of two teenaged daughters, assisted her husband with the business, looked after an aging mother, exercised daily, and was remodeling a home for retirement. The new home was a two-hour drive from where the family lived. Looking after all of this left her barely a minute to herself. In therapy, we talked about how tired she felt, the break she'd like to take, and what she would need to do to get that break. Each week, she set an intention and plan for taking a break to catch her breath. Yet, the following week she told me why she was unable to follow the plan. She also told me of falling asleep during the movie when her husband took her on a date, of oversleeping and being late getting her daughters to school, and other annoying consequences of being tired and overworked.

After three months of this, I received a phone call from her husband. The wife was unable to come in for her appointment because when returning from the retirement home she was remodeling, another driver sideswiped the car, causing an accident. With a broken clavicle (collar bone), doctor's orders were, "Stay in bed and rest."

I decided to visit her bedside that week asking: "Do you think there's any connection between your repeated statements about needing a change of pace, not creating it, and this accident?"

"Definitely," she replied. "This accident is forcing me to slow down. I believe that if I had slowed down before, I would not have had this experience."

When this woman didn't listen to the "slow down" lesson to which her attention was drawn by her tiredness and yearning to rest, the opportunity to learn it was repeated and repeated. Negative consequences such as falling asleep on her date and being late for appointments occurred. Each time the consequence got a little harsher, until she was in the accident.

This happens when we don't listen and follow the messages offered. Something, or some force, appears to be insistent that we learn lessons that come up in our lives. There is something deep inside each one of us that moderates our learning in the way this woman's lessons were brought up and repeatedly presented to her. No person outside of us is doing this; and it's vital that we heed whatever is brought to our attention.

Depending on our beliefs, we may perceive that "something" as a deep or higher part of ourselves guiding learning. Or we may see it as fate, as "bad things" happening, or it's the Universe wanting us to learn. To improve our life, it's less important to know what guides this process than to understand what is happening.

Take some time to observe life. Particularly when looking back, see that when something comes up in life that requires change, that message comes up over and over again. When we don't pay attention, and learn, we get more and more imperative reminders. We don't have to learn the lesson that arises, but we pay a price for not learning it. It's the way the system is set up.

I've observed this thousands of times with hundreds of people. When my clients go a while without heeding the message and making the change, I comfort them: "It's okay. You don't have to change. Just realize now that the lesson is pointed out, the Universe will not give up until you learn the lesson. Remember: Each time the lesson comes up, it's connected to a harsher consequence. You have the choice about how long you take to learn, and even whether you choose to learn the inherent lesson at all."

This understanding is very motivational for most people. When we know the system is set up this way, life can work better as we learn to embrace the lessons and changes immediately rather than avoiding or procrastinating on that learning.

Every time we have an experience, it's connected to emotion, which offers us a message about what action(s) to take.

For example, we may feel angry with a neighbor or co-worker who has taken over, without regard for the hard work we've already done in a particular area. Anger suggests we:

1) take a look at what has happened,

2) accept that we need to make a change,

3) identify the change(s) we think will work, and

4) make that change(s).

One of the messages of anger is: "Take action." If we don't listen or take action, our lesson is more and more harshly repeated. But, what can happen when we embrace the learning, follow the steps, and make change?

2

REALLY GOOD NEWS ABOUT OUR GIANT SCHOOL

Here's the good news: The instant we learn the lesson, we're done. Finished. No more repetitions. No on-going harsh consequences. It's over. We're free to move on to other things.

It may seem unbelievable, but having experienced this myself, and seen this happen thousands of times during the last 50 years, I know it's true. This aspect of our Giant School seems intended to encourage us to learn lessons as soon as we're made aware of them. Don't learn the lessons: Repetition and increasingly harsh consequences. Do learn the lessons: Immediate completion and relief. When we understand the system, then we will learn to immediately embrace and learn lessons that come up.

WHAT MAKES EARTH A GIANT SCHOOL?

If we're going to build a school to attract people to attend, which offers a curriculum with lessons that will go on for a lifetime and learning that will last a lifetime, how will we set it up?

Chances are we'd have an initial idea about what and how we'd like to teach, and then we'd design an attractive place for students to learn. We'd need to decide how students will learn.

Lecture? Socratic questioning? Experiential? Of course, we'd look for the way we think people learn best.

We'd recruit the best teachers. To the extent possible, we'd tailor lessons for each individual student and learning style. To avoid overwhelm, people need to complete basic lessons before going on to higher-order lessons. We'd make sure students pursued lessons until the work was complete. When our students completed the lessons, we'd want to provide an immediate and satisfying reward.

We can guess this is the process followed to result in our world operating as a Giant School. It's pure conjecture to identify the initial idea about why humans need to learn, and what needs to get taught. Yet, after half a century of watching what happens, what we're postulating here seems a very possible scenario.

For all of us, there are major lessons in this Giant School. And then there are the individual lessons. In my lifetime, I've learned to understand a few major lessons, which include:

- Learning about LOVE, including the unconditional giving and receiving of LOVE

- Learning how to learn

- Learning how to treat one's self and one's fellow human beings

- Learning to care for and about others (empathy and compassion)

- Forgiveness

- Humility: the ongoing recognition that there is something larger than self

- Gratitude

I don't know why these lessons are important, yet I've seen them all brought up and repeatedly offered in the lives of the people with whom I've worked.

OUR LEARNING ENVIRONMENT

Another part of setting up an effective school is selecting a proper environment. Let's take a look at the environment selected for our Giant School, beautiful planet Earth. Space explorations have revealed the beauty and specialness of Earth. It's a very attractive place.

In addition to this beauty, Earth is special because it's concrete. We all know that concrete is hard. When something falls onto concrete, or runs into it, the concrete has a powerful impact on it. As humans, what we're talking about when we say the Earth is a concrete environment is that it's structured in such a way that when we act, we get a definite and often immediate response. Another word we use to describe this is: Feedback. Whenever we speak or act, we get definitive feedback on verbal and physical levels, on an emotional level, between people, and between us and our physical environment.

On Earth, whenever we say something, choose a path, make a decision, move our body, or interact with other humans, animals and nature, we have an impact; and we're impacted in return. Our action leads to reaction. The quicker we receive feedback, the faster we can grow and change, as we experience, observe, feel, react, and make adjustments, while simultaneously developing relationships with the people and things around us. Because Earth and the environment are concrete, feedback is fast, making learning potentially fast, too.

If I stick my finger over a flame, I get feedback that is destructive and painful to my finger. If I fail to keep my attention on a woodsy path I'm walking, I can trip over a rock and cause myself to fall down, giving me feedback about my inattention. If I feel angry with someone, and hold that anger inside, it won't be long before it starts to boil over into my life, giving me feedback that holding onto anger isn't really a good idea. If I invest money, I soon find out if it is an investment that will grow or shrink. If I say something sarcastic to someone I love, I'll quickly realize that I have passed pain on to them. They may also become angry with me, and share that anger with me. Every day we have instances of getting feedback based on our decisions, statements, actions, inactions, and choices.

More than 40 years ago, I heard this quote made on a recording from the Spiritualist Church, "Creation exists so that Love may become aware of itself."

Think about this quote for a minute. Consider what it means. One of the things I think is remarkable, is that this way of looking at "God" or "All That Is" allows humans to envision, "That Which is Greater than Humans" in whatever way we want. At the same time, it leaves room for us to acknowledge that there is something or someone much greater than ourselves. We all need this. It's difficult to have a life based only on the minutiae of the material world. Otherwise when something goes wrong we have nothing dependable to hold onto.

One of the things that makes studying the human brain difficult is we have to use it to study itself. It's difficult to study something inside of us, similar to a fish studying the water in which it is swimming.

What if the Universe is created with a problem similar to this?

If there is an overall creator, or creative force, and we're all part of that force and creation, how do we become aware of what is happening in that creation? How can we learn or move forward if we cannot observe the process?

What if the solution is to divide creation up into smaller units—say humans—with each one living a life that demonstrates how a human expresses and works with the creative force of love, for example?

Much like the father in the Bible who entrusted Talents to his sons going off to seek their fortunes, each of us goes into the world to do what we perceive we can do. In the case of the father in the Bible story, two of the sons invested and multiplied their Talents. One son returned with the same Talent, having buried it to preserve it, out of fear of losing it. This father was not happy with his cautious son, sharing with him that even with only one Talent, the expectation was for him to invest and create as much with that one Talent as possible, rather than doing nothing, especially if was motivated by the fear of losing what was given.

Many scholars and teachers interpret this Bible story as an allegory for what humans are entrusted to do during our life-times. When we add to this allegory the notion that Earth is a Giant School, prepared to help us learn during our lifetime, we see that humans are in creation to help that creative force to better perceive how the "experiment" of creation is going, based on what each of the units (humans) is doing. By embracing the lessons that come to us, accompanied by emotion, we assist this creative force in becoming aware of itself. At the same time, we move forward more smoothly, comfortably, and successfully with our lives. If we didn't have experiences and get feedback, it would be like living in an on-going *Groundhog Day*, where the same experiences occur over and over again. With varied experiences and feedback, and especially when we add awareness and learning or growth spurred by emotions, Earth becomes a magnificent and interesting residence and learning environment for each of us.

We're on Earth to learn to experience and see beyond what we can see. Ultimately, if we view the Universe operating on Love, then each person on Earth is experimenting with love. Both Love and Not-Love allow us greater awareness. Becoming consciously aware of the love and not-love we're experiencing and spreading in the world promotes tremendous learning.

Our life experiences and how we deal with each sends reports back to the Universal Dashboard, offering information about *love* and *not-love*, as encountered by each of us. In this way, we grow individually, and the Universe (including all people) also grows. In any school, it's important the students advance. As any great teacher will affirm, teachers also learn from the students. This scenario is occurring all the time in the Universe, and in the world in which we abide.

MY PERSONAL LABORATORY

As a child, did you ever steal anything? Most everyone does—it's part of "experimenting" in life, finding out what happens when we steal. What do you remember most prominently if you were caught in your experimenting? Most adults I've surveyed remember more about their parent's reaction than they do about their own beneficial learning.

My son started a new school in third grade. Scarcely three weeks after the start of school, I received a call from the manager of a local convenience store telling me my son was caught stealing a candy bar. Having taught him that our Earth is a Giant School, such that every time we have an experience it's an opportunity to learn, he was not at all surprised when I asked him, as he walked in our front door: "So, son, I understand today was the day you decided to learn about stealing—is that right?"

He hung his head, but nodded "Yes." It was clear he was full of remorse.

"What did you learn so far?" I asked him.

"Stealing is not worth it—it's definitely not worth it!"

"I've never known you to steal before," I continued. "How did it happen that you stole the candy bar?"

"There were two boys who told me they stole candy bars and it was fun. They said it would be fun for me, too. Except I got caught and they didn't!"

My mind was racing with the thought: *How can I turn this experience into a profitable lesson for my son?* I wanted to be sure we focused on his emotional experience rather than mine. It was clear this experience was a powerful one for him.

I continued my questioning, "So, what you're telling me is that there were these two boys, I mean these two voices outside of you, saying stealing would be fun; and you listened to them and did what they said. Is that right?"

He nodded.

"Was there ever any other voice you heard?"

He nodded.

"Whose voice was it; and what did it say?" I continued.

"I think it was my voice, and it said 'don't do it; it's not a good idea."

"So two voices from outside said stealing a candy bar would be fun and you did what those voices said. And a voice coming from inside of you said 'don't do it; it's not a good idea," and you didn't listen and do what it said. Is that right?" I asked him. He nodded.

"Tell me something. If you could go back and live today over again, would you make the same decision, or would you make another decision?"

My son was crying, and told me through his tears "I'd make another decision. I'd listen to my own voice. In fact, from now on, I'm listening to my own voice and not to voices coming from outside of me!"

Putting my arms around him, I told him this: "If you learned today that stealing is not worth it, and that it's better to listen to the voice coming from inside of you than to voices coming from outside, then I think you had a very valuable day. And I'm proud of you!"

Checking with him years later, I learned that this was a one-time learning; my son never stole again. Not only did he learn to listen to his own inner promptings, but he learned the lesson of stealing and never needed to have that experience again. He also helped me parent more sensitively.

We immediately embraced my son's experience as a "lesson," yet because we were in a long-term relationship (parent and child), the "lesson" was for both of us.

YOUR PERSONAL LABORATORY

Think about when you stole as a child. If you were caught, how did the adult(s) around you respond to your experiment?

Do you remember most about your own learning experience, or theirs? (Most adults I've asked about this remember their parents' reaction, along with their reaction to their parent(s), instead of recalling their own powerful learning.)

What might you have been attempting to teach yourself through your experience with stealing? Have you forgiven yourself? If not, will you do so, now?

Do you still steal? Feel okay about it? If not, what might you need to learn, now, so you can be finished with this long-lasting experiment?

Write the answer to these questions (privately), recording what you have learned—or are still learning—in your Personal Laboratory.

3

LEARNING FROM LONG-TERM RELATIONSHIPS

In this Giant School, we get most of our powerful lessons through interaction with others over the long term. Our love relationships with parents, children, and long-time friends and enemies are the best teachers. This is because we're together during the long haul. How we behave, the choices we make, how we allow each other to treat us, the needs we help each other to fill—all of these, over time, can impact us more than a similar interaction with someone we only know peripherally. We're in each other's lives to help each other grow. Often, the people who irritate us the most are also powerful teachers, though thankfully, the more we cooperate with the system, the less often we'll run into people who hurt us or drive us crazy.

Think about how things could be different if we saw our children as teachers, or our most irritating friend as our "guru." We teach each of these people; and each is working hard to teach us, too. We all teach and learn just by being ourselves, by being who we are. When we're in another person's life over time, we have greater impact on each other.

What's also important to know is that in this Earth School, we humans are designed to solve and resolve every issue, challenge, and problem. If you've ever felt overwhelmed by circumstances and problems in life, think about this: We're designed to solve the problems we encounter. This is important to know when the problems we experience push us to our limits. We may need to learn something in order to resolve the issues—things like making a change, altering our perspective, setting aside ego, being truthful, or learning to ask for help. Always remember: We can resolve the problems and challenges of our life because that's how things are designed.

In my experience, understanding that our world is a Giant School is a most effective way to resolve all problems and challenges we encounter. As soon as we realize we need to learn something, seek out that learning, and then accomplish it, not only is a particular problem resolved, but our whole experience of resolving problems becomes easier and easier. Another thing is that the same problems don't keep coming up over and over again. Life begins to flow more and more smoothly. It's like turning problems into puzzles, which makes solving them more fun and possible.

What follows is an example of how one woman allowed this system to help with an on-going problem with her husband.

POWER STRUGGLES WITHIN LONG-TERM RELATIONSHIPS

Amanda felt angry toward her husband after a heated discussion about Dan's insistence, "It's my job to save Amanda from making mistakes." Amanda believed in learning from errors and told him, "I don't want you to take mistakes from me; I learn from my mistakes."

Dan believed it was important to live as error-free as possible, and in pointing out potential errors and speaking up whenever Amanda made a decision that was not a good one, according to Dan, was helping Amanda to stay on the best path.

Amanda and Dan went through this disagreement a number of times during their marriage. Neither was willing to change position. This time, as Amanda flounced to the spare room, she said: "He doesn't respect who I am!" With that, Amanda felt even angrier, sat down heavily on the sofa, reviewed her anger, and said, "Dan is messing up our lives with his controlling behavior."

I learned from Imago Institute founders Harville and Helen Hendrix that early in any relationship, we start engaging in power struggles. Another way to look at these power struggles is that we early-on start offering lessons to each other, including challenging each other to revise erroneous ideas, change behavior, and explore our relationship with personal power. Power struggles are an affirmation that our long-term relationships cradle us and our growth, and do this more deeply and profoundly than our shorter-term encounters. To better understand this, let's look at two different ways Amanda could deal with this situation.

THE TRADITIONAL WAY COUPLES HANDLE DISAGREEMENTS

As Amanda stewed over Dan's meddling, Amanda felt enraged: "He's not respecting me." For a time, she went over all the proof of this from recent interactions, demonstrating how Dan presumed superiority, along with his unwillingness to respect Amanda enough to live her life her way. "I need to get him to see what he's doing! He'll never stop doing this if I can't get him to see how his actions are hurting me."

When the time felt right, Amanda broached this subject with Dan. She wanted Dan to see the damage done and wanted an apology for his blatant disrespect.

"Dan," she began. "You know I love you. I know you love me. But I need to talk with you about how your efforts to save me from making mistakes are painful and hurt me."

That's as far as Amanda got before Dan interrupted and said, "You're right! I do love you. And because I love you, and I'm your husband, it's my job to keep you from making blunders. You think what I do is painful and hurts; I don't even want to give you the chance to find out how much pain and hurt you'll feel if I don't try to help you this way!"

It didn't take long before Amanda and Dan were running circles around each other again, angry at the perceived stubbornness of the other person. Amanda left the conversation feeling both helpless and hopeless. For just a minute, Amanda even entertained thoughts of, "Why am I with this man?" before remembering how important the "for better or worse" clause in the wedding ceremony was to her.

EARTH-AS-GIANT-SCHOOL WAY COUPLES CAN HANDLE DISAGREEMENT

As Amanda sat in the spare room and thought about Dan's lack of respect, she remembered learning that such a clash was offering the participants a glimpse at something they themselves needed to learn. This situation wasn't so much about Dan as it was about her. Since, as Amanda had come to accept, we're all here on the Earth to learn and grow, she felt it was important to focus on finding her lesson. She had to swallow a little ego in order to shift direction to look for her own learning, but understanding better how things work in the world, she knew the effort would be worthwhile.

After Amanda brooded for a while on how Dan could change, she asked herself: "What can I learn from this? What's the lesson for me?" At first she felt stymied. No answer came to mind. Then, Amanda recalled that in this Giant School, other people act like mirrors, reflecting ourselves back to us. That meant (and she hated seeing this part), if Dan wasn't seeing her for who she really was, then most likely Amanda wasn't seeing herself for who she really was either. Even though a big part of her wanted to assign all the blame to Dan, Amanda's efforts to get Dan to change told her that continuing that path would only create more frustration. She decided to focus on getting her own learning done, even if he wouldn't do his.

Amanda began to examine her life to see if she could find ways in which she didn't respect herself. She found many ways she hadn't noticed previously.

Just cleaning the house Amanda realized she first cleaned up every other part of the house except her own (and Dan's) room. She constantly put herself last in this way. Amanda realized this spilled over into her interactions, where she would drop something she was doing that was important to her, to listen to or help someone else. Her behavior demonstrated that everyone else was a more important recipient of her energy than Amanda.

She thought about her professional life. For many years, she had watched others with less insight, less talent, and less drive than she had zoom past her, becoming better known, more successful, and making more money. Why? "Because," Amanda thought, "I don't respect myself enough to speak up, to let people know what I really think, to take credit for ideas I generate, or to ask others for help." This inquiry was showing Amanda how much she disrespected herself. Amanda knew she was worthy. She felt worthier than most of the people who had passed her by at work, yet she had not received a promotion in five years, nor a pay upgrade in three years.

Amanda was stunned at all she was discovering about herself. She decided to take the energy of the anger she'd felt toward Dan, and use it to take action on her own behalf. She made a mental action plan, then wrote it down as a reminder:

1) Every morning, remind myself: "I'm a shining star, full of great ideas, strong work ethic, and wonderful abilities."

2) At work, tell others when an idea is mine, draw attention to what I've accomplished, and what I'm good at.

3) Allow others to see my worth and give me compliments, which I'll receive graciously.

4) Get promoted and a pay raise within six months.

Then Amanda looked at her relationship with Dan. Why was she protesting Dan "looking after her" by stepping in with critiques and warnings about potential disasters? In truth, he had acted this way since she met him more than 20 years ago.

She considered: How about letting Dan be who he is? How about living the life she wanted to live, even when she believed Dan was attempting to interfere? Instead of becoming angry with him, Amanda decided to step in close to him, give him a hug, and say, "Dan, I appreciate how much you care about me!" Amanda decided to do that every time, then proceed with her life in the way that was right for her, with attention to not hurt Dan.

Amanda's signal to apply this solution was when she started to feel irritated with Dan. Instead of allowing him to irritate her, Amanda would use his behavior as a signal to focus on being loved by him, being loving to him, and being respectful of herself.

At first, things seemed to remain static. But within the first week, Amanda noticed herself feeling less irritated with Dan. She was happier at work, which helped her to be better at her work. Within six months, when she got a promotion and raise, Amanda could barely remember that Dan ever corrected her. As she stopped feeding energy to Dan's mistake-correcting behavior, Dan began to do less and less of it. Instead of having to confront him and pressure him to change, Dan was somehow creating the change she wanted all on his own.

USE THE MOST POWERFUL WAY TO CREATE CHANGE OFTEN

As we can see from these two approaches, the most powerful way to actually create change—even with others who are in our inner circle—is to focus on changing our self, learning the lesson that our experiences point out to us. As Amanda learned, focusing on changing herself instead of her husband made things easier in the relationship, and also left room for the changes for which she yearned to occur.

This is the power of accepting our Earth as a Giant School. When we do, we have the opportunity to become enthusiastic learners, to be grateful for the experiences, and to embrace change. One of the best places to learn is in our long-term relationships.

MY PERSONAL LABORATORY

My daughter was nine; her brother was almost three. Those were the days of my "independent parenting" (single parenting), so it was my job to get everyone up, bathed, dressed, fed and out the door each school morning, to get to school by the time it started. This was not always an easy task.

One morning, my daughter changed her pattern. She appeared in the kitchen with her hair brush and asked me to fix her hair. I had no problem fixing her hair; but I did have a problem with doing it in the kitchen. I lectured her about not fixing hair in the kitchen, telling her to not ask me for that particular service. Instead of heeding my advice, she kept bringing the hair brush to me in the kitchen, asking me to fix her hair, day after day. I was feeling angrier and angrier, yet still it took nearly two weeks before I consciously realized that the whole time I was lecturing her, I was actually fixing her hair in the kitchen. Though I was telling her it was something that "should not be done," it apparently didn't really bother me.

"Whose voice is it that says, 'No hair brushing in the kitchen?" I asked myself after returning from the run to school. After a while, I heard my Grandmother's voice saying "I don't want a hair in my kitchen!"

When I was five, I lived with my grandparents for a year on their farm in South Georgia. It was such a healing experience to be their "only child," and to be able to develop a close relationship with these loving grandparents. I'm sure this time saved me from having a much worse life. Each morning, my grandfather—whom I called Papa—and I went to the barn to milk the cow. While he milked, I leaned against her leg, because she was warm; and it was cold in the early mornings. On our way back to the house, where my grandmother—whom I called Mama—was fixing breakfast on her wood range, we stopped by the smokehouse.

The mother cat and her kittens lived in the smokehouse. Papa gave them the top milk, pouring it from his brimming bucket. I took the opportunity to pick up the kittens and love on them.

When we arrived at the back porch of the house, Mama sang out to me: "Now, Ilene, you dust yourself off and wash your face and hands. Because, I don't want a hair in my kitchen!"

My daughter's sudden requests for me to fix her hair in the kitchen revealed this long-held belief to me. Hair didn't belong in the kitchen. I realized beliefs I held could belong to someone else, not me. I also realized angry emotions that came up in me didn't really reflect me, yet they played themselves out as if they were mine. I was floored. For reasons I'll likely never know, my daughter took on the task of helping me to see that I was carrying my grandmother's "should," leading me to feel angry in my present, 32 years after I spent that year on the farm.

My daughter and I were in a long-term relationship. She was doing her "job" as a child, pushing my buttons so I could realize an area of growth that was still "open," that I needed to complete. I was grateful to her, as well as to myself for catching on, using the framework of the Giant School. I thought doing the opposite would help me to heal. I instructed her that from then on, she had to bring me the hair brush in the kitchen to have her hair fixed.

How many more times do you think my daughter brought me the hair brush in the kitchen? None. Zero. Nada. You see, when we learn our lesson, we're immediately finished with it. It doesn't arise any more. A week later, I went to a family home to teach a parenting course. When the mother of that home left to take her children to school, I needed a rubber band or tack. I pulled open a couple of kitchen drawers, hoping to find what I needed. In one of the drawers—to my total surprise—was nothing but hairbrushes.

YOUR PERSONAL LABORATORY

Have you ever gotten emotional about something happening in your life, only to realize that upset didn't seem to be yours?

Perhaps, like me, you kept doing something you believed was not supposed to happen, not realizing this meant that what you were upset about didn't originate with you.

Look for such an experience now. We often "borrow" emotions from parents and grandparents, especially developing ideas about what "should" or "should not" happen in life. When you find one, write about it.

Did anyone with whom you were in a long-term relationship do something that brought this to your attention?

If you followed the idea of "Earth as Giant School," how would you have dealt with the emotions that arose in you?

What do you intend to do "next time?" Write your intentions, and then "next time," fulfill them, to the best of your ability.

4

ONE IMPORTANT THING ACCOMPANYING EVERY LESSON IS EMOTIONS

There is one thing that is part of every experience we have on Earth: Emotions! They're part of us from birth and stay with us 24/7 throughout life. Even if our brains stop working well, as with dementia, we still have emotions. Emotions are with us each time we make a decision, take an action, try something new, let go of something (or someone) that's been with us a long time, or take a chance.

For generations humans have demonized emotions, pushing them down or away, attempting to ignore them, denying we have them, thinking there is something wrong if we have them, or believing we have done something wrong because emotions have shown themselves. It's not clear when this negative relationship with emotions began, but it's clear it keeps us from using emotions as intended. Demonizing emotions creates a view of emotions as a "problem," instead of as "support," which they are designed to be.

Think about water running through a stream bed, much like emotions run through us, starting when we're young. All is well until extra amounts of water are added during a heavy downpour. Then the stream can turn into a raging torrent, tearing out the stream banks, overflowing into homes, and creating havoc. Starting with temper tantrums in our early years, we can see that emotions do a similar thing. As adults, when we lose our job, experience a parent dying, lose our home in a fire or flood, or are robbed, emotions can turn into a major torrent, ripping out our foundations, leaving us feeling anchorless, helpless, and hopeless.

We've pushed emotions away for far too long. Read or watch any news report to get affirmation that emotions are running through all of humanity like a major torrent. It's time for a change.

Most people have not learned a positive way of working with emotions. We haven't learned why we have them, what they're intended to do, what to do with them, how to work with them, whether we can keep them under our own direction, or how to turn them loose without harm, once the emotion has served its purpose.

For nearly half a century, I've studied emotions, working to develop mastery over the emotions coming up in me, and passing this learning on to people who seek my help. The primary motive for writing this book is to share the amazing things I've learned about emotions and how to work with them, so they become helpful partners, instead of the scourge of life. Emotions make sense, have a purpose, and working with them is not difficult.

Emotions are given to us as messengers designed to help us more easily navigate our lives, for our entire lives. Emotions function brilliantly when we partner with them. Each emotion has a different, unique message, which I will share in more detail. I want to introduce emotions in a way most people likely never encountered until now.

MY PERSONAL LABORATORY

This experience speaks to the issue of how we start off in life and illustrates the phenomenon of trapped emotions and how we can work with them.

My youngest granddaughter was born with an Apgar score of 4 out of 10. The Apgar score rates the well-being of newborns.

She was blue and floppy. A respiration therapist encouraged her to breathe. Then the baby was rushed off to the Neonatal Intensive Care room. Her mother (my wonderful daughter-in-law) encouraged me to go with her.

I had several times practiced a ritual with the newborns in my family, including this child's older sister. I got to tell each new arrival where they are in the world, who the major players of life are (mom, dad, siblings), and who I am. Then I provided a "report on the state of your body," sharing the wonderfulness of the body they're occupying (none of my grandchildren, thankfully, had vital things wrong with them). I call this ritual: *Orienting Newborns.*

This ritual was what I intended to do with my newest grandchild, too. As I did, she reached her little hand out and wrapped her fingers around my pinkie. I held her fingers there with a light pressure of my thumb.

"Welcome! You're in Northern California. Your mother and father are both here. You have one sister, who is already here, too. I'm your grandmother, Ilene."

She listened in an intent manner. There were no other babies in the room. She was connected by wires and sensors taped to her body. The information on her blood oxygen saturation level, blood pressure, rate of breathing, and other vital pieces of information were sent to one side of the room where a nurse monitored the readouts.

That's when I remembered a program I featured on my Internet podcast, *Full Power Living.* It featured Chiropractor Dr. Bradley Nelson, who worked with what he called "trapped emotions." His idea was that we all have emotions trapped in us, because we don't notice and work with them at the time they occur, causing us difficulties as life goes on. Trapped emotions might also get passed down from parents and grandparents.

This granddaughter's birth was challenging. As I began to muse about what emotion might get trapped from such a birth experience, potentially causing a lifetime of difficulties, I realized

25

if I had gone through the experience my newborn granddaughter had gone through, I might not feel safe.

I talked with her, "That was a very rough landing you had after your trip through the birth canal! You might not feel safe right now, but I want you to know it's over. You are now safe. In fact, you don't ever have to go through that again in this lifetime! You are totally safe. We all are working to keep you safe. All you have to do now is pay attention to occupying your body. Make your breath go in and out evenly, allow oxygen to mix into your blood, relax and give yourself a proper blood pressure. It's time for you to let yourself occupy your body. Just remember you are safe; you never have to go through that again!"

During the years that followed, people shared thoughts about what happened. Did this newborn infant understand my words or did she respond to the tone of my voice? Was it possible for a newborn to understand such ideas, even though she had no way of knowing the language I was speaking? My own belief is that I was talking to my granddaughter's essence and she heard me loudly and clearly. Regardless of the explanation, when I got to this point, the nurse looked up and said: "Whatever you're doing over there keep it up. Everything just went to normal!"

To release emotions that may have gotten trapped inside, rummage through the experiences of life and ask the questions I asked about my granddaughter: "What would I feel if I had this experience? Is it possible that feeling is trapped in me? If so, I'm ready to release it. Please help me release this feeling if it is trapped in me."

Naming the emotion, stating the intention to release it, and asking for help starts the process of dislodging the stuck feelings. Personally, I believe tiny babies, animals, people who are demented in older age, very young children, and others do understand what is said, when it is offered in love and as help. This has to do with our spiritual connection with the Universe and with each other.

Our tiny newborn started her emotional learning during and just after birth, and had a chance to undo potentially damaging emotional issues from the beginning. Not all of us have this opportunity. Yet, all is not lost, because the way our Giant School is set up, we have our lifetime to make connections, corrections, and release energy we no longer need. As I often say: "If you get it the day you die, you've done it!" The primary reason to complete learning earlier than the day of our death is to make life easier, happier, and better.

YOUR PERSONAL LABORATORY

Pick a challenging experience from your life. Take time to remember it and write it down. Now ask yourself, and write your guesses and insights down, too: "What could I have been trying to teach myself by having this experience?" "Is there anything I would do differently?" "How might I have felt differently, and how might my life have been different, if I perceived this challenge as a lesson and did my best to learn from the experience right away?" Finally, ask yourself: "Is there any emotion that is still with me, that may be trapped in me, as a result of the experience I'm remembering?"

Face the facts by stating the responses out loud, and through your increased awareness, allow the emotions to move up and out of you.

5

MY PERSONAL JOURNEY WITH EMOTIONS

INTRODUCTION

It wasn't until I became a single parent at the age of 28 that I realized how important emotions are and how much they impact every minute of life. I found myself blowing up in anger at my toddler daughter, who didn't deserve it. I felt unable to control my outbursts. Even though I vowed never to hit my children as my father had hit me, when my daughter moved into the "Terrible Twos" I started hitting her whenever she crossed some imaginary line. (We tend to repeat the same behaviors we experienced, even if consciously we don't want to do it.) Anger surged through me. This was totally unacceptable, so I was desperate and searching for a solution.

Through therapy I realized how my early childhood experiences formed my emotional landscape, the one that was now interfering with my ability to support and love my daughter. I worked with a very talented therapist who pointed out that my daughter was in the "me, mine, gimme" phase of life. What was really setting off my anger was that even though I wanted to do the best for my daughter, due to mostly absent parenting, the little girl inside of me never had a "me, mine, gimme" phase!

When I was my daughter's age, there was no adult to help me, so every time my little girl put herself first (as was age appropriate), it set off a rage inside of me.

We devised a way for me to fill that empty hole inside. I felt a lot better and things improved. Yet it wasn't enough to fully curb the anger. I needed to do even more work on my early childhood experiences.

After the neglect and trauma of the first two years of my life, my father (whom I had never seen or met before) came and took me away from my birth mother. There was a loud argument and he gave my birth mother a bloody nose as I watched. As was customary in those days, no explanation was given about why my life was changing or how I could deal with the emotions of terror, anger, and grief I experienced. My father proved my birth mother's neglect in court, and as a single father, he won sole custody of two daughters, ages three and five. Such an outcome was unheard of in 1945.

He enrolled us in boarding schools during the week, bringing us to his apartment on weekends. He did a heroic job for which I'm grateful, but at the first boarding school, I endured the anger of a washerwoman. A chronic bedwetter, I was required to bring my urine-soaked sheets to her each morning. I was barely three. Having had almost no adult supervision up to that point, no requirements had been put on me, and there were no rules. Now people were upset at me for bed-wetting, something I didn't know was unacceptable. Without explanation and understanding, I was living in a world unlike anything I had known.

I was given rules I was expected to follow, which was bewildering. Nobody seemed to take into account that I'd never been asked to follow rules or procedures. Living in those boarding schools was like being sent to another world where everything was punitive and crushing. Nothing, and no one, was familiar. I was separated from my older sister, who continued to be my most reliable mother figure. I was a mass of emotions: terrified, rejected, lost, angry, hurt, abandoned, and daily chastised and shamed by the washerwoman in the basement.

The second boarding school was a little better, but had its own list of horrors for me.

My father remarried when I was almost four, giving me a beautiful step-mother who was intent on raising my sister and me as an act of repentance for the loss of her own child (whom I believe died of SIDS at the age of 3 months). She wanted to do a perfect job, and tried. Up to then, she hadn't parented longer than three months, yet was taking on two young children who had known no limits and were used to running their own lives. My sister, for example, invented her own language and taught it to me. She frustrated our parents by speaking to them in this language, instead of English, especially when they were seeking answers when mishaps occurred. She and I chatted unceasingly in this language, especially during times of family crisis, driving our parents crazy.

My father was a career officer in the Air Force. This meant our family moved every 18 months to 3 years. By the time I left for college at age 17, I had lived in 12 different homes and attended 15 different schools. These moves built resilience in me, but because of the dysfunctional nature of my family, it also left me feeling ashamed and different, with low self-esteem, and disconnected from my peers.

Add to these feelings the abuse that occurred in my family. Physical abuse included hair pulling, spankings with electrical cords, and slapping. Emotional abuse included telling me I was "the daughter of a prostitute" (my birth mother). Ironically, my father never admitted he was married to one.

Financially, I was deprived of all personal money, including the money I earned as a teenager, working six evenings a week as a babysitter for neighbors.

Social abuse included refusing to allow me to accept the lead in our high school play, *Time Out For Ginger*, using the excuse that we were going to move to Turkey. We didn't move for two years. I wasn't allowed to go to school dances, to stay overnight with friends, or to attend sports events held by my high school.

I was also sexually abused by an older male relative, between the ages of 12 and 14 years old.

When I left for college at the age of 17, I never went home to live there again. The final act of abuse was my parents insisting that I attend college, but after enrolling me in the College of William and Mary in Virginia, refusing to pay tuition starting the middle of my first semester freshman year. Years later, I discovered they did the same thing to my older sister. If I was to get a college education, it was up to me. Fortunately, at the time, in addition to being determined to educate myself and move away from my family, I connected with a fellow-student, whose family had a different kind of deep dysfunction. We married at the age of 19, helping each other through those early years. Together each of us earned a bachelor's and a master's degree.

I built up hurt and anger for my entire childhood. These emotions were too dangerous to express and I pushed each one down until I was no longer aware of its presence. These emotions grew bigger and more powerful during those years I repressed them.

I became a very dedicated victim and angry person, the predominant themes for my everyday life. I feared rejection, abandonment, and criticism. From the time of my foot injury at age two, I became terrified every time I heard ambulance sirens. I had little character, no ideals, and no principles of my own that I could use to guide my life. As I neared the end of my teens and escaped the control of my parents, the emotions I repressed began to get brazen about finding ways to escape into my everyday life.

WHAT'S IMPORTANT ABOUT THIS STORY

As I entered adulthood, I was sure few people had a childhood as painful and traumatizing as mine. Sadly, I've discovered there are a lot of people who also had painful and traumatizing childhoods. However, from the stories I've heard as a psychotherapist, I discovered only a small fraction of people had things worse than me, thankfully.

As my emotional landscape developed, things played out like a video game, with someone firing at me every time I left cover. Yet, there was also a benefit to this series of experiences: I strongly empathized with others and could offer help from the position of someone who had been there. As I moved into my life-long career as a psychotherapist, having that awful childhood set me up to be a stronger person, and a more compassionate therapist. For that, I'm grateful.

It took a long time before I discovered that many souls who come to the Earth, and especially those coming here since the early 1980s, have taken a similar trajectory. I discovered why we put ourselves into awful conditions, so challenging it sometimes seems like it's not worth staying here. It's because we came to Earth to do a job, one that requires strength, persistence, and an ability to handle adversity. The challenging childhoods we may have created for ourselves were designed to get us ready for the work we've come to Earth to do. Having those painful experiences sucks, I know. But that's what it's about.

Once I learned this, I marveled at and was grateful for having gotten through it without becoming addicted, alcoholic, or schizophrenic. I wanted to make changes to live my life as if I never had these challenges, traumas, and problems. I didn't know if it was possible, but I determined to do it if it was.

In 1972, I had completed a Master's degree at the School of Social Welfare, University of California in Berkeley. My daughter was two years old. My husband left us when she was 10 months old saying he wasn't ready to be a father. This was the tipping point that allowed all the anger I stored for 28 years to begin spilling over, dumping into my life, and onto everyone around me. As this occurred, I sought a way to quell the anger I experienced. Observing the anger in me spill over onto my child, I concluded there was more I needed to know about anger. I set out on my quest to learn all I could, believing that was the only way to save my life and the life of my child.

I went to the School of Social Welfare library, in 1972, before there was an Internet. I was not taught specific things about anger during my psychotherapist training, but I was sure there was information. I wanted to know:

- What causes people to become angry?

- Is it possible to stop being angry?

- What does it take to stop experiencing the kind of anger I felt?

- Is it possible to work with and get in charge of emotions?

- Any- and every-thing else I could learn about anger to allow me to take it off center stage of my life.

What I discovered was (drumroll): Absolutely no information to answer these questions.

At that time, therapists learned about emotions through engaging in their own psychotherapy, by seeing that a particular emotion was involved with a specific mental illness, and from whatever was learned in personal life. Individual emotions were not addressed separately during their training.

This meant people were prepared to professionally help others deal with the emotions causing trouble in their lives, yet were totally unprepared with an agreed-upon understanding of the cause of emotions, what they're for, and how to work to bring them under control.

In fact, in 1998, 25 years later, I had someone from my office call 37 colleges and universities that prepared therapists for licensure and practice in the state of California. We asked this question: "Do you now, or have you ever, offered a stand-alone course on anger?" Not one of these 37 institutions of higher learning answered: "Yes." One said it was currently offering a class on forgiveness, which addressed repairing anger, but offered nothing to answer the questions I had in mind. While I was dismayed that more specific attention was not focused on this emotion we all experience every day, I was not surprised. It was clear I had to find the answers for myself.

I embarked on a personal study of anger, sharing the findings with my therapy clients. My search led me to study most other emotions, eventually developing into a comprehensive understanding regarding emotions, their intended function in our lives, and best ways to work with them. I discovered it's possible to work with emotions so they don't have to be constantly monitored. I learned emotions make sense, as long as we take the time to understand them. Eventually, and contrary to popular opinion, I learned that working powerfully and masterfully with emotions is easy.

GETTING PROFESSIONAL HELP

Working full-time as a privately-practicing psychotherapist gave me the advantage of moving my learning along with greater speed. I observed how what I had learned worked in different lives and situations. I was developing my knowledge about anger and other emotions, and what I discovered I paired with ancient, universal principles. I offered my learning to clients as something to experiment with, to see if what I learned would work for others. Considering that no therapists were taught a comprehensive way of approaching and working with emotions at that time, my clients were delighted to be offered tools that worked better than what they had. What I offered did work, creating amazing changes. My reputation as a therapist who could help clients make fast and lasting changes brought more and more deeply pained people to my office.

A police officer worked with me for several months. He was slated to have surgery to remove gall stones. The operation would occur in one month. I asked if he'd like to experiment. Based on my learning, I theorized that anger played a part in the development of gall stones (this was before the first modern book pairing physical illness with emotions). We experimented with my techniques, working with anger's energy in his weekly sessions.

Daily he repeated aloud the words: "I'm angry. I'm angry. I'm angry." in a slow cadence, pausing only to say what he was angry about, whenever such thoughts arose. This allowed him to Face Fact, setting him free of whatever anger might be stored in him.

We also did an internal personal search, together, for all anger he might carry from the past, both professionally and from childhood. At the end of one month, he reported for the surgery, but the examination showed the gall stones were no longer present. He didn't need the surgery.

Shortly after this experience, Louise Hay published her work, *Heal Your Body*, which connected emotions and physical illness. The publication further validated what I was accomplishing in my life and helping others to do in their lives.

Using the "experimental" approach, I started asking people I worked with if they'd like to "try for a week" a different way of working with particular situations. By experimenting with willing clients under conditions that did not have negative risk, such as with the police officer, my professional work as a psychotherapist began to feed into the construction of an overall understanding of how anger works, and how to work with anger in easy ways, creating profound outcomes. It was both amazing and rewarding to observe that when we worked with anger, using this understanding of how emotions work, people started making faster progress, developed tools, and found ways for them to side-step the usual repetitiveness of anger-involved situations. The professional side of my work dovetailed with the personal. People began to flock to my office.

It wasn't me. It was the development of a way to work with people's emotions that we could understand, work with ourselves, and that was effective in ending the emotional rat race most people were experiencing. That's what drew people to work with me. My efforts at understanding and working with anger, as anger behaves naturally, were paying off. A comprehensive theory and way of working with anger was being developed, and it was effective for me and others. This comprehensive theory is what I'm offering in this book. Start experimenting with it yourself, today.

After almost 10 years of studying and experimenting, I started talking with people about what I'd learned. In my Conscious

Parenting classes, I taught parents how to work with children's emotions, how to teach children to deal with those emotions, and how parents deal with their own emotions in the process. In eight years of teaching continuing education classes for California Probation Officers, we found the material was useful when dealing with recalcitrant clients on probation. I also taught continuing education classes to adults and teens in local high schools. I had opportunity to teach in other places in the United States, Australia, China, Ireland, and appeared on radio programs and on U.S. national talk television. The reports were heart-warming. People were able to take this simple understanding and approach, and make lasting changes in relationships and life situations that had plagued them for years.

I BECOME A REAL PIONEER

One of the fun things I've played around with during the years, is the division of human beings into "Pioneers" and "Settlers."

I'm a Pioneer. I like to explore, travel, go to new ideas in my head, meet new people, and take risks.

Settlers, on the other hand, prefer to stay at home, explore only a little bit (and with others), may like a small amount of travel, prefer to create and follow rules, and behave conservatively, which minimizes risk. Pioneers and Settlers are both vital in the world. Pioneers open up new territory while Settlers create culture and stability in those new territories.

In 1994, I actually did become a pioneer. I was approached to write a series of manuals for parents, sharing how to help children understand and work with 7 different emotions. The manuals allowed me to become a Pioneer in the developing Emotional Literacy movement. The movement was for schools to include Emotional Literacy in the curriculum, therefore, the books were distributed to schools and local libraries. From 1994 on, I expanded what I had learned about how emotions work, combined that with the research I'd done to write the manuals, along with the results of the experimentation my clients and I did. The result is a comprehensive system that answers those early questions:

- What causes people to become angry?

- Is it possible to stop being angry?

- What does it take to actually end the kind of anger I felt?

- Is it possible to master emotions?

- Any- and every-thing else I could learn about anger to allow me to take it off the center stage of my life, so I could be a more loving, patient, and supportive mother.

I call this system *Emotional Mastery*, which is taking charge of our *Emotions in Motion*. Not only does it give a working picture of emotions and individual emotions' purpose, but it also gives specific approaches and tools for working with all emotions. *Emotional Mastery* offers a way of working with emotions that creates lasting change. We don't have to keep going over and over the same issues or the same emotions. Instead, we can hear the emotions' lesson, finish the learning, release the emotion, and move on. This system is for everyone who wants to do more than struggle with emotions for a lifetime.

MY PERSONAL LABORATORY

As I came more fully into living life as an Emotional Master, one of the most delightful things I noticed was a huge upsurge in optimism. Don't get me wrong, I've been a glass-half-full kind of a person most of my adult life, with only the darkest of times taking that stance from me.

However, I never fully trusted my optimism. I'd been criticized for it. But when we're emotionally masterful, we're more developed spiritually. And the more spiritually-developed we are, the more we trust inner urgings. An incident from 2008 stands out in my mind that illustrates this.

My husband, Bob, had talked about going to Bora-Bora for years. When I came into some money unexpectedly I told him, "I'm using this money to take you to Bora Bora!" He was delighted, but felt he wasn't physically up to that trip. Instead, we planned a two-month trip that included a month on a cruise ship crossing the Pacific ocean, and another month touring New Zealand and Australia. Our trip was planned down to the last detail, and we were having a wonderful time. This trip turned out to be a highlight of Bob's life. I was glad I spent the money and did this, because by 2011 he started developing illnesses, which debilitated him and led to his death in 2016.

The night we stayed in Adelaide, Australia, I realized I had made a mistake with our flight reservations. We were scheduled for a tour in Sydney the next day, Monday, yet our flight to Sydney was for Tuesday. When I told him my discovery, he reacted with upset and worry. Seeing this I told him, "Why don't you just keep working at your computer and let me work my magic?" He assured me, in no uncertain terms, that my "magic" wasn't going to work for this one.

My first efforts, talking to plane agents in Australia, didn't work. Bob was even more distressed when I shared these results. I announced I'd call our airline in the states, using Skype. He assured me Skype wouldn't work, that all was lost and our trip was ruined. (Do you get that Bob was a glass-half-empty kind of guy?)

I connected with an agent in Arizona, where it was midnight. I was grateful she was working. She was able to work things around for us to catch a flight the very next morning (Monday), just one hour different than the flight I thought we had. Not only that, we got a small refund on both of our tickets.

Glass-half-empty people have a hard time accepting that people of the opposite persuasion pull off the magic they envision. Bob told me the change was pure luck, unexplainable, but certainly not due to anything out of the ordinary that I had done. By that point, however, I had learned to accept a single thought: "It will all work out. Even if I can't see how, I know it will all work out." I asked for help, set up my Skype, and "Presto, Chango." We arrived in Sydney with plenty of time to connect with our tour.

It wasn't really "magic" of course. I was working with myself, the emotions, and intuition that arose in me, in addition to my brain, my computer, and the airline representative. The "magic" was that I asked for help, and knew that things would work out. Unlike in years earlier, I actually believed things would work out, even though I couldn't see how.

YOUR PERSONAL LABORATORY

Have you ever made a mistake you knew would have a negative impact on your plans or what you wanted to do? Find one to work with now. Write down:

- What was your error?

- What emotional reaction did you feel when you discovered your error?

- Did you believe you could make changes to reverse the situation?

- Did you quit, or move forward?

- Did you believe you could ask for help—even if a person was not present?

- Did you ask for help?

- If you kept moving forward, how did things turn out?

- Is there something you didn't do you think would have helped?

Once you look at how things occurred, look at how you might do things differently, next time.

Write down:

- Will you allow yourself to be human and make mistakes?

- How many mistakes will you allow yourself in a year? Write this figure down!

- If you make a mistake, will you forgive yourself?

- What might happen if you focused on the idea that things will work out?

- What will you need to do differently inside yourself to make room for this idea?

- Will you ask others to stand back, so you can see what magic you can wreak?

- Will you keep trying, with as little stress or pressure as possible for a solution?

- When you (co-) create a solution, will you savor it and allow yourself to feel happy?

- Will you express gratitude to yourself, those who help you, and to the universe, for the great work and outcome!

Congratulations for conducting your life in these ways. You're moving into living as an Emotional Master.

SECTION 2

EMOTIONAL DEVELOPMENT

6

WHAT WE KNOW ABOUT EMOTIONS

OVERVIEW

How much thought do we give to the emotions that arise in us? Many people feel overwhelmed by emotions, others believe emotions are out of control when we feel them. I've had opportunity to work with many people who report not feeling emotions at all.

Almost all of us were taught to hold emotions inside, but doing so can create problems. Holding anger, the most active emotion, inside long enough can kill us. We've heard the saying that holding onto anger is like holding poison inside of us, expecting it to destroy somebody else.

Holding on to emotions causes them to become "negative," and is one of the worst things we can do, because emotions are energy. Emotions are made to move. It's vital we discover how to allow the emotions that come up inside of us to move through and out of us, so the energy of those emotions doesn't linger.

Before we go into more depth on this, there are some things we know about emotions that are important to remind ourselves about, including:

1. *We are born with emotions.* Newborns cry, get red-faced, startle when frightened by a loss of physical support, and react when uncomfortable.

2. *Everybody has emotions.* No exceptions. We cannot get rid of emotions.

3. *Not everybody experiences the same emotions regarding the same things* that happen in life (not even people in the same family). However, there are certain life experiences that bring the same basic emotions (such as sadness or love) to everyone, all over the world, regardless of ethnicity, age, or culture.

4. *Emotions are always with us.* There are no vacation days for emotions; and no off-duty hours.

5. *Most people don't really know much about how emotions work and how to work with emotions.* Instead of being masterfully in charge of the emotions we experience, most people attempt to manage emotions in a futile effort to keep them under control. If that doesn't work, and the emotions become frightening or overwhelming, the person may sink or turn to medication or other numbing agents.

6. *We develop our emotional landscape early in life, when we are still children.* We learn a majority of what we know about emotions from our parents, caretakers, and siblings, including how to react to and interpret our early-life emotional experiences.

7. *Emotions can't tell time.* If something happens in our life today that stimulates an emotion we had earlier in life, that emotion will come forward.

8. *Emotions are at the bottom of many of our most difficult human issues,* such as relationship difficulties, murders, abuse, work or school failures, communication challenges, physical illness, addiction, and parent-child problems.

9. *Humans don't have an agreed-upon understanding about emotions.* This makes working with emotions in our life a more difficult experience, because we don't all understand emotions the same. This can block clear pathways for healing that works for the majority.

10. *Most people believe working with emotions is very hard.* Many believe that emotions are inherited and are not changeable. Neither has to be true.

UNANSWERED QUESTIONS ABOUT EMOTIONS

There are many things we don't know about emotions, such as:

1. What are emotions?

2. Why do we have emotions?

3. What causes emotions to come up?

4. How and when do emotional landscapes develop?

5. What do humans do that make working with emotions more difficult?

6. Do we have to keep working with emotions over and over again?

7. Why are some people better at working with emotions than others?

8. Is there one thing that can lessen the power of emotions?

9. Why do emotions keep coming back?

Questions like these have driven me for years in my quest to understand how emotions work. Sharing what I discovered can give us a common understanding, enabling us to work more effectively with emotions. When we become more proficient, we develop new pathways for emotional mastery, thus adding to our knowledge and well-being, as well as to a satisfying life. Let's look at the answers to these questions.

MY PERSONAL LABORATORY

My new stepmother officially joined our family when I was almost four. To me she was Mom. She worked very hard to be a good mother, having taken on two little girls who were difficult to work with because they hadn't been properly civilized up to the time she became Mom.

Mom carried a lot of anger of her own. In a deep conversation Mom, Dad and I had once when she was in her sixties, I realized she must hate men (something I spent some time in psychotherapy working to divest myself of). I asked her: "It sounds like you hate men. Do you?"

"Yes," she said immediately, taking little notice of my Dad.

"How did it happen that you came to hate men?" I asked.

"My mother hated men," she said, matter-of-factly. "I thought about the reasons she hated men; and I decided to hate them, too."

As an aside, note that I was three years old when I encountered her, carrying this belief, and clearly downloaded it from her brain into my own youthful brain. Until that day, I could never figure out where this came from, because I felt I loved the men in my life.

Years later, after my father died and she remarried, we were talking on the phone. She began to share with me the story of how her brother had taken something from her that her father had made for her. She felt robbed. I'd heard this story many, many times. This time, I said to her, "Mom, I really don't want to listen to you tell me this story. I know you will feel very, very angry when you tell it. You have a heart problem. I don't want to be present if you give yourself a heart attack while you tell this story to me."

"Well," she started, sounding like that would be okay with her.

"In fact, Mom" I inserted as quickly as I could, "it's not necessary for you to keep being angry about this situation. Do you know that I'm an expert about anger, and that I can help you end these angry feelings in your life? Would you like to do that? I'd love to teach you what I know."

She considered my offer for quite a while. Then she said to me, "You know, I've been angry about this for a long time. I think I'll just keep on being angry!"

We all experience emotions; they're with us all our lives. We can know we experience them, and do so for years, even if they cause us pain. We can certainly choose whether we deal with them and move on, or whether we keep our same relationship with emotions that have the power to eventually kill us.

YOUR PERSONAL LABORATORY

Do you carry anger around with you? Write for how long you've done this.

Is there an emotion you know has been hanging around in your life—maybe for years—that causes you pain whenever it arises, yet you still retain that emotion and think of it as "yours?" Write what the emotion is. Write why you think you remain loyal to keeping it around?

If you realize this emotion is connected to someone you love (like my Mom's anger was connected to her mother), who is it? Look squarely at this situation. Will you hurt this person in any way if you release this emotion and don't stay loyal to keeping it around? If you decide the other person won't feel pain from your actions, choose to let the emotion go, and then let it go.

Write what happened as a result.

Go to the section of this book that talks about the emotion in question. Learn more about it, including what it may be costing you to keep it in your life. Again, let it go.

Express gratitude to yourself for lightening your emotional load.

7
WHAT ARE EMOTIONS?

OVERVIEW

Emotions are energy, famously and frequently referred to as "energy in motion" (*Emotions in Motion*). Like other forms of energy such as wind, electricity, and water, emotions are designed to move. In fact, emotions are designed to show up, deliver a message, and move on.

As energy, emotions obey the laws of energy, which are what we refer to as "old physics." These laws include such things as: "Energy can neither be created nor destroyed," "energy constantly seeks a way to move," and "resistance to the movement of energy creates pressure." The principles from Quantum physics that very small particles like quarks don't exist until we pay direct attention also applies. For example, when we get more upset or angry the more we think about a particular situation. Or perhaps we didn't realize we were angry until someone suggested we should investigate the emotions inside, which resulted in finding a lot of anger.

To understand emotions-as-energy better, think about water trapped behind a dam. The water stays behind the dam unless there is even a miniscule break in the dam. Then, the water is assisted by the pressure it exerts on the dam and slowly breaks through. Note, too, when the dam bursts, the water tears through relentlessly, until it flows freely again. We cannot stop the water's energy. We can attempt to channel it and control it; but we cannot take away its energy and drive.

It's vital to notice that when we try to control energy like water or wind, it's impossible to do perfectly. Energy is constantly seeking a way around, through, or out. One tiny break and the control is over. The same is true for emotions. We can provide a channel for the energy, allowing it to move through the area where we are. We can even get it to work for us (as with wind or water turbines) as it passes through. Emotions work in the same way that other familiar forms of energy do.

Unfortunately, what we were taught to do over generations ignores these laws. Instead of helping emotions to move through us, we learned to stuff, stop, and hold onto emotions, thus trapping the energy inside of us. Just like water held behind a dam tends to pile up and get deeper, emotions held onto tend to grow in power.

It's not so bad when we hold onto the emotion of love. To have it grow inside of us is great. Even so, when love grows enough, we feel compelled to share it with others, to let it out. But think about what happens when anger or fear grow. Anger grows in power, intensifies, and can turn into hate or rage. Fear can grow to incapacitate us, as it does in mental illness.

Most of the problems humans face occur because we hold onto emotions for a long time. We resist emotions, not allowing movement. The work emotions are designed to do cannot be accomplished. The emotion grows so we're now both filled with the emotion and are fearful of letting it out. Often, we fear the emotional release will destroy us. We live in an on-going bind of wanting to release the emotions' energy, while living in fear of what releasing the emotion might do to us or the ones we love.

The truth is, if we've been holding a specific emotion inside for a long time, when first released it will burst out and create havoc. If we decide to do this, it's important to have an expert standing by. Have a psychotherapist or a coach, who thoroughly understands how emotions work, to stand by and help during the time you're releasing long-held emotions. While these emotions are breaking through, we may be concerned that the rampage will never end. I advise my clients to tell people participating in long-lasting relationships that they're releasing long-held-onto emotions, giving those people permission to stand back until the release is complete. It is usually too difficult to stay close. Since every person's release time is different, we need also to tell others that we don't know how long this will take and we will advise them when the release is complete.

How will we know when the release is complete? First, remember that just like the water bursting from behind the dam, those emotions will at first feel savage and powerful. Eventually, however, enough water runs out that it begins to stay within the bounds of the waterway, flowing like a stream or river. That is also what happens with long-held-onto emotions. Emotions also drain out enough to come into natural bounds, flowing, and moving according to their design. We will start to feel calmer. Once released, I've never known anyone to allow emotions to pile up inside of them to the same extent again.

When I released the stored anger in me, it raged for two years. I really needed someone to help me continue to allow the release of all that angry energy, because I felt crazy and frequently felt hopeless that it would ever be over. Therapist Shirley Luthman stood by for me, encouraging me that there would be an end. And, there was. I finally ran out of stored anger, and was able to lead a more balanced and peaceful life. I was comforted to learn that once released, anger would never build up like that again.

To ease the rampage, we can also work with tapping, with color, meditation, or physical exercise. These can help modulate the force of the releasing emotion(s). Identify the message of the emotion before tapping or meditating it away.

Many people want to reach for medication to help ease the rampage. While we can do this, it's my observation that all medication does is make the process take longer. Medication does not get at the root of the problem; it only dulls our emotions. Staying on psychiatric medication over a long period of time is not advised. When we stop taking the medication, we still have the issues related to the emotion we're storing and still need to deal with those emotions. Why not go ahead, right away, and deal with the emotion, rather than dragging the process out and taking up lots of our time?

Once released, emotions are allowed to more freely meander through us, without causing problems. The principle is: Once the mind grows to a new place, it cannot go back. Releasing emotions held onto for a long time allows us to restore the emotions we feel to a natural state.

MY PERSONAL LABORATORY

Emotions are energy. Human beings are energy beings. As a group, humans are learning a lot more these days about our ability to work with energy. This story from my Personal Laboratory of 1972, is how I very accidentally discovered that energy can be quite specifically conveyed. I believe we can all do this, yet it took a powerfully painful experience for me to create the evidence of this movement of energy.

In 1972, my marriage ended. My husband moved out. I began my life raising my 10-month-old daughter, attending my last year of graduate school (and then starting my own psychotherapy business), and tending to our home with its 22 fruit trees.

My estranged husband had a very curious habit of calling me, almost every day, to tell me how much he loved me. Tearfully, I would challenge him: "If you love me so much, why aren't you here?" He could only tell me "I can't be." One night, we were having our telephone conversation, when I realized something was different about him. "You've met someone," I said to him.

"Yes," he replied.

"Who is she; what's her name?"

"I'm not going to tell you," he said, "I'm afraid you'll use what I tell you against me."

"Please, " I begged. "I won't! I just need to know the facts!"

Still he refused. When I didn't relinquish my quest, he said, "goodbye" and hung up the phone.

I was lying in my bed. I cried, and cried, doubled over in agony. When I was a snotty mess, I fell asleep.

During the night, I had a dream I was talking with my husband, explaining to him that if I just knew a few facts, I could relax and let the situation go. He repeated his concern about me using the information against him, yet told me her name was Marie.

"How tall is she?" I continued.

"Not as tall as you, by about two and a half inches."

"Is she blonde, brunette, or redhead?" I inquired, gaining confidence.

"Her hair is a lot like yours, though it's a little darker," he said. My hair is blonde.

"How old is she?" I asked next.

He started to answer. Somehow I had the idea that she was about my age, but was a tad older. The garbage collector was stopping at our house and awakened me from this dream. I wrote down what I remembered.

Later that day, I had an appointment for psychotherapy. My therapist worked in the same facility as my husband. I arrived early, asked him if we could talk, briefly, when he passed me in the hallway. When the door was closed, I asked:

"Is her name Marie?" He blanched.

"Is she shorter than me by about two and a half inches?"

"Who told you?" he demanded.

"And her hair. It's not really dark, but it's darker than mine, right?"

I was about to ask more, but he turned abruptly, look me straight in the eye, and said, "You psychic bitch, get out of my life!"

While this encounter was painful, still I was amazed and gratified. My husband hadn't wanted to tell me this information, yet I got it anyway.

I'd never had such an experience. I never, to my knowledge, got specific information about something or someone when I wasn't actually told it by somebody.

Looking back, I saw the intensity of the pain and emotion I felt as I dropped off to sleep. It was great. I was focusing on needing to know those answers, had asked for help in getting them, and proclaimed I was ready to hear them. They didn't come from my husband, but did in my dream. These are the kinds of things we can do in order to have the emotions that come up in us help us out, direct us, and relieve our suffering.

YOUR PERSONAL LABORATORY

Have you ever had an experience like mine, where your emotional pain was so great that what you felt you needed to see or know was given to you, even though the person you wanted to tell you refused to do so? Write it down. Perhaps you have known someone for whom this occurred. You can write about them if you don't have an example of your own.

Can you see in this story, the demonstration of emotions as energy? Where did those answers come from? Look for answers you have come to know, when nobody actually told them to you. Write them down.

To develop this ability in yourself play games. When someone draws your attention, imagine that you are that person. Voice aloud what they might be telling you, feeling, or thinking. If you can, get verification about the veracity of this information.

When your phone rings with a ringtone you haven't programmed, before you look, guess at who is calling you.

Whenever there is a question about something, pause and ask yourself: "What is the answer?" Then, as events unfold, check the information you "received."

Since the experience that had me called a "psychic bitch," I've learned we all have the capability to know, get information, and realize things that come, largely, through emotions. Consider that a possibility for yourself; then play around with your abilities.

Write down what you discover.

8

WHY DO WE HAVE EMOTIONS?

I f we were sending someone dear to us to a challenging school, we'd send them off with something that might make the experience easier. We might pack a lunch, provide a backpack, paper and pencils, and give a bit of advice.

As discussed, we're all in a Giant School called Earth. We came here with things to make the experience easier for us. One of the most important is emotions. Emotions are devised as messengers, each offering a signal we can use, if only we learn the signal of each emotion, then look for and take time to recognize and work with that signal when emotions arise.

What if we send that special someone to school with our advice and the items to make school easier, and that person doesn't use what we give them, with backpack kept closed, and pencils, paper, or lunch not accessed? What if that loved one is afraid to open the backpack, because the belief is the backpack is both dangerous and overwhelming, or will cause them to go berserk? Tools were given, but not used, not even looked at, not understood, and even demonized. What was given to make things easier becomes totally useless.

Over generations people were advised never to open the "backpack" containing emotions. Emotions were demonized. The few times people tried to look in the backpacks proved overwhelming, with the emotions inside pushing and shoving to get out, running amok, and re-affirming negative beliefs.

The time has come for us to open up our backpacks, allow the emotions inside to emerge, and figure out how to work with them. It's time to claim our birthright. To make this easier we're feeding the brain some information, before we open that virtual backpack, so we'll be better prepared for what we find there.

MY PERSONAL LABORATORY

My second husband, it turned out, was afflicted with a mental illness, Bipolar Disorder. Even during the days I attended graduate school to become a psychotherapist, Bipolar Disorder (in those days termed Manic-Depressive Disorder), was viewed as something severe, for which people were locked into psychiatric hospitals. I never realized people with the disorder wouldn't be incarcerated. I'd never seen the behaviors associated with Bipolar Disorder, or related them to the diagnosis. In short, I got involved with this very unusual and fascinating person, without realizing that many of the unusual things about him were a mental illness.

We did our best to have a relationship, and then a marriage, that lasted for more than seven years. Then, I asked him to leave. I'd taken care of him in almost every way during those seven years: I invited him to move into my home, had a child with him, supported his business ventures, and made almost all the money to support our family of four. When I was pregnant with our child, in fact, I needed to work extra hard (I was self-employed and had no savings, but that's another story) in order to stop working long enough to deliver my child. He told me he couldn't find work that suited him, so he earned no money. Under the circumstances, that was something I couldn't understand.

When he left, I immediately felt relieved. For three months, I felt wonderful. He went on to develop a relationship with a woman named Jane who lived in our same town. When he came to spend time with our child, he would tell me things about Jane.

Three and a half months after he left, I suddenly became enraged. I was so angry, I was having trouble breathing. By that time, I had learned a lot about anger, so I used every approach and technique for quelling anger that I'd learned. Nothing was working. The only thing that gave any relief was to meditate, breathing in love, breathing out anger, coupled with an urgent request for "whoever is out there" to help me release the anger.

After two weeks of this agony, things began to fall into place, allowing me to literally catch my breath. I began to realize the incredible coincidences occurring in my life.

My birth mother's name was Jane. This was the name of my husband's new woman, too.

My father always told us he met Jane in a dance hall. My husband's Jane, who had driven her car to my home on a couple of occasions, had a sticker on its window that said, "I'd rather be dancing."

My birth mother, to my understanding, never fought for me. She just let my father take us and I never saw her again. Though I asked my husband to fight for me, our family and our child, he didn't. He just moved on.

My father held me and my sister responsible for the consequences that resulted from his marriage to our mother. When I was an adult, he sent me a bill for several hundred thousand dollars. He said my sister and I "owed" him for fighting for us in court, thus depleting the family resources and leaving the family he made with my step-mom less monied. My husband told me everything that went wrong was my fault, too.

In this Giant School, the experience I was having with my estranged second husband was very similar to the insults I experienced when I was almost three (and beyond), and my father took me away from the only home I had ever known (even though it was a home in which I was severely neglected).

The emotion of anger was paired with this incredible lesson. As a young child, I was only allowed to express anger toward my father (for taking me away from my home) for a very short period of time. Now, my husband was taking himself away, devastating my home, and I was free to let that anger out. It was nearly overwhelming; yet it was not so powerful that I couldn't deal with it in the end.

What appeared to cause anger to come up was the close replication of the circumstances I had endured 35 years previously. Once again, a person in long-term relationship with me was the catalyst for my experience; and the experience was offering me an opportunity to learn, accompanied by the emotion of anger. When I untangled things and addressed the anger toward the real culprits, my birth mother and father, I learned the lesson and the anger moved through and on.

YOUR PERSONAL LABORATORY

What experience have you had where you felt strong emotion you thought you had already dealt with, when you couldn't figure out why it was so strong, or what it was really connected to? Think on it, then write your experience.

Ask yourself: "Are there any similarities in this situation with something I've experienced in the past?" Take your time. Write down what you discover.

When you find such a parallel situation ask: "What do I need to learn from this coming up in my life again?" If you're not coming up with an answer, ask for help. "Help me to see what I need to learn from this experience. I'm ready to learn. Whatever it takes, I'm ready. Please, help me."

Listen.

Explore the answers that come to you. Allow yourself to free associate, seeing where there are connections that have meaning for you. Write this down.

Your experience may be subtler than mine. Don't dismiss what you get because it's subtle. Be grateful for this learning. Write what you're aware of learning.

9

WHAT CAUSES EMOTIONS TO COME UP?

Cognitive Behavioral Therapy, which is very popular today, teaches emotions come from thoughts. This idea makes sense when we're observing adults; but it doesn't explain why an infant experiences anger or fear. Humans experience emotions before they're shown to have thoughts.

Research shows we're born with the ability to experience emotions. We may experience emotions while in the womb. Animals such as whales, higher primates, elephants, and porpoises are also shown to have emotions, including compassion.

Recent research to help autism patients in England demonstrated that our connection with our body, in particular our ability to listen to our own heartbeat, enhances our ability to feel emotions. Emotions start with the body. Scientists suggest that experiencing emotions is part of having a body: You get a body; you get emotions. Perhaps we don't need deep thought so much as we need a body and heart connection in order to experience emotions.

Another bit of research coming from England tells us everyone does not relate to or see the same emotion based on how another person's face looks. Instead, we learn to interpret emotions, even learning to pair specific emotions with different stimuli.

It turns out we perceive emotions based on what we're taught; yet we feel them based on our ability to be in, and to feel, our body and heartbeat.

This is very important because if we wish to feel more, we need to take more time to relate to and feel our body, particularly our heart. If we don't like our emotional reactions, we can start examining how we perceive those emotions, and what we connect to in our perceptive network. First, feel the emotion and only then look at how we think in relation to it. Drawing from our earlier discussion of how important it is for us to have experiences, so we can get outside of our own existence enough to perceive what is going on, the next step of connecting particular emotions to our experience becomes easier. Part of getting "outside" is to identify and name emotion.

Did you ever get bitten or attacked by a dog when you were young? If so, what was the emotional reaction of the adults nearby? How do you feel about dogs now? Usually, parents get quite upset. Parents can even teach a child to fear dogs following such an attack. The result is that we either don't like dogs as an adult or we still feel fear when a dog approaches.

When my son was four years old, he was bitten in the face by a dog while we were visiting friends. The bite required stitches and a tetanus shot. I was calm, inviting my son to participate in making the decision to go to the ER, to take the tetanus shot, and even to hold still without the usual little-child restraints while the doctor stitched his face. Afterwards, we returned to the dog, where my son forgave the dog, learning from me that it was just "dog behavior" that caused the dog to snap. Nothing either my son or the dog had done was wrong. My now 42-year-old son has never feared dogs. In fact, when he was five years old, he insisted we foster a dog with a reputation for biting small children, just more than a year after he was bitten. With my young son paying particular attention to show her his love, Tracy the dog lived with us happily and without biting for nearly eight years.

My son's openness and receptiveness to dogs throughout his life is also based on the perception that the dog attack was reasonable (given how dogs behave), and could be repaired, learned from, and released. He was encouraged to forgive the dog (forgiveness means to "let go"), which he did.

For those who feel aversion or fear, and had the experience of a strong and/or fearful parental reaction when attacked by a dog, the event was likely interpreted as full of fear, negativity, and something awful. That is very likely still a part of the perception. As we move through life, how we perceive situations affects what emotions arise (and whether emotions do arise) in our lives.

Let's also take a minute to notice the perceptions we have are based on past experience. If we developed a fear of dogs, we will recoil when a dog runs up to greet us, all based on past experience of being attacked by a dog (or seeing someone else attacked). This dog today may be friendly and happy, yet our reaction is fearful, as if this dog, too, will attack us, as we've seen or experienced in the past.

If we see emotions as signals, then the complicated system involving our primitive brain (referred to as "The Limbic System") is set up for emotions based on experience. Part of that experience is the thoughts we have related to that experience. Our thoughts regarding experience are most often based on the beliefs we have developed during our lives. Beliefs result from similar thoughts that occur repeatedly, over time, in our brains. As advertisers know, when we repeat a message often enough, our subconscious mind takes it as true, even without objective proof. We also learn our beliefs from the people (especially caretakers) around us as we grow up.

In other words, emotions arise in us which may or may not be true and most often come from the past. We have an experince. The experience is accompanied by emotion(s). We generate thoughts about our experience, making it appear that thoughts create emotions, because they are so closely connected. In fact, emotions occur in our body, and our brain interprets the emotional experience, based on past experience and beliefs. Unless we examine and change the beliefs stored in our subconscious mind, we repeat similar experiences, accompanied by the same emotions, ad nauseum, throughout life.

This explains why some people can have a different emotional reaction to a particular situation than others. A classic joke that illustrates this is the story about a child who finds Santa Claus left a pile of manure for him. While most children would become upset about this gift, this child gives a whoop, a big smile, and grabs a shovel to begin digging in the pile of manure. When asked what he's doing, he says exuberantly, "With all this manure, there has to be a pony in here somewhere!"

This child has a belief that there is good buried; and that the good can be found. When given a pile—even of manure—his mind goes to the best possible thing, rather than to the worst. In his experience, he has found things he wants buried beneath things most of us don't want, so he reacts with joy rather than with anger or sadness. He believes good comes to him regardless of the form in which it is delivered.

The question remains whether this child's reaction is a result of nature or nurture. Did someone teach him to react emotionally in this manner or did he arrive on Earth with a particular way of responding to life that takes him in the positive direction? Are the emotions we experience part of our basic nature or did we learn how to interpret what our body experiences, using our brain to interpret those feelings, based on past experience? Or both? The fact is, we really don't have a definitive answer to this question.

Based on my clinical work, I believe it's both. We can make some changes to our basic nature (what we were born with). We can change everything we have learned since our arrival on Earth, if we choose. Yet, whether we're a basic pessimist or optimist seems to be part of who we are at the moment we arrive.

When looking at our family, do we see more of one emotion that was paid attention to rather than other emotions? For example, in my family, a lot of attention was paid to anger. As adults, my siblings and I get angry first when something happens. Some of the people in the generations after mine have also developed the "anger first" response. With my work to become a "Recovered Angry Person," this pattern has changed for me, and is changing for many in the subsequent generations after me. I know other families that have a "love first" response in life. In large measure, we learn to experience the emotions that are most paid attention to by the people intimate to our early lives, people with whom we have long-term relationships.

Once we have a tendency to focus on a particular emotion, then we surround the emotion with our thoughts. When we go looking, usually in adulthood when those people who helped form us are not around, we see the thoughts, not the exposure and training. We believe our thoughts create our emotions.

It's more realistic to think of our thoughts as supporting the emotions, which we have already learned to pay attention to.

This is important because, in attaining Emotional Mastery, we don't need to change our thoughts in order to change the emotions we feel. Instead, work with those emotions directly, heed the message and lesson, and then release. That way, we'll master the emotion, learn, and evolve. Interestingly, we will also change our thoughts, because we begin to pay attention to different things.

Because our thoughts arise from our perceptions, developing the ability to perceive a bigger picture is also effective in working with emotions. If we become angry at other drivers who cut in front of us on the freeway, for example, we can open the door to lessening the anger experienced by changing our perspective. We can perceive that it's not only the driver in front of us who is cutting in, but about 35 percent of all drivers do that. Once we have an expanded perspective, we'll experience less anger, because when a driver cuts in line ahead of us, we'll know: "Oh, you're part of the 35 percent of drivers who cut in front of others!" This change in perspective makes the offense less personal and more readily released.

MY PERSONAL LABORATORY

Speaking of not listening and partnering with your emotions, during the time I've been working on this book, I had a powerful demonstration of "not heeding."

I made a reservation for me and my RV in a national forest area of Arizona. There are nearly 40 slots for RVs and tent campers in that park. I had stayed there previously. The rules allow people to stay up to two weeks, which was my intention. Usually in such parks people are friendly to each other, but come prepared to live independently.

My goal was to edit and approve the editor's suggestion, then read aloud my entire manuscript, doing my part to get my first full-length book published.

About mid-morning, someone knocked on my RV door. My stomach was tight; but I didn't pay attention to it, or to the fact that my little dog was barking in a particularly animated way. There stood an older man, dressed roughly, dirty and walking in shoes that barely functioned as shoes. He told me he'd been charging his battery pack at another camper's RV, but they weren't home. He asked if I had some way for him to charge his battery.

Showing him the electrical plug on the outside of my van, I told him he could plug in there. The only place for him to sit was on a hard cement bench, which he told me he'd been sitting on for days, causing him much pain. I pulled out my folding chair and set it up for him. I then excused myself, telling him I had a lot of work to do, closing the door to my van while he stayed outside.

Within half an hour a hail storm arrived. He just sat in the chair. I didn't want him and the chair to get too wet, so I opened my RV door and offered him an umbrella, which he accepted. When the hail subsided, he complained that he was cold. Realizing I wasn't going to invite him into my RV, he told me he knew someone else who had allowed him to come in out the cold before; he was going there. I told him he could take my umbrella, because hail was still falling.

When he returned a couple of hours later, again knocking on my door, I was on the telephone with my son in Northern California. As I closed the door, he said, "That man has terrible energy! You need to be careful around him, Mom!" My son and I have this kind of relationship, in which we share our emotional and intuitional reactions with one another. I assured him I was having minimal contact.

The next day, the man came by my van, knocking on my door, at least five times. I opened the door, talked with him, then returned to my work. I found his presence annoying. I knew he was aiming to use me (manipulation), and gave him only minimal attention, because I just couldn't be mean to an older man who was polite but down on his luck. Later that day, I left the campground to move to another town.

During the night, I had the most horrendous nightmare, in which people were unceremoniously killed, cut up, and debased. When the nightmare awakened me at 3 A.M., my first reaction was, "That man has poisoned me! This is his energy, not mine!" It had been many years since I had a nightmare of any kind.

I grabbed the chair in which he had sat, and threw it and the umbrella out the door. I cleaned my aura (something I learned to do many years ago), told the negative energy to get out of my van, and returned to sleep.

Two days later I called my son, who had been frantically trying to contact me to find out if I was okay. I had neither cellular nor Wi-Fi service in my new location. He told me he had a strong premonition that man was going to murder me. Fortunately, with my move, that opportunity was negated.

I had felt the emotions and body tension, but hadn't paid attention to them. Both my dog and my son attempted to tell me to "pay attention!" Focused on my writing and editing tasks, I didn't listen. I don't know what would have happened with one more day at that location, but enough happened in the night once I left the man's presence that I realized, once again, emotions are constantly attempting to give us messages, to get our attention, and to guide us regarding what actions to take.

YOUR PERSONAL LABORATORY

Have you ever put yourself in danger because you didn't listen to emotions that were coming up in you? Recall any incidents in which this was true. What happened? Did you eventually avoid serious repercussions, or did something painful or hurtful happen? Write what you remember.

Now, looking at one of these incidents, identify what you felt. What was it that came up in you that you didn't pay attention to?

If you had that experience to live over again, from the beginning, would you do something different from what you chose then? What?

Take time to imagine the incident, this time with a different ending, based on what you believe you would do differently.

Check with yourself to make note of what you're feeling. If you feel better and lighter, be grateful to yourself.

Listen. Explore the answers that come to you. Allow yourself to free associate, seeing where there are connections that have meaning for you. Write this down.

Your experience may be subtle, but don't dismiss what you get because it's subtle!

Be grateful for this learning. Write what you're aware of learning.

Make a decision about listening to body sensations and emotions you experience. If you intend to listen to them and take action on the basis of what you experience, set your intention now to do that, should any similar experience occur in your future.

10

HOW AND WHEN EMOTIONAL LANDSCAPES DEVELOP

In looking at why some people are better at working with emotions than others, we need to understand how the emotional landscape develops in each of us.

We're equipped with emotions at least from the time of birth, if not before. During the first seven years of life, our focus is on having experiences and getting to know emotions, developing our patterns for what kind of relationship we'll have with the emotions inside us. We come to associate emotions with experiences, trauma, power, safety, and love. We're getting to know everything we can, including how others want us to experience and deal with emotions. Ideally, we also learn which emotions we prefer, how to partner with emotions, how to utilize emotional messages, and how to turn emotions back to the energy pool.

Little children study the people around them, so in addition to what we're taught about emotions from our caretakers, we develop emotional reaction patterns that are copied from others. Children whose parents are afraid, or who express anger and upset, for example, will learn to become fearful or can develop personalities filled with anger. Very much like putting a program into your computer, children's brains (up to the age of 12) "download" their parents' emotions, reactions, and beliefs. Then, they hold onto them, believing these as reality.

66

In 1490, adults believed the Earth was flat. A parent in all earnestness passed this "truth" on to the child. By 1495, word had reached a lot of the world that through maritime exploration, the Earth was determined to be round. Now the adults of the time taught the children the "truth" that the world was round. Much of what we're offered as "truth" about emotions, however, is how a small handful of the nearly eight billion people currently on Earth relate to the experiences and emotions that arise in life. These are not necessarily true in the larger sense; but may be true to the people who are a great influence on our development.

We also learn not to tell the truth about the emotions we're experiencing. When we're very young, we get lots of directives:

"Don't be scared; there's nothing to be afraid of."

"This is your nice grandmother. Give her some love!"

"Be brave, little man."

"Be sweet and loving, little girl."

"Be polite!"

"You tell this person you're sorry for what you did!"

Usually, those giving the directives aren't very concerned with whether we're feeling fear, anger, love, or regret. Instead, we're given the message that emotions are felt at will. This is a method for teaching us to doubt ourselves and our experiences. We can make ourselves state emotions we don't really experience. And when we comply, we're taught to lie about what we're truly feeling.

We also learn to judge some emotions as "bad" and others as "good." Certainly, we learn which emotions are acceptable in our family and with those we depend on to love and support us for our life. Over time, we learn to manage the emotions that come up in us, making sure we show certain emotions and don't show others. In short, we stop telling the truth about what we're feeling, instead substituting a socially acceptable version of the emotions we experience. Eventually, a lot of people lose the ability to tell what is really true for them emotionally.

The brains of young children are open, not good at discriminating what is best or whether something learned is beneficial or will cause difficulties. Children load on the "programs," indiscriminately developing mental and emotional landscapes. By the age of seven, when the thinking brain kicks in, these land-scapes are formed, needing only to be filled in more fully, like coloring in a drawing that has already been outlined in crayon.

Over time, the information we download, our experiences, and the interpretations given to those experiences begin to coalesce into beliefs. We don't really notice that we're forming the beliefs. We don't realize many of the beliefs we form are not accurate. Yet, because we believe something, we can experience it repeat-edly, and will argue vehemently that it's true, based on our own experience. How does this work?

As a psychotherapist, I talked with many women interested in a romantic involvement with men. When I ask for a list of the qualities wanted in a man, I've found most women believed men didn't cook, and weren't interested in cooking. After getting involved, many of the women complained about being expected to cook, because "men don't know how to cook!" Very few of this group found a man with an interest in cooking.

One of the women was young, attractive, and never learned to cook. When it came time for her list, she insisted any man in her life had to cook. Her belief was "men know how to cook; I don't." Every man this woman dated cooked, and loved to cook.

When we believe something, we involve ourselves in what is called "selective perception." We see what we need or want to see, place our attention there, feed it energy, and participate in creating it. The women who believed men didn't know how to cook focused on the ways in which men were inept in the kitchen. After a few such evidences, the talk turned to: "Joe has never been interested in cooking." Even if Joe could cook-- which was often the case-- Joe saw no point in letting on about it, because Joe enjoyed being cooked for. When asked, the woman in Joe's life could point out experiences of taking over the cooking because of how little Joe knew about cooking. The woman saw what she believed.

The other young woman, by contrast, focused attention on every little thing a man she met was able to do in the kitchen. She affirmed the man's capabilities, was thankful, and didn't make an effort to take over or take up any slack. This young woman saw and experienced what supported her beliefs, too.

Unless we consciously look at, identify and question our beliefs, and listen to the messages brought to us by the emotions that arise in us, we will follow the emotional blueprint as first established. This could be a fabulous, workable blueprint; or it could be a terrible, crash-and-burn blueprint. Regardless, we'll adhere to it, believe in it, and use the blueprint to form the ways we think about ourselves and our world.

Remember, we're designed to come to Earth, get what we can call our "homework assignments" during our early years, then use our adult lives to complete and resolve those "homework assignments" in our Giant School. The assignments are designed for us to work out. But we must know about the system, listen to and heed the emotions we experience, and dedicate ourselves to resolving the "problems/assignments" we encounter. It's a powerful system, that when used as designed, is arguably the most effective learning system ever devised.

MY PERSONAL LABORATORY

When my son was two years old, he moved very fast. He frequently bumped into things, fell down, or knocked himself sideways. When he did, he said very firmly: "That chair made my fall down." "That doorway pushed me." His dad and I, after validating his experience, showed him how his own actions had caused him to bump into the chair or run into the door jamb. We taught him how to avoid such catastrophes.

When we are two, emotions come into us with a roar. Many people say "s/he's going through The Terrible Twos." There are reasons besides the fact that emotions are bursting into a child's awareness for the Terrible Twos to occur, but in my observation the biggest reason is that emotions come in with a whoosh, are nearly overwhelming, and are so new our child doesn't yet have any kind of a handle on them.

I also believe they look real to small children. That's when children can suddenly scream and start to run, yelling: "He's chasing me!" We look, and nobody is there. We call it an imaginary playmate. I don't think what young children are seeing is always a playmate at all.

When my son was that age, he would sweetly sit in his crib at night, poring over his books. He no longer wanted me to read to him. He had memorized them and would read them, aloud, to himself.

Occasionally, however, he would call me into this room, complaining: "People are talking in my ear!" Or, "Bad people are here and they are bothering me." I took those to be the apparitions of emotions, and believed that to my son they were real. I treated them like they were real. I would rush in, dish towel in hand, fling open his windows, and wave my towel around, "chasing" those horrible people out of his room, proclaiming their need to "leave my son alone!" He would be satisfied with that and either return to his reading or lie down to sleep.

We experience emotions from the beginning of life. We become aware of emotions near the age of two. How parents respond to their children during the time those emotions are populating the child's awareness really matters a lot. As parents, who are we to believe our child's experience is not real? Why not consider it real and help our child as an ally (like emotions do for us). Children who are supported in their emotional development in such ways grow up to be unafraid of emotions, to have some idea what to do about them, and to be more trusting.

If you, like me, didn't get this kind of support, start giving it to yourself. Now.

YOUR PERSONAL LABORATORY

What emotions still plague you in your everyday life? Take yourself back in time, in your memory, and discover the first things you remember about one of those emotions in your childhood.

How did the emotion impact you?

How did the adults around you respond to you experiencing that emotion?

What help did you get with dealing with it?

If the help was not adequate, give that help to yourself now. If you don't feel you can do it alone, get help from a therapist, coach, or spiritual counselor.

Write about what you've discovered, what emotion was involved, what learning was available to you, and how you're feeling, now that the healing has been done. Savor.

11

WHAT WE DO TO MAKE WORKING WITH EMOTIONS MORE DIFFICULT

The most challenging thing we humans do routinely, regarding emotions, is to resist, which means to fight against, ignore, or refuse to learn the lesson.

For example, when situations of grief arise, it is accepted that the first thing a person experiences is denial or resistance, which is refusing to accept the reality of the situation. This natural response allows us to slow things down, so we have opportunity to absorb and allow what is happening, without getting overwhelmed. This is normal human behavior when we face obstacles that seem big to us, because we need to slow things down in order to handle them emotionally.

Because humans have demonized emotions, working to push away or hold them down inside of us, most people are in resistance to emotions most of the time. One of the biggest issues humans have with emotions is our resistance to recognizing their presence, feeling them, and paying attention to their message. The more a person is in resistance to emotions, the less the person can effectively use and move the emotions that are making life difficult. Conversely, the more a person accepts and works with emotions, the more easily life will flow.

Recall that emotions are energy in motion, designed to move. When we go into resistance to the emotions that arise in us, we slow down or stop the progress of that emotion's movement through us, obstructing our learning and often making it more painful. Most suffering in this world is due to people's resistance to what is happening, rather than to the actual events. For example, when a person refuses to forgive, think about how much energy they hold and continue to carry.

A person who welcomes emotions as friends offering a message, and embraces and follows the message, works far more effectively with emotions than one who is in resistance.

Finally, we turn to physics to look at what happens with another form of energy, electricity. Here the definition of resistance says, "the degree to which a substance prevents the flow of an electric current through it." With emotions, which are also energy, we see resistance as the degree to which our pushing emotions away prevents the flow of emotions through us. In other words, where emotions are involved, we're the substance that prevents flow. And preventing flow keeps electricity from doing its work, and from moving on to do work in the world, just as preventing flow with emotions keeps those emotions from doing work, and from moving on to do work in us and in the world.

When we resist allowing emotions to arise in us, resist allowing our experience of emotions, or push emotions away, we block the movement of the energy of those emotions. We already know blocking that energy sets the condition for the energy to grow in volume, power, and force. To keep that emotional energy from breaking through (like water building up behind a dam), we must focus a lot of our personal energy on keeping that emotion in check. Resistance to emotions focuses almost all of our energy on that emotion as we struggle to keep it contained (even as we're not consciously aware of our efforts).

When we allow the emotion to arise in us, give it room to move through, listen to its message and partner with the emotion in comprehending and utilizing that message, we can then turn the energy of the emotion loose. We no longer need to stay on top of that emotion, making sure it doesn't escape.

To become an Emotional Master, we need to face the fact that emotions are in us, and will be coming up and moving through us. Our best stance is to be both welcoming and great listeners. It's simple. Like floating in a canoe down a stream. The stream may be bumpy at first, but only because of our long-stored resistance to emotions. Remember to get help with working with long-stored emotions, so the response is neither horribly frightening, nor overwhelming. A therapist or coach can keep track of everything else, while you learn to float your canoe over every type of rapid. Once the long-held-onto emotion is fully released, the stream will become a peaceful, smooth stream on which we can drift happily.

One of the most famous quotes from Walt Kelly's long-running comic strip, *Pogo,* is "We have met the enemy, and the enemy is us." When talking about why some people can work more effectively with emotions than others, we conclude that in working with emotions, we can easily be our own worst enemy. Our resistance to step into flow, to allow life to happen as it happens and to feel the emotions that accompany our experiences, nurtures problems with emotions. The simplest step in developing Emotional Mastery is to get out of resistance, accepting ourselves and life just as they are, and being grateful for it all.

MY PERSONAL LABORATORY

My son's godmother was a direct voice medium. I met her when I was part of the Spiritualist Church, then studied meditation with her for three years after we both left the church. When I was pregnant with my son, only my husband and I were still in the meditation group from the original nine members. When the group was nearly over, we were told that all three of us would have a lot of contact with people and could help a lot of them— each in our own way—so through the group, we were brought together to strengthen and educate ourselves, in order to do the best job possible.

Long after that group ended, she offered get-togethers in her home, which I attended. I often brought people I knew, too. During those get togethers we would each pay a small fee. Then, in the group, she would deliver a message to each of us. When the message-delivery was over, we all socialized as we ate the pot luck dishes we had brought. A simple gathering, yet sometimes very profound.

At one of these meetings, she said that Simon (whom she channeled) wanted me to "think globally about fame."

"Do I have to?" I asked.

With only a brief pause, the answer came back, "Yes."

The next day I was clearing some brush on the hillside in my yard, thinking about her message. "I don't want fame!" I complained aloud.

I loved being incognito, not having to worry about my appearance when I went to the store, or having to meet anyone's expectations. I made one more statement.

"I don't want to be famous," I said. "God, if you want me to be famous, you set up the conditions, do the work, and make it happen! I like my life the way it is."

"Set and forget," I thought.

Five years later, as I began my worldwide podcast radio program, I remembered this message. "Okay, God," I said. "I'm ready. If you want me to have fame, I accept."

Apparently God's idea of what would happen in "fame" was not as terrible as I thought. Some people around the world know me or of me, but I still enjoy being incognito and not worrying about my casual appearance when I go out. Fame, if that's what it is, hasn't been so bad. We'll see what happens as I keep writing.

Emotions bring us messages that tell us what is best for us to do. If you accept the idea that we're souls here on Earth in human bodies, you may also be willing to accept the notion that we set our life up for ourselves; and we are in a constant process of doing this as we live life.

I made the accomplishment of my fame more difficult by not accepting it, and by resisting the entire idea. We do the same when we resist the emotions that arise, slowing our progress and increasing the difficulty of our lives. Here's hoping you, like me, will eventually come to the point of accepting the message and opening to the actions. The consequences of acceptance may be as gentle as mine have been.

YOUR PERSONAL LABORATORY

Here are some questions and actions for you to consider to help yourself give up resistance to emotional messages.

Make a list of emotions you see creating difficulties for you.

Ask: "What's the worst thing that would happen if I opened to embrace this emotion, learn from it, and follow its message?" If what you get is not too bad, embrace it.

Go one step further, if it fits for you, ask: "What do I intend for my life in having this emotion (or memory) arise in me now?" "How can I profit the most in dealing with it?" Listen. Take action on the response.

Keep working with yourself in these gentle, supportive ways. Embrace the emotions that arise as friends, setting your intention to partner with them to accomplish their mission. Then, be grateful to the emotions and to yourself. This will enable you to reach the promised Joy in life.

12

Common Misunderstandings About Emotions

We have already talked about how the same emotions repeat for us when we have not learned the lesson inherent in any experience and its accompanying emotions. We don't have to keep working with the same emotions, and the same set(s) of problems over and over if we learn the lessons. There are a few things that get in our way, especially in the ways we understand and relate to emotions, such as thinking of certain emotions as negative and believing all emotions are real. Let's look at these issues.

Emotions are Not Negative or Positive

Almost everyone who teaches or writes about emotions discusses "negative emotions" and "positive emotions." Even in the last several years, when more and more people are paying attention to emotions, and teaching others how to manage them, there's a judgment about "positive" or "negative" emotions. In my learning, there is no such thing: Emotions are emotions. One is not more positive or more negative than the other. Each emotion is a different form of energy designed to deliver messages and help us navigate life. Anger is as positive as love, because it draws attention to actions we need to take and changes we need to make in how we see our world. Fear is as positive as hope, because it alerts us to things we need to handle with special care. One emotion is not more "negative" or "positive" than another. Emotions just "are."

Emotions can behave negatively in our lives. This happens when we hold them inside of us (resistance), and the energy grows to powerful intensity, which is painful when we hold onto it, and painful if we're able to release it. This is when we think of emotions as negative. Guilt, hate, and shame, for example, can behave negatively when we hold onto them. No real emotion is inherently "negative." Real emotions become "negative" when held inside of us, allowing them to grow in power, enabling those emotions to create havoc and pain in our life.

EMOTIONS CAN BE "REAL" OR "SYNTHETIC"

Even though almost every human accepts emotions as real and may wrestle with them for a lifetime, certain emotions are not real. Real emotions have both positive and negative aspects. In a sense, emotions are balanced. Love, for example, is positive when we share it happily with others who want to share it with us. But have you ever had someone profess love that was unwanted by you? Or they told you they love you, but you couldn't believe what they were saying? Many of us have. That part of love doesn't feel good. The negative side of love is when it's given, and isn't genuine, and/or isn't wanted.

We all know the negative aspects of anger, which can include pouting, rage, accusations, abandonment of others, or verbal or physical attack. The positive aspect of anger is it pushes us to take action and shows us where we need to change our perceptions and expectations. Anger has positive and negative aspects; it is a real emotion. Each "real" emotion has positive and negative aspects. "Synthetic" emotions such as guilt and shame have only negative aspects.

THE SYNTHETICS OF GUILT AND SHAME

Accepting emotions like guilt and shame as "real," tends to engage us with those emotions and creates struggle. Knowing that guilt is a form of anger and shame is telling us there is something wrong with us (an idea we either downloaded, inherited, or were taught through harsh experience), allows us to refuse and not become influenced by these synthetic emotions.

Guilt: Name what is positive about guilt, for example. Some people think it serves the positive purpose of helping us keep ourselves in line, acting somewhat like a conscience. In fact, it does not behave like a conscience. Our conscience reminds us, prods us to look at what we're doing. It does not condemn, stifle, or punish us the way guilt can. Conscience does not freeze us in the past the way guilt does. In fact, we have another emotion that fulfills this conscience function better: Remorse.

What guilt does is keep us frozen in the past, keep us from taking action. We draw on our past experience (which can lead us to feel guilt) to keep ourselves from taking present action. Guilt stops us from listening to our heart and stifles creativity. Someone who abandoned her family with a very young child once told me: "I'm afraid to meet with my son. I have a hard time offering him my love when I see him." This is what guilt does. It freezes us so we cannot be present in the now. Furthermore, it's almost impossible to become "un-guilty," because about all we can do with guilt is drop it; and that's difficult to do.

Guilt is a synthetic emotion. There is nothing positive about it. It's created by the human mind and doesn't come with us when we're born.

This is how we come to have guilt in us. During our childhood, we're inculcated into the "Society of Guilty Persons," mostly by parents, advertisers, coaches, religion, politicians, and teachers.

"You're going to feel terrible if you hit that child!"

"You'll never get over this mistake!"

"Don't do that or you'll feel guilty!"

"God will take revenge and you will suffer!"

"Everybody has guilt."

Many years ago, there was a television ad for laundry detergent that promoted guilt, admonishing homemakers: If you have "ring around the collar" you're not doing a good job with the wash, and therefore aren't a good homemaker.

Another ad, aimed at men, reminded: Protect the family with insurance provided by "The Rock." If you don't, you're guilty of not caring about your family, and by reference, aren't a good husband, father, and provider.

The promotion of guilt is everywhere. We think of guilt as a positive factor in life, helping us to walk the proper path. We believe it's a real and good emotion to uphold. It's not. I no longer "do" guilt, because it hurts people, keeps them stuck, and slows learning and evolution. When I learned guilt isn't a real emotion, I dropped it from my life. Since then, I'm happier and healthier.

In listening to and working with the emotions that arise in us, we can have a less error-prone life, creating very little remorse. The remorse that arises comes from not following our true emotional guidance in the first place, and can be dealt with easily and immediately by taking responsibility for choices, and making better choices the next time.

When feeling guilty, ask: "What is this feeling doing for me?" If it's not doing something positive, consider moving past guilt and do learning powered by another emotion (such as remorse) that can help with our growth.

Shame: Shame results from a belief that there is something wrong with us. This, too, is taught to children growing up. We're shamed by adults and download the shame of significant adults into our brains. In fact, there is nothing wrong with any of us. There may be things we don't like about ourselves, things we need to change, or things others fear or don't like, but there aren't inherently things that are wrong with us. We're all here in this Giant School to grow and evolve. We don't need to feel bad in order to grow. Like young children we can grow through joy, curiosity, and adventure.

THE WAY OUT: WE NEED TO BECOME CONSCIOUS

Unless we become conscious of what has been inserted into our emotional landscape, we will maintain the same emotional programming for our entire lifetime. That's why so many of us repeat the same emotional issues over and over often with a different cast of characters, but with the same story line.

Margery Ann looked back at three marriages, all ending in divorce, to see if she could see patterns to change. Imagine her surprise when realizing that all three former partners had difficulty expressing love, were quite self-centered, immature, and depended on others for basic needs like cooking and cleaning. Each former partner had wonderful qualities, too, yet this configuration of not-so-wonderful qualities is what led Margery Ann to give up trying.

Ed had experienced two business failures. He had started off with incredible ideas, found amazing and talented partners, and yet had failed in creating the businesses he had envisioned. Both of Ed's former partners stepped in and forced Ed out of the businesses he started. He could see in hindsight how the partner had hung back and allowed him to do all the formative work. Ed was quite frustrated that the partners didn't help him more. He spent hours meeting and discussing the issue with them, but never asked them to leave or found another partner. At a certain point, when the business took off, at last earning money, the partners stepped up and took over, forcing him out.

In these examples, both Margery Ann and Ed repeated patterns relating to interacting with others, which led to similar results each time. It may take a while to catch on, but when we have repeated painful experiences such as these, it's the signal there is an emotional block in us that needs addressing. Margery Ann discovered she carried a belief that she was not lovable, so each time she selected a partner, she rushed in to show that partner how valuable she was, earning their love (she hoped). Picking people who didn't know how to express and share love, however, made this scenario a no-win for Margery Ann.

Ed, on the other hand, was sure other people were as dedicated and giving as he was, and did not face facts during the long months when he was doing all the work. Talking with his partners didn't do it, because Ed didn't take the action he needed to take, the action that feelings of frustration, anger, and hurt were telling him to take. In retrospect, he could see that he had followed the exact same pattern regarding his partner in both business ventures.

Another principle we can see at work here is: When hindsight becomes foresight, we have true insight. The trick is to stay as aware as possible in the moment so we face fact regarding the experience. We also need to take the action the emotions we feel are suggesting we take. Staying aware gives us the chance to see patterns before, and while, they are happening, enabling change.

A big part of the message is this: It's possible to change our internal emotional landscape. We can develop our relationship with emotions so the emotions serve and help us, cooperate with us, and lead us to the wonderful life we envision living. As an Emotional Master, we take charge of emotions in the present moment, and paint our own emotional landscape. We can develop the ability to put anger, guilt, worry, jealousy, loneliness and even fear under our direct authority, having mastery over those emotions and ourselves.

We have emotion-related experiences in our current life that reference directly back to emotion-related experiences from our past. It's important to know that we don't actually have to single-handedly heal emotional experiences from the past. Instead, we're set up to offer ourselves opportunities to heal emotions and emotional situations from our past. We're set on "auto pilot." Our built-in, personalized Mentor is always on the job for us. All we need to do is utilize and work with the information when it comes up on our personal "screen."

We will not keep going over the same experiences and the same emotional responses if we relate to ourselves as learners, not people with things that are wrong with us, harshly influenced by so-called "negative emotions."

MY PERSONAL LABORATORY

Gardening is my passion as an adult. I've had the good fortune of having a garden, ever since my first outrigger tomato garden outside my houseboat, grown on the surface of Lake Union in Seattle, Washington, in 1963. These were planter boxes that floated on a platform on the water's surface. As the tomatoes became heavier, the boxes tended to turn over. My inventive husband created an "outrigger" system he nailed onto the boxes so they would stay upright. Growing up on my grandparents' farm gave me a relationship with growing things and a taste for freshly-picked vegetables.

In the 1980s, I was living in Marin County, California, in the small town of Fairfax. It was time to till the garden for the Spring. I read in *Organic Farming* magazine about a study that showed fewer weed seeds germinated when farmers tilled the soil in the dark. So, I decided to use my two-cylinder rototiller, which made quite a bit of noise, to till my garden after dark. I started about 8:00 P.M.

After tilling for more than an hour, I was nearly finished with my small plot, but my rototiller ran out of fuel. As it died, I heard my home telephone ringing and ran to answer it. It was my neighbor, a man who was always pleasant, nice, supportive, and caring.

"Are you out of your mind?" he yelled at me. "Turn that engine off! No loud noises are permitted after 8:00 P.M.!"

After I gave him my apology, he told me he needed to arise early the next morning for work. And that night, it turned out, was the first night of the "summer sleeping" he and his wife did each year. This meant moving their bed onto the outside deck and sleeping under the stars. They were attempting to sleep right above where I was rototilling.

Every day for the next three days I thought about completing the job of rototilling my garden. Even when I knew this neighbor was not home, I found myself unable to turn on the rototiller, much less run it long enough to complete the tilling. On the fourth day, exasperated with myself, I sat down for a self-to-self talk.

"What's going on?" I asked myself.

"I'm afraid to turn on the rototiller. I don't want Bill to yell at me like that again."

"Bill's not even home," myself argued.

"I know, but I can't stand him yelling at me like that. It's like my father yelled at me. I don't want that from anyone. I'm an adult now, and I don't want to be belittled."

"Understandable," replied my kind self.

This got me thinking. My neighbor yelled at me the way my abusive father yelled (at least it was reminiscent, happened when I didn't expect it, and felt harsh). I felt immobilized, the way I did as a child. My reaction was way out of proportion to the event, which I knew was a sign this experience tied back to my past, to something I hadn't completed and released. This was one of those times, when what was happening in the present was tying in to something in my past, giving me an opportunity to complete it and release it, so I no longer carried it with me.

I knew there were two ways to accomplish this:

1) Go into the past through my imagination. Recall this same type of pain as I experienced it in the past. Take someone strong with me in my imagination for backup. Speak to my father and tell him how his behavior had affected me for the past 40 years, followed by setting limits on my willingness to ever have him speak to me that way again. This was taking power over the past.

2) Take power in the present. This meant going to talk with my neighbor, setting limits with him about how he could talk to me, requesting him never to yell, "Are you out of your mind?" or anything like it at me again.

I had learned the importance of taking back my power. This meant getting in charge of what happens in my life by telling others what I will tolerate and the kind of behavior I want them to exhibit toward me. I decided to talk to my neighbor of more than 10 years.

We agreed to meet. I went to his home. His wife was also present. I realized the words were nearly choking me, but gently insisted to myself to say what I had come to say. "Bill," I began. "Have I ever given you a reason to believe I will not cooperate with you if you ask me for a change?"

"No," he said.

"Then I have something I want to ask you. I'm aware you don't know that my father was abusive. Because of that I'm very sensitive to how people—particularly men—address me. The other night when you wanted me to stop running the rototiller, you said 'Are you out of your mind?' instead of just asking me to stop what I was doing. The way you talked to me was stunning and painful. I'm here to ask you never to talk to me in that tone of voice or with those kinds of words again. Will you agree not to talk to me that way, ever again?"

"Of course," Bill assured me. "You have made the change I requested—we've got no problem together. In the future, I will just ask you to make whatever change I need from you."

He apologized for speaking so harshly, remarking at how frustrated he was during the hour my rototiller roared and he was unable to reach me to ask me to stop.

"Thank you," I offered, feeling incredibly relieved. I again apologized to them.

The three of us talked for a few more minutes. Bill revealed that he knew about the hours for not making excessive noise because he had violated that rule some years earlier. Someone got upset with him for the same thing.

It was Saturday. I knew for a fact that Bill and his family were home. I went immediately to my garden and finished the rototilling and planted my seeds. By taking power in the relationship with Bill, and having him cooperate with me instead of remaining belligerent the way I experienced with my father, I healed the current issue, and also healed myself emotionally from the past. I had no further problems with my neighbor, Bill, who continued to be his supportive, kind, agreeable, and pleasant self.

Remember, when we complete a lesson, we're finished with it forever. While the issue of being spoken to in harsh and abusive ways was with me for 40 years, when I had this experience with Bill, in the subsequent 35 years (as of this writing), I haven't experienced such a tongue-lashing again.

YOUR PERSONAL LABORATORY

Record an experience you had in which the emotions you felt during it: 1) reminded you of similar emotional experience(s) from your past, 2) brought you to an "out of proportion" reaction to what was actually happening, and 3) in which you felt at least partially helpless.

Once you identify how the more recent emotional experience was like the earlier one, make note of whether you want to heal this type of emotional experience. If you do, will you heal it through your imagination or by directly talking with those involved in present time? For healing through imagination, write what you want to say, what or who you might bring along for added power. Take the action. For healing through the present, talk with the person(s) involved and ask for what you want. Take power. Note what happens in the situation, and most especially, in you.

13

WHY ARE SOME PEOPLE BETTER AT WORKING WITH EMOTIONS?

We're familiar with the idea that different people arrive on the Earth with different talents, things we do well, and do well with little effort. In a similar way, some people are born to work better with emotions and have a natural talent for doing so.

We also learn how to work with emotions. Either we're taught by caretakers and teachers, we figure out what works best, or we copy what we see others do. Some learning is more suited to the task of working with emotions, and some is not; hence some people develop a better ability to work with emotions, and others develop less effective ability. How we're responded to when we're learning makes a difference in how talented we become in working with emotions.

In working with emotions, practice makes us better. Like driving a car, the first few times we drive, we're shaky. We feel afraid, unfamiliar with what we're doing and don't know the limits or capabilities of the car. Yet, with practice, we not only drive, but listen to music, engage in conversations, talk on the telephone, argue with others, eat or drink, put on makeup, and many other things. All because now we're familiar with what we're doing so many of the tasks we accomplish are habitual and feel easy to do. We don't have to overcome fear each time to have this experience.

As we develop our ability to work with emotions, we don't feel shaky about acknowledging, feeling, and working with those that arise in us. As with driving the car, our relationship with emotion becomes a little bit more automatic, so we can work with emotions at the same time we live our life. With emotions, experience in working with them makes working with them more automatic and easier.

Whether we have an affinity or talent for working with emotions (ours and those of others), we've learned how to do it, or we've practiced over and over again, some people will be better at working with emotions than others. Note that some people can't balance a checkbook, design a rocket ship, perform surgery, cook a meal, or teach a lesson as well as some others can. We're all good at different things.

Remember, we can all be at least good at working with emotions. After all, as we live our lives, we have opportunity to get to know and work with emotions every day. Since we're already doing the work, why not aim for becoming the master of emotions, allowing emotions to do the work designed for them to do, helping us live satisfying, easily-flowing lives, without working harder than we need to? This is what Emotional Mastery is all about.

MY PERSONAL LABORATORY

One of the things I have taught people in my workshops on emotion is that others can feel and react to the emotions we hold, even if we don't speak them aloud. To demonstrate this, I devised an exercise.

First, demonstrate. I choose a partner, and tell them I'm going to test their arm strength. On their dominant arm, I place one hand on the shoulder and the other on the wrist. When I say aloud "ready, resist," I put pressure, two times on their wrist, with the instruction that they're to resist this pressure as much as they can.

After they lower their arm and shake out their hand, I resume the posture. This time, I think in my head three times, something negative about them. It doesn't have to be true. I repeat it in my mind each time I put pressure on their wrist.

Another lowering of the arm and hand shaking, and another two attempts to view their arm strength. This time, I think three times a positive thought about them, which also doesn't have to be true.

Then we talk. During the first round of two downward pressures, people usually keep their arm strong and steady. During the second round, people lose strength, and remarkably so. During the third round, their strength returns, and is sometimes better than in the first round.

I explain to them what I was doing in my mind, then ask them to pick a partner and repeat the exercise.

Even when everybody knows what is being done, the partners still lose strength in the second round, when something negative is thought, and regain strength in the third round with positive thoughts. What we have in our mind definitely affects others. We know that what we concentrate on also brings up emotions, which are, in turn, affecting the person's arm strength.

In one workshop, no matter what, one man didn't follow the pattern. He was surprised at this. We worked with it as a class. I asked him: "Did you ever make a decision, as a child, that you were never going to let anyone get to you?"

He started laughing immediately, saying his relationship was so bad with his father that he made this decision when he was quite young.

The power of all emotions was reduced for this man, as a result of making an early-life decision not to let anyone "get to him" emotionally. We can do this, too. We lessen the power of emotions when we refuse to accept them. We can restore ourselves to better functioning just by remaking the decision, opening the door for others to connect with us emotionally.

YOUR PERSONAL LABORATORY

The decisions we make as children can have great longevity.

Are you struggling because you can't seem to break through a challenge, even though you really want to? Ask yourself if you've ever made a decision that you would "never do" or "never have" whatever it is you're wrestling with.

When you find old decisions it's easy to reverse them by making a new decision. I do it in this form: "From this moment on, I give myself permission to allow others to get through to me, whenever I decide." The last phrase, "whenever I decide" is to assure you that you're still in charge, and won't open yourself to the hell that caused you to close yourself down in the first place. You can also use the phrase "whenever I'm ready."

A dear friend of mine asked me to help her through the last stages of her life. She was a very strong person, in mind, body, and spirit. She had an illness which she knew was in the process of killing her. She rejoiced the day she was able to make the decision to "allow myself to die, whenever I and my body are ready."

One winter night, she was taken out to a celebratory dinner. She came home very happy, and went to sleep. She never awoke. That night, she and her body were ready.

It's that powerful. Look at decisions you may have made as a child. If they're now working against you, remake them and say your new choice aloud.

Write what happens.

14

IS THERE ONE THING THAT CAN LESSEN THE POWER OF EMOTIONS?

Is the real question: "Is there one thing that can keep emotions from turning my life upside down?" Or is it: "Is there a way to cut back on the role emotions play in my life and weaken emotion's power over me?"

To answer the second question: "No." Emotions are always with us, forever playing a role in our lives. Emotions have the power over us that we allow them to have. We cannot get rid of emotions. We cannot legislate when emotions arise in us. We cannot refuse any specific emotion. As stated before, working with emotions is like working with the energy of water, electricity, or wind. We can't make these things go away. We cannot end them. We cannot even reliably regulate when they have power. What we can do is channel this energy, direct it to do work or to move through without harm. This is also what we can do with the energy of emotions.

As to the first question, the answer is: "Yes." There is one thing to lessen the control emotions have and that is to accept the presence of emotions similar to the way we accept the presence of our right hand, pancreas, eyes, and legs. Accept that emotions are there, are what they are, and arise in us to perform a function to make our life work well for us.

Once this idea is accepted, we can do more things. We can learn the message of each emotion, develop ways of partnering with the emotions that arise, and focus on learning the life lessons connected to our experiences (which are always accompanied by emotions).

When we:

- Accept emotions as an omnipresent part of life.

- Allow emotions to arise in us.

- Learn and understand the message of each emotion.

- Partner with emotions to listen and learn, which will end our resistance to feeling the emotion.

- Learn the larger lessons accompanying the emotional experience.

- Are grateful and turn the emotions loose to go on their way.

Then emotions will play a far less powerful or disruptive role in our lives. In fact, we can develop the ability to experience, feel, and resolve incredibly powerful emotions within minutes, with minimal upset. This is what is possible when we step into the realm of Emotional Mastery.

MY PERSONAL LABORATORY

In the 1980s, every week there was a drop-in volleyball evening at the high school in my town. Most of the people who came to play volleyball called themselves Sprockets, because they worked for George Lucas in his studio doing special effects. They were nice young people. I enjoyed going as often as I could to play volleyball with them for a couple of hours.

Over the weeks, I became aware that men and women played the game differently. If two women had a chance to hit the ball, they often stepped back and allowed it to fall on the floor between them. If it was two men in the same situation, they would knock each other down while trying to get the hit. When a new man joined the group, he soon noticed this, too. In an effort to improve the game, he would yell at the women: "Get the ball, Girlie!" Most annoying.

While all the women were bothered by his approach, no one seemed to be willing to speak to him about what he said. After three weeks, I talked with him. "Hi," I said, extending my hand. "I don't think we've met. My name is Ilene. If you would use my name when you see a ball coming my way, I think I'll respond faster. Will you do that?" He readily agreed.

The next time the ball headed my way, he dutifully yelled "Get the ball, Ilene!" My message was not strong enough to alert him to his behavior however. For all the rest of the women playing, he continued to yell: "Get the ball, Girlie!"

Since accepting emotions strengthens our relationship with them, it was important for me to use the annoyance and anger I felt toward this man to help me create what I wanted: Not to be called "Girlie." Once I accepted the emotion, and respected him enough to allow him to just be who he was, without making him bad or wrong, I came up with a solution that worked beautifully for me.

YOUR PERSONAL LABORATORY

Is there someone in your life who is not talking to you the way you wish to be spoken to? What emotions does it stimulate?

Are you embracing those emotions, and using them to help you come up with a solution that works for you?

Find the situation. Identify the emotions. Partner with them by asking them what they want you to learn.

Imagine the best way to implement the advice.

Take action.

None of us is fully conscious. We don't know, some of the time, how we're impacting those around us. If someone is impacting you in an uncomfortable way, partner with the emotions that come up in you to help you devise a way to let them realize their impact and ask them for what you want instead.

15

WHY DO EMOTIONS KEEP COMING BACK?

Briefly, emotions return because we're not complete with them. Human beings are like onions with layer upon layer of emotion packed on top of one another. We can work a very long time to remove layers of our emotional "onion," only to discover after a time that there are still more layers that need removing. Sometimes, it seems like the number of layers is endless. But in my experience, personally and professionally, there is an end to the number of layers. Fortunately for us that "internal something" that helps us to complete life's homework assignments has a lovely way of not giving us more than we can handle.

What this means is we can work diligently, even for a period of years, and resolve dozens of issues. We then have a period of time where life flows smoothly and we feel peaceful and complete. Then something happens. Suddenly, it feels like the rug was pulled out from under us. We're confused and angry, because our belief was we were finished peeling off the layers. The fact is we still have some layers to go. What we've been doing, during this time of feeling peaceful and resolved, is building strength and depth, so we can handle the next layers, which are usually much more intense or difficult. We need breathing room and extra strength, which we obtain through this quiet time.

MY PERSONAL LABORATORY

I had a lot of wounding from my childhood. As an adult, I became aware that I was constantly anxious, fearful, filled with anger, depressed, held low self-esteem, maintained a very low self-concept, feared taking chances, was shy, feared rejection, and was terrified of being hit or abused. To mend myself, I went to therapy for six and a half years, during an eight-year period, starting at the age of 22.

My last therapist was social worker Shirley Luthman, co-founder and co-director of the Family Therapy Institute in San Rafael, California, where I later took a professional Advanced Family Therapy course. Working with Shirley, I thought uncovering emotional traumas and problems would never end. No matter how much I worked on issues or with particular emotions, they kept coming back.

Shirley assured me there was an end, and that some deep part of me was monitoring and directing my growth. She said this part of people never gave them more than they needed in order to grow. She described the process like this:

1. Problem is presented and is very intense: Resolve and move on.

2. Quiet period. Life seems better for a time, for months or years. Inside, these changes are being sorted into their proper "cubbyholes" for safekeeping.

3. Problem is presented again, this time a deeper and more painful part of the issue or emotion. Resolve and move on.

4. Quiet period. Life seems better for a time, for months or years. Inside, these changes are being sorted into their proper "cubbyholes" for safekeeping.

This process, it turns out, repeats and repeats, until we get to the absolute bottom of the issue, when we finally finish it and it doesn't return again.

Seven calm and happy years after my last therapy session with Shirley, my life started to turn upside down. I was irritable, with anger escaping in every direction it could, as often as it could. I was also exceptionally fearful, not at all centered, and watching everyone for the "significance" of their actions and statements toward me. In short, I was paranoid and felt like I was thrashing about. I told my husband to stand back, because something was happening and I was going to let it happen so I could find out more about it.

After all that therapy, what emerged was the awareness that my entire life had, up to that time, been lived on the basis of my fear of rejection. I finally saw that my life occurred in three recurring segments: Being rejected, getting over being rejected, and getting ready to be rejected.

All that time in therapy, and this had never emerged, even though it was a pillar of my life. I realized this information was so profound and painful, I couldn't have handled it earlier in my life. Now, I was ready. I accepted this information and began working on ways to release the fear of rejection forever. I realized that my birth mother, who had taken such poor care of me early in my life, never rejected me. She was just focusing on herself to the extent that I became non-important to her, except for every once in a while. I realized, I had never been rejected. I had just been forgotten. Both hurt, but being forgotten was easier on my psyche. My fear of rejection, I realized at last, was not real, because I never had been rejected. Realizing this, I let it go; and it has never returned.

If emotions or challenges keep repeating, keep working on them. That "special something" deep inside of you, is guiding you to total release, precisely when you're able to handle the deepest part of that emotional state or challenge.

YOUR PERSONAL LABORATORY

Is there an emotional issue or challenge that has plagued you for years? A worry that a loved one won't come back home one day? A deep fear that your children will get hurt irreparably? A concern that you're never equal to tasks you're expected to complete? The "I'm not good enough (for you, for anything)" syndrome? Take some time now to identify your deepest emotionally connected challenge.

Talk to this "something deep inside." If you're ready, tell it aloud: "I'm ready to complete this learning around not feeling equal to any task or situation. Please show me all that I need to learn in order to finish this issue. Thank you." Keep asking this question until you reach an "aha" moment regarding this issue. Write about it.

If this task is overwhelming, please find your own coach, counselor, psychotherapist, or spiritual counselor who doesn't have personal connection to you and thus can be neutral (and you don't feel you have to take care of them).

Embrace the learning that's there for you to complete. Keep working on it until, like me, the core of the issue shows itself and you can at last put it to rest.

Once completed, appreciate and be grateful to yourself and that "something deep inside" for what you are able to do.

16

SECTION SUMMARY OVERVIEW

We've taken a long look at emotions. In order to make different choices in life, behave differently, and change what was given in the past that doesn't really work, look at the emotions that arise. Use the process I call: Facing fact—looking squarely and honestly at "what is." Let's do a brief summary of what we have "faced fact" about.

- Emotions are part of us and are part of life. Emotions don't go away. Our resistance to feeling and working with them underlies most of our problems.

- Each emotion is a different form of energy, each form aiming to give us a message about how to navigate life. We human beings are here on Earth to learn and progress, aimed, overall, at creating a better understanding and relationship with love. Emotions work to keep us on track.

- Emotions don't belong to us, but arise in us. Relating to "the emotions I feel" or "the emotions that come up in me" allows us to separate enough to work fully with emotions

- We learn through experiences. Emotion is part of every experience. We can either accept the emotion, heed the message, learn, and move on; or we can refuse the message (resistance), not learn from it, and stay stuck. Stuck emotions can get unstuck if we give up resistance and deliberately work with the emotions.

- We develop our internal emotional landscape during the first seven years of life. Unless we examine and/or change that landscape, we'll continue to have the same kinds of emotional experiences and issues throughout our lifespan. We'll have similar emotional experiences, over and over, with only the characters and circumstances changing.

- Emotions are provided as part of the navigational system for life. Emotions are energy and follow the laws of physics that govern energy. The message each emotion brings inherently tells us the best actions to take and paths to follow in our situation.

- Emotions held inside tend to grow. Some can eventually explode or create havoc in our lives. Anger held onto long enough can kill.

- Emotions begin in the body, usually arising as a combination of body experiencing and thinking. Emotional reactions and experiences also develop as a combination of nature and nurture. We have innate reactions to emotional experience and we also learn our reactions.

- Emotions are neither positive nor negative. We experience emotions as negative only as a result of holding emotions inside of us over time.

- Some emotions are real, some are synthetic. Real emotions have both positive and negative aspects. It's important not to be taken captive by emotions that aren't real.

- Resistance determines our ability to handle emotions well or less well. Resistance is one of the most pervasive and difficult emotional issues, when we refuse to allow ourselves to acknowledge, feel, or deal with the emotions, and accompanying experiences, that arise in us.

- Our internal self is constantly working to help resolve and put to rest emotional experiences and issues from the past. This is how we grow and evolve. Emotions constantly work to help this resolution. All we need to do is allow ourselves to have and feel emotions and identify and cooperate with their message, to successfully navigate our life.

- It's possible for us to get in charge of the emotions we experience, finishing with particular lessons, and going on to other (usually easier) lessons.

This is the process of Emotional Mastery—getting in charge of directing the energy of emotions, rather than having emotions dictate our life and experiences. Know that Emotional Mastery is possible. Stop pushing emotions down. Instead, kick Emotions Into Motion, thus leading a more conscious, fluid, and fulfilling life. Having our Emotions in Motion is what being alive is all about.

SECTION 3

EMOTIONS

17

INTRODUCTION TO EVERYDAY
EMOTIONAL STATES

In this section, I give you basic information about emotions, along with the signals of nine everyday emotions and emotional states. Some emotions are combined with others that are closely similar, so we will really learn about 12 emotions and emotional states. This short overview of each emotion gives some of the salient facts to help with recognizing and working with each emotion at an introductory level.

For each of the emotions of anger, guilt and depression, hurt, fear, anxiety, stress, intimacy and love, loneliness, jealousy, and shame and remorse, I give information about:

- Cause/Origin

- Signal/Message

- The Lesson: How to find it

- The Lesson: How to release the emotion and move on

I offer basic information to allow us to start thinking about, understanding, and taking definitive steps to change our relationship with a particular emotion, as well as with all the emotions we experience in life.

Remember, we don't own the emotions that arise in us. A major thrust of my life work is recognizing that emotions aren't designed to own us either. Emotions are tools. Every human being has access to these tools. In its magnificent design, however, each of us has a very personal relationship with emotions, just as working with a Mentor. The Mentor is the same person working with many clients, yet each client has assignments and support that are custom-made for each person's challenges. We experience the same basic emotions, yet our relationship with those emotions, how powerful the emotions are, which emotions we feel most often, what kind of consequence or benefit each emotion brings can be different for each of us. Even children in the same family experience anger over different things, as anger is always tailor-made for the situation and learning of each child.

Humans are in the midst of making a change, from living in a three-dimensional, material world, to understanding that all that is material is energy. Today we're busy changing our understanding of reality from material to energetic. Recognizing that everything is energy allows us to make better sense of things. Learning to work with this energy, partner with it, and use it as intended, can open us to amazing, spectacular lives, in addition to allowing us to become the leader of our lives, staying in charge of directing the energy of the emotions we experience.

We also cannot control energy. We can direct it, work with it, and understand its abilities and limitations. It's also vital for us to accept these basic "laws" or "rules" about all energy, including emotions:

- Controlling the energy of emotions is impossible.

- Energy (emotions) can neither be created nor destroyed.

- Energy (emotions) is designed to move.

- Blocking the energy of movement (movement of emotions) creates resistance.

- Built-up energy (emotions) can be destructive.

This means we can't get rid of energy (emotions). It's vital to keep emotional energy moving, because if we don't, it builds up and can get destructive, exhibiting our resistance to its flow. Despite our best efforts, the emotional energy we try to hold onto seeks a route for escape. This can make us miserable and detract us from the life we really want, whether we're struggling to hold onto the emotional energy or we're enduring the destructive aspects of its explosive release.

Remember these things about the energy of emotion through this brief overview of common, everyday emotions.

My Personal Laboratory

In my first marriage we had cats. When we lived on the Presidio in San Francisco for a year, our cat Freddy was hit by a speeding jeep and killed. We were on vacation. Our kindly neighbor wrapped his body and kept it in his freezer for us, so we could say good-bye and bury him on our return.

Ready to dig a hole for his little body, I realized I was terrified of death. I didn't want to touch Freddy's body. My husband, who was also a psychotherapist, urged me to just touch him, which I finally did. His fur was still soft. Though his body was stiff, he was still our sweet Freddy. With my husband's help, I faced the death of a creature I really loved. I had feared death my entire life.

When we feel fear, we often walk away from it, trying to ignore it so the fear will go away. In studying fear, I've found this never works. When we close fear out, it doesn't really disappear. When it shows up, initially, it's in front of us, where we can see and deal with it. When we walk away, the energy of the fear circles around, and allegorically, when it comes back again it hits us over the head, from behind. This makes it much more difficult to deal with the fear.

The first step to dealing with fear is to face it directly, as I was helped to do in facing Freddy's dead body. I call this "stepping into the fear." Inevitably, our experience of fear is much less difficult than our fear of the fear. Confronting Freddy's death taught me this.

YOUR PERSONAL LABORATORY

There are basic things in life with which all of us feel challenged. Birth, death, loss, and change, for example.

Pick the one from this list that is most challenging for you. Identify the emotions that arise in your body when you think about the challenge.

Pick one of these emotions to address. Ask yourself and your body questions such as, "What about this challenge frightens me?" "What's the worst thing that could happen if that occurred?" "How capable am I of dealing with that worst thing?"

For most people, this is enough to encourage them to go ahead and deal with the challenge effectively. (If this isn't true for you, it's your signal that it's time to get help!) Focus on the emotion you've selected in this section and deal with it as described. When you feel resolved, release the challenge and the emotion. Let them go.

Facing your challenge and its accompanying emotion is a big job. When you've cleared this issue for now, savor your feelings and be grateful to yourself.

Record your experience.

18

ANGER

Ever notice how different people in the same family get angry about different things? We get sensitized to focus on different emotions based on our experiences, especially those in the first seven years of life when our Emotional Landscape is forming.

A major influence is birth order. The oldest child tends to get angry about people getting into their things. That's what younger siblings do. Oldest children believe this shouldn't occur. The family's youngest child tends to get angry about being told what to do. That's what everybody who came before the youngest child tends to do. I'm a middle child. We get angry about being ignored or not getting noticed, which reflects our early life experiences when we're neither the first-born, nor the cutest.

Keep in mind that all the emotions we feel are Messengers working to draw our attention to things we need to notice, work with, and change.

ANGER'S UNIVERSAL CAUSE

One of the first things human beings do is develop a way to keep the world from seeming chaotic. We do this by observing, drawing conclusions, and lumping our thoughts and conclusions together into beliefs, which are housed in our Subconscious mind, out of the way, and out of our conscious awareness. Nature has invented an ingenious way of helping us find our beliefs, going by way of emotions.

Anger results when the idea we have about how things are supposed to work in the world is violated. Another way of seeing this is we become angry when our beliefs about the world are shown to be untrue.

We organize these beliefs in the form of "shoulds." We totally believe these shoulds are correct and will never be violated.

"Mom should always give me a hug and say 'hello' when she comes home." If Mom doesn't do that, we get angry.

"Dad shouldn't talk to me with a loud voice." If he does, we get angry.

Each of us carries a list of "shoulds" and "should not's" around with us. These form the basis of anger that arises in us. Some people have more "shoulds" than others. They feel angry a lot. Our "shoulds" are formed in the first seven years of our lives, and can be "borrowed" or "downloaded" from others, too. Almost everyone feels some anger when another person butts in line or takes the last cookie without sharing. These are "shoulds" most of us learned in Kindergarten.

The interesting thing is that if the expectations in our "shoulds" were correct and true, those "shoulds" would never get violated. Yet, they are violated. This means that our "shoulds" are incorrect. As adults, we need to update these "shoulds" and it's anger's job to alert us to this need and to identify precisely what needs to change.

Anger attempts to draw our attention to places where our ideas about reality are rigid and incorrect, so we can update these beliefs.

ANGER'S MESSAGES

Most emotions offer a single main message. Anger offers us two.

1. Your idea of how things are supposed to work in this world is incorrect. Update it.

2. Take action.

Do you remember the movie, *Network*? It's famous for the line, "I'm mad as Hell; and I'm not going to take it anymore!"

This is a perfect demonstration of the power of anger's message. We experience anger, and we no longer wish to accept things as they are. It's also a statement about anger pushing people to take action.

Anger's ability to push us to take action is one of the great things about anger. It won't allow us to accept the status quo. Because we experience anger, we feel both a need and a right to take action. Too frequently we wait until anger builds up in us, so when we take action we're forceful, more negative, or more hurtful than we might otherwise allow ourselves to be.

Unfortunately, when we do something new, we're often not very steady in our actions. Once we take the action a few times, though, we get smoother and kinder. Anger can lead us, eventually, to take action without needing to become angry first. To do this, we need to decide to take action the instant we're aware of starting to feel upset or angry about the situation, knowing anger is signaling us we need to make change, and setting about to search for and identify that change. Here's what anger is designed to help us do:

- Feel
- Identify the signal
- Find the change needed
- Make the change
- Move on

Anger comes up to tell us we're viewing the world incorrectly and need to change as well as to push us to take action. Whenever anger comes up, stop and look for what we think "should" or "should not" happen. Take steps to update these ideas. Then take the action needed in the situation, as gently as possible.

Consider following this Principle: Get anger out of you, but not onto others.

When we dump the anger we feel on others, there's a tendency for others to get angry back. If we're living responsibly, we'll need to stay around to help work all this anger out, which can take a lot of time and effort as we repair the relationship. Instead, when you notice you're angry, go off alone for a few minutes. Blow off steam before returning to interact with others. Identifying what we may feel hurt about is a tremendous help in dealing with anger. We'll save ourselves a lot of grief and time by also working with the hurt that's present.

FINDING ANGER'S LESSON

In addition to the signal, the anger we feel is bringing to our attention something we need to learn. Searching for the lesson, and learning it, completes our experience with particular angers, so they don't have to keep coming around to draw our attention to the same lessons.

Madelyn was angry with her husband Joe for years, because when the toilet paper roll emptied when he was in the bathroom, he never replaced it with a new roll. She tried talking reasonably, instructed him on how to replace the roll, complimented his meager efforts, begged, and fumed. Nothing worked. Relationships often "stick" on small points like this one.

Madelyn's " should" was that whoever emptied the toilet paper roll would be the person to replace it. Her should was incorrect, because Joe didn't share her imperative. It was Madelyn's idea of how the world was, not Joe's. Instead of being angry with Joe, Madelyn needed to learn to change her expectation. If she did this by reminding herself that: "Some people never change the toilet paper roll when they empty it; and Joe is one of those people," she would feel less angry. She would also be accepting him just as he is. Because replacing the roll was important to Madelyn, she would need to take responsibility to replace it. She didn't have to; but since it was vital to her and not to Joe, it was up to her.

The inherent lesson was this: Madelyn was disrespectful of Joe. Respect is one of the seven skills of love, the act of accepting others as they are, without needing to change them. Her many efforts to get Joe to change demonstrated not accepting him as he was.

Madelyn also wasn't taking full responsibility for something that was important to her: Replacing the toilet paper roll. She attempted for years to shift something that was important to her onto Joe, without being responsible for what was vitally important to her, and was not actually Joe's responsibility.

In this way she was disrespectful to herself. She'd endured years of getting upset, never making sure what was important to her actually happened, regardless of who did it.

Joe could have learned to put the roll on out of love and concern for Madelyn, but that's another discussion.

If Madelyn changes her shoulds and takes responsibility for replacing the toilet paper roll, it often happens that Joe will start complying with her wishes. The pressure is off. Joe has more opportunity to act out of love and concern, no longer feeling disrespected and pressured by Madelyn pushing for how she thinks he should behave.

Every time anger appears in life, it's offering us messages and giving us opportunities to learn lessons. It's up to us whether we take the opportunity. If we decline, it will come up again. What- or who-ever is the creator of our world doesn't quit until we learn the lessons that arise, no matter how long it takes.

RELEASING THE ENERGY OF ANGER

Just the act of heeding the message and learning the lesson anger brings, releases its energy a lot. For what lingers, the best things to do are:

- Forgive ourselves for the erroneous ideas and actions that anger has shown were in us

- Be grateful to anger for helping us to grow

Almost always, under anger is hurt. Identifying and dealing with the hurt is a marvelous way of releasing anger's energy.

MY PERSONAL LABORATORY

Soon after I asked my second husband to leave he moved in with Jane. They stayed together for 12 years. He came to my home to pick up our son once when I was not at home, and afterwards I saw evidence that Jane had been in my home, even though she had never accepted my invitations to come in when I was there. I certainly felt violated and angered by her intrusion, and told my ex about it.

On a hot summer day a few months later, my ex-husband came again to pick up our son. Jane stayed in the car, which was parked in our driveway, the hot sun beating down. I knew she must be uncomfortable.

A mutual friend of ours, Gene, was visiting me. My ex got into a lengthy discussion with him, all the while Jane was sitting in the car. As I made myself some iced tea, I had an idea. Opening the door, I said: "If Jane doesn't want to come in, would she like to sit in the yard and drink some iced tea?"

"Not with you that angry!" he responded, saying good-bye to Gene and leaving abruptly.

I was stunned. I was totally unaware of feeling angry, so where had that come from? I asked Gene, "Did I seem angry to you when I invited Jane to come into the yard?"

He said, "Yes."

I was stunned even more deeply. Was I angry? I couldn't find any anger.

After a long examination, I came to this conclusion. When I went to the door, I was full of enthusiasm about my idea. When

I stated it aloud, there was a lot of force and power in it. That force and power, I realized, seems like anger to a lot of people when it comes out of me. I was not angry, but I had expressed myself fully and powerfully. I watched myself regarding this for a few years, realizing I affected people in this way in many different situations. I learned to modulate this part of me, explain to people that I was not angry when I saw a certain look cross their face, and also started to become a "less angry" person.

The people in my life knew all about my relationship with anger, so it was natural that my ex would experience my expression as motivated by anger. I knew clearly it was not in that instance, yet by looking at it I discovered a part of myself I'd never paid attention to previously.

When we carry anger, we cut our personal power off at the knees. Since it's our most active emotion, always working and attempting to escape, we use a lot of our personal energy trying to keep it in line. Then, when we express ourselves with great force and power, this can be experienced by others as an outburst of anger.

YOUR PERSONAL LABORATORY

How does anger impact your life?

Do you have a lot of it, like I did, and need to constantly work to contain it? Does anger hardly ever arise, so people tell you they feel angry about situations you experience, yet you don't feel angry? Is the anger that rises up in you well-modulated, so it continues to give you messages, yet doesn't take over your interactions and your life? Find out by spending time with yourself looking. Write what you find out.

Note when my ex accused me of being angry I didn't get defensive. Instead, I became curious and sought feedback from another source. It's okay to ask others how they're experiencing you. Good friends will tell you the truth, no matter how uncomfortable it makes them.

We're all here to learn more about who we are and who we can be. Every experience, every emotion, and everyone in our environment is here essentially to help us with this task. Ask, ask, ask. Ultimately, it's all a plan to get to know Love in all its permutations. Especially if it feels like "not love," get curious and find out more about what you're carrying around, and what comes out of you.

19

HURT

Hurt is an unacceptable emotion in our world. A man who says he feels hurt is often viewed with disdain or labeled a "Woos." A woman who says she feels hurt is most often judged: "Isn't that just like a woman? Poor thing, she's hurt!" (said sarcastically). Even though we all feel hurt at one time or another, it's not acceptable to claim that emotion.

Interestingly, hurt is usually under anger. One of the fastest ways to release anger is to find and acknowledge the hurt that is underneath.

Anna dated her fiancé for six years. During that time, he spoke frequently about intending to marry her, about what they might do when married, and how happy he was to think of her being his wife. Yet, no steps were taken to ask or to set a date for the wedding. Her fiancé talked so much about marriage she was certain his proposal was imminent. Though she needed a new kettle to warm water for her morning tea at her home, she postponed purchasing one, believing it unnecessary because her fiancé already had a very nice one which would be theirs to use, once they were married.

Then one day he said, "I've decided to wait another year before asking you to marry me."

She felt crushed and hurt. Without any explanation, he did what to her seemed like an "about face" on marriage, asking her to wait even longer than the six years she had already waited. Though she decided to accept his decision without further discussion, Anna felt hurt. The hurt caused Anna to step back from the relationship, which her fiancé seemed not to notice. She considered that perhaps this was not the man for her.

If it was acceptable to claim feeling hurt, Anna might have had a deeper discussion with her fiancé. Two years later, after they were married, Anna learned that his sibling, with whom he was very close, had questioned whether he was fully ready for marriage, and exhorted him to wait. It had nothing to do with Anna; yet she was given no reason to know that. Over time, the hurt came out in bits, through disagreements, which never elicited the full explanation until long after the wedding. How different things would have gone if Anna felt free to register the hurt, moving the energy of the emotion, and getting all of this out into the open at the time it occurred. Hurt takes a long time to heal, because part of hurt is a loss of trust.

Women may deal with hurt differently than men. Many men react to women reporting hurt feelings as manipulative behavior. Hurt is a little more acceptable emotion for women to experience than for men, yet is most often disparaged if identified directly. Men often have difficulty acknowledging hurt. Society teaches boys and men to keep a stiff upper lip. It's okay to get angry; but not to behave "like a girl" when feeling hurt.

What if Anna had postponed the wedding without explanation? Likely her fiancé would have said nothing, also stepping back from the relationship and asking himself what else he could do to persuade her of his love. He wouldn't talk about it with others, but would keep a stiff upper lip. It's also likely the relationship would end completely, the man giving up, believing that he "was not enough" for this woman, who, it appeared, was difficult to please.

Holding hurt in, because it's not an acceptable emotion, can wreak havoc with relationships, promote the repression and non-movement of anger, and make us miserable.

HURT'S SIGNAL IS ABOUT TRUST

Especially in long-term, intimate relationships (such as with partners, spouses, and children), trust is very important. When we can trust our teenager's word, know our partner will do what is promised, and rely on our partner/spouse having our best interest at heart, first and foremost, each person in the relationship can relax, enjoy, and move forward in life together.

When trust is broken, for example, if a partner has an affair, our teenager lies, or our partner fails to follow through with promised actions, it takes a very long time to heal the trust. In these cases, it gets difficult to believe the other person will operate with integrity, so we become reluctant to relax and rely on what we're told or promised.

Why does it take a long time to trust again? Because once trust is broken, it becomes harder to tell what the real truth is, and what is not true. We no longer know when to check the veracity of what we see and hear, and when we can relax. Especially if the other person was deceitful, paranoia steps in: "Can I trust what they say, or do I suspect every single word and action and check it out before trusting it?" Humans need a lot of proof before we allow ourselves to trust again, once we've experienced hurt.

Another thing about trust is there isn't a specified time, or a specified action or promise, that restores it. Each of us is different and each transgression carries its own pain, and its own time frame for healing.

For example, if my spouse of 30 years insists on not coming to the hospital when I lie close to death, how long will it take to repair the trust? Indeed, how possible is it to repair such a breech? Repairing trust takes as long as it takes. The person who has broken trust bears the burden for the repair. The person who has felt betrayed needs to both maintain boundaries and standards for repair, while looking deep inside to forgive. A successful repair of trust is in the eye of the one whose trust was violated. There is no specified way or time for that to happen.

When we feel hurt, it's our signal to look at how trust was broken and decide for ourselves what we'll need for it to be restored. To accomplish this, we need to:

- Acknowledge the hurt,

- Decide what we need to heal,

- Ask for what we need,

- Stand behind personal requirements for the restoration of trust, and

- Look to forgive from within and offer the forgiveness when ready.

HURT AND ANGER

Under anger is hurt. One of the fastest ways to release and move past anger is to acknowledge and express the hurt.

Jacob was excited about Christmas the year his son Ken was four. He purchased toys Ken would love and got them wrapped a few days before Christmas, excitedly laying the packages under the tree. Hours later, returning from errands, Jacob noticed the carefully wrapped packages appeared re-wrapped by a four year old. Jacob nearly popped with anger. For several minutes he thought angrily about what he would say to Ken when he got home from nursery school. Jacob had never been so angry with Ken before.

With nearly four hours before Ken's return home, Jacob had time to remember he recently learned that under anger is hurt.

"What am I feeling hurt about?" he asked himself. Immediately his head filled with the pictures of Christmas, when Jacob would see the surprise and joy on Ken's little face once he saw what Jacob had given him. Now, he realized, Ken had already seen the gifts. Jacob had missed one of the most important parts of the Christmas giving process, seeing Ken light up as he opened his gifts. Jacob felt hurt that he had been deprived of that wonderful experience.

By the time Ken returned home, Jacob was ready to share hurt, not anger. Jacob told Ken, "I was really looking forward to seeing your face light up when you saw what I'd gotten for you. I'm sad that I'm not going to get to see that happen at Christmas this year."

Ken was stunned. "I didn't know!" he told his father.

Jacob snuggled him, forgave him, then told Ken he would wrap the presents again, differently, so Ken wouldn't be able to tell which present he was opening. That was helpful to Jacob and more fun for Ken, too. The learning was so profound for Ken that he never cheated with family presents again.

Christmas morning the men in the family knew what had happened, but they no longer needed to concentrate on remorse, hurt, or anger. Instead, they enjoyed the journey together of making the opening of gifts a time full of fun, surprise, and enjoyment.

By acknowledging the hurt, Jacob dissipated the angry feelings. He was then able to share his personal truth with his son, bringing them closer together and finding a solution for the situation that worked for them both. Trust was re-established and Ken learned a valuable lesson that lasted for a lifetime.

FINDING HURT'S LESSON

Inside of each experience is a lesson that we have an opportunity to realize and learn. How do we find the lesson in any experience? We ask. Jacob identified his lesson by being willing to ask and answer the question, "What could I be feeling hurt about here?" The answer revealed to him a loss that he hadn't previously noticed. The real lesson for Jacob was to realize what he had lost, allow himself to know how important it was to him, and take action to repair and restore that value.

The lesson of hurt is to realize the love we have for our self, then both give it to our self and ask for it from the other(s) involved. Trust is restored when we again have a solid platform for our life.

We experience the greatest hurts in those first formative seven years of life, when we don't have the cognitive ability or the communication skills to speak up, remedy the pain and restore the trust. Because of this as adults we often feel helpless when hurt arises.

"They won't care. There's no reason to say anything," we tell ourselves. We also experience what feels like extreme vulnerability, "Is this hurt worth taking the risk of facing such vulnerability when I tell them how I really feel?"

Dr. Fritz Perls was a psychiatrist who taught the world about the importance of "completing the gestalt." "Gestalt" is a German word meaning "whole" or "totality." What Perls discovered is a person can be counted among the "walking wounded," psychologically speaking, if carrying around open emotional wounds, most of which we carry from the time of early childhood. When we're "walking wounded," our energy is tied up in holding onto the pain and attempting to keep it from leaking out into our life. Over time, most of us aren't successful in curtailing this leakage.

Dr. Perls developed processes for us to go back in time and express our hurt and helplessness, taking our personal power back. Using these processes allows us to feel better, while regaining the personal energy we use to carry this pain and hurt around. The process is like the one I used in talking with my neighbor, Bill, about how he spoke to me over the phone. Speaking our truth into the past, amazingly, restores our personal energy and improves our quality of life.

RELEASING THE ENERGY OF HURT

From Jacob's story we see that acknowledging the hurt and finding a way to express and work with it allowed the energy of hurt to move on. By the time Jacob and Ken were working out a way to repair the situation, Jacob was relating constructively and lovingly with his son, neither feeling angry nor hurt. This is the power of "Facing Fact."

Remember "Facing Fact" is the process of looking squarely at what happened and how we're feeling about it. It's not always easy to do. "Facing Fact" means for us to look squarely at what happened, how we feel, and where we want to go next. Hurt urges us to Face Fact.

Jacob looked at the situation and discovered: "I'm really angry about this." Then he realized: "I'm really hurt, and this is what is hurting me." Jacob then decided what he wanted to do about the hurt feelings: "I will share my hurt feelings with Ken and discuss with him a solution that eases my pain." Finally, Jacob talked with Ken, forgave his son, and implemented a personal solution for making the feelings better.

If Jacob had not "Faced Fact," he would not have completed the process. "Facing Fact" is the road to freedom. We look at what is happening and we're free to address it, change it, and move on. "Facing Fact" is really important with the emotion of Hurt. The pain so many people experience regarding hurt comes from being unwilling, or unable, to face the fact we feel hurt. It's the result of our resistance to acknowledging and feeling hurt. If we're unwilling or unable to see or acknowledge hurt, it takes even longer to heal.

MY PERSONAL LABORATORY

When my first husband was transferred by the Army to serve at Letterman Hospital on the Presidio in San Francisco (now where George Lucas' Film Studios reside), I was in the middle of earning my Master's degree in Social Work. I chose to drop my studies in Seattle to accompany my husband. Hence, when I arrived in San Francisco to look for a job, I was equipped with only half a master's degree. As I often said, that's like being lower than dirt!

I looked for three months for a job. Finally, at Travelers Aid Society, located at the juncture of Mason and Market streets in the Tenderloin district of San Francisco, a man was working who had attended school with me in Seattle. He was aware of my abilities and persuaded the head of the Traveler's Aid office, Clarita, to hire me—even with only half a master's degree. In that office our job was to help people who had run into difficulties while traveling. We had one hour to assess the problem, decide on a plan to help fix the problem, call people to help with resources, and move the client out the door. Despite having only half a master's degree, I was good at doing this.

Clarita had just returned from Washington, D.C., where she had spent three years working on a special project. While she was gone, she rented out her furnished house in San Francisco's Bay Area. One Monday morning, when I asked how her weekend had gone, she told me it had been rough, because the tenants in her home—a doctor and his wife—had moved out, and she had been unsure they would do so because they really wanted to stay. That was 1969. I had no idea how important that doctor and his wife would be to my life; and didn't find out for 25 years.

The second year of my employment, Clarita asked me to be in charge of selecting, training and manning the satellite stands at the Greyhound Bus Station and the San Francisco airport. I recruited, trained and supervised volunteers manning these stands. I had never done such a thing, yet grew to enjoy the work and did a good job. Those stands for helping and referring people were always manned with good people, and many travelers were helped.

During that year, I became pregnant, due to deliver in July of 1970. In March, I decided I wanted to stop work in May, so I could get myself ready for this momentous occasion. I advised Clarita of my end-date, giving her two months' notice.

At my next personal conference with Clarita, she told me, "I don't think this agency owes you anything. I have already placed ads in the journals looking for your replacement. If someone applies that I want to hire, you will be let go immediately."

Stunned and hurt, I said nothing. I couldn't tell her how hurt I felt, because even though I was a practicing therapist, I knew expressing hurt would make me look weak. At that moment, I didn't want to offer her any fuel to make things worse for me.

It was Friday, and I had the weekend to share this with my social-worker husband. He immediately expressed anger saying, "She is threatening you!" He advised me to go in on Monday morning and quit, right then. He promised to stand behind me. I was frightened to do so, worried we wouldn't have enough resources to care for our baby, because his contract with the Army was ending in June. He persuaded me, and I went in on Monday and resigned. I was required to give two weeks' notice, so I still had to go to work during that time.

Tuesday, however, I met with a friend of mine who was working for the Army Education Center at the Presidio. She introduced me to her boss after telling me they were short on people to help soldiers who were mustering out of the army in droves. The Vietnam War had ended; and people were returning to civilian life. The army wanted to give them some help in figuring out what to do with themselves after leaving the service. They needed psychological testing people to do this.

I'd never administered a psychological test in my life, but I applied because my friend explained to me what I needed to do and I was confident I could learn it quickly. I was hired to work half time. The office was one-and-a-half blocks from my home on the Presidio. I was to work half time, on a two-month contract, earning the same salary for half-time work as I had earned full time at Traveler's Aid.

When we pay attention to the hurt that accompanies an experience or challenge, it can lead us to amazing outcomes. In this case, with the help of my young husband, I was led to exactly what I needed at that time. When I shared my hurt feelings with him, he was able to guide me to what I needed to do to bring the next great thing in store for me. Usually, I've learned, when something is removed from our lives like this, there is something even better heading our way.

By the way, the doctor who was living in Clarita's home, whose wife died in 1985, became my husband in 1998, 29 years after Clarita was simultaneously his landlady, and my boss. Their wonderful, gorgeous, smart, and amazing daughters are now my stepdaughters, whom I love beyond measure.

YOUR PERSONAL LABORATORY

When someone does or says something that feels hurtful, what do you do? Do you recognize the hurt feelings, honor them, share them, get help in dealing with them?

Right now, think of a time when you felt hurt. Note what you did about it at the time. If you did nothing about those feelings then, you can complete them now, like I did in the situation with my neighbor Bill that I shared previously.

Make a plan now. If you had this same situation occur again, what would you do differently regarding your hurt feelings? Write this down.

What did you do to rebuild trust after the hurt? In my case, I moved on, and found I could trust the universe to bring me something even better than what was in my life when I experienced hurt.

Make another plan that addresses how you intend to rebuild trust, should you ever experience hurt again. Write this down.

Finally, give yourself permission to experience hurt when it arises. State aloud: "I give myself permission to feel hurt whenever it arises, whenever I decide."

Write about what you've learned about hurt.

20

LONELINESS

Loneliness is an interesting emotion. Most people associate the emotion of loneliness with being alone, but in fact, we can feel lonely in a marriage or in a large group of people. Loneliness is not about being alone. It's a message about how we need to work with ourselves and our energy.

Marie had felt lonely throughout her childhood. An only child, she had complained to her parents about feeling lonely. Aside from arranging a few additional playdates, the parents did little to help Marie with the loneliness. Marie chalked her feelings of loneliness up to a lifetime of doing things alone and came to believe there was something about her that was not attractive to others. Perhaps, as an only child, she became too selfish. Even psychotherapy hadn't helped. The therapist told her to reach out to others more. When she was with others, Marie often felt lonely. Since the therapist didn't help, Marie concluded there definitely was something wrong with her, and had been wrong since early childhood. As time went on, Marie found it less painful to spend increasing amounts of time alone, lost in her stamp collection and music where she felt less alone, but her actions still didn't take the pain of a lifetime of loneliness away completely.

Tom, too, often felt lonely. He chose to escape the dullness of other people's conversations by being alone. It hadn't stopped him from having times when he felt profoundly lonely. When those times hit, Tom grabbed his "To Do" list and kept himself busy doing chores. With listening to his music as he worked, Tom felt less alone, feeling better because of what he was able to accomplish. Tom didn't think there was anything wrong with him. Loneliness was the price he paid for his high intelligence and interest in having real, not banal, interactions with others.

We all feel lonely at times. It's human to feel lonely. We're programmed to be together with others, yet face the issue of being in separate bodies, having separate lives, and living in cultures that reward our independence and separate accomplishments. The question is, can there be a cure for loneliness, one we can use whenever loneliness hits us, that causes us to feel less lonely, and lasts for a long time?

THE UNDERLYING CAUSE OF LONELINESS

Doing research, as I prepared to write 10 emotional literacy manuals for parents in 1994, I came across this information, offered by Concept Synergy: "Loneliness occurs when you have more energy going out than coming in."

This means there is no specific time, configuration of people or relationships, or other condition to account for us experiencing loneliness, except for the condition that we have more personal energy going out than coming back in to ourselves. The signal of loneliness is that we have a deficit of energy coming into ourselves. Loneliness is about what is happening with our personal energy, not about what others are doing or not doing for us.

As I discovered, by further research and personal and professional experimentation, each person is in charge of bringing energy back into ourselves, thus ending loneliness.

The best ways to bring energy in are through doing things for which we have a talent. Marie clearly has a talent for stamp collecting and music. Whenever she engages in these activities, she feels better. A talent is something we do well, almost without thinking. When others say, "You're so good at that!" in admiration, we often respond, "Oh, it's nothing—anyone can do this." But they usually can't. Whatever we're doing is a personal talent.

We can bring energy in by asking others for attention. This is a less reliable fix than getting energy through ourselves. It's okay to ask someone to take a walk, go to a museum or movie, or get coffee.

Even though loneliness is not really about being alone, our brains still associate loneliness with being alone. Because of this, a profound fix for loneliness that works for many people is one I discovered in 2017: Remind yourself that in this universe nobody is every really alone. If we have a belief that there is something, or someone, greater than ourselves, and that this energy is loving, then it's impossible for us to ever to be alone. In this approach, loneliness is seen as the result of forgetting we're always connected to this loving, something-larger-than-ourselves being/energy/force. Try saying out loud, when experiencing loneliness:

"I'm never alone. No one is ever totally alone. I'm surrounded by loving energy that is always with me, always caring about me. I'm part of that energy; and I can give loving energy to myself, right now!"

Let the experience of loneliness disappear. Each time we remind ourselves of this, loneliness will fall away more quickly. Soon, it will hardly be an issue.

Simple things we can do to help bring loneliness to an end in our life include making a list of the things we believe will feed us energy and will make us feel good. Then, the next time we experience loneliness, consult the list and do one of these things. Note what you're feeling before taking the action and after. If we've chosen something that feeds us, we'll likely feel much better afterwards, and perhaps not lonely at all. And if we want to knock loneliness out of the park, keep remembering we're never really alone and are constantly bathed in the Love of the Universe!

WHAT IS THE MESSAGE OF LONELINESS?

Clearly, the message of loneliness is that we need to take more energy in. As an energy being, we're running on close-to-empty when we feel lonely. On a larger level, the message is: "Remember you're always loved. God/Energy is always available to you. Remember our connection. Call on us for energy. You need more love right now!"

FINDING THE LESSON LONELINESS REVEALS

What are we paying attention to when we allow our personal energy to fall below the levels that feed us? Usually, we're paying attention to people and experiences outside of ourselves. To remedy the situation, pay enough attention to ourselves to make sure we're fed the energy we need. With this in mind, what is the lesson loneliness offers us?

We're not paying enough attention to ourselves and our needs. We're not taking full responsibility for taking care of ourselves, allowing ourselves either to drift without full care, or to allow other's needs to take precedence over ours. Another way of seeing this is that we're not loving ourselves enough, which is why connecting to that "something-larger-than-ourselves" works so well when we're drawing on the love of the Universe. It's fine to love and attend to others. Yet, the only person who is always and fully going to look after loving and attending to our needs is us. Loneliness reminds us we've lost track of this and need to re-focus our attention.

What amazing things emotions are! Every day, our emotions are checking our personal energy gauge, working to let us know where we need to focus our attention, when we need to top up, and when we're doing okay. What a blessing that we have such indicators. By paying attention to the emotions that come up in us, such as loneliness, we're told what we need to do to make corrections for our life, so things go better for us. All we need to do is allow the emotion to come up, know its signal, heed its advice and put it into use in our life, and learn any lesson that comes with our experience. I get tickled when I see just how lovely and simple this system is.

RELEASING THE ENERGY OF LONELINESS

Once we follow the lesson and signal of loneliness, and start bringing energy into ourselves, the energy of loneliness dissipates. We really don't have to work at it. By heeding the message that we need emotional (energy) nourishment, and taking action on it, the energy of loneliness leaves on its own, replaced with the energy of love.

When we approach loneliness from the larger level—of reminding ourselves that all the love of the Universe is constantly available to us and wants to be with us—loneliness drops away incredibly fast. In my experience, continuing to focus here allows loneliness to fall away, almost permanently. We're always connected. We need to remember that.

MY PERSONAL LABORATORY

My son was 7 years younger than his sister. When he had just turned 10, she left for college, coming back for only two more semesters of school before leaving home forever.

Our home was in a lovely, forest-like setting, high up on a hill in a little town in the San Francisco, California Bay Area. It was a lovely place to raise children. The road leading to our house from the downtown area was narrow and winding. With few children in the neighborhood, and even fewer in my son's age group, he was left with lots of hours of his time, alone while his mother worked. I worked at home, with my office in our back yard, but because privacy was vital to the conduct of psychotherapy, I needed to leave him alone in the house while I worked, just 50 feet away.

My son's father had left our home when he was two-and-a-half years old. I worked very hard to keep them seeing one another; but his dad didn't usually work, had no money, and lived about an hour away from us. I encouraged their relationship, but with his dad's bipolar disorder, visitation was episodic, and not something to count on.

When my son was 12, his dad grew weary of having to contact me to set up times to get together with him. Making a few negative statements about me, my ex-husband announced one day, as he was bringing our son back from a weekend together, that he was no longer going to contact me to arrange visits. He told our son he was old enough to arrange visitation for himself. When my son came into the house, he told me of this new arrangement, then followed the telling by saying, "I told him it's not my job."

From that time to age 14, our son saw little of his dad. He was angry with him, and felt manipulated when his dad sent letters but did not request to see him.

I knew my son was lonely, I arranged for him to be assigned a Big Brother. Nice as the man assigned to my son was, he was not right for him. My son became uninterested in trying that route a second time.

One summer night I had arranged for my son and me to cut down a tree for my aging next door neighbor. After gathering my tools, I went out and started work, expecting him to join me. An hour into my labors, I went into our house to find out what was keeping him from helping me, only to find he wasn't there. He didn't come home until nearly 10:00 P.M.

I was frustrated and angry with him, not only for failing to help me cut down the tree, but also because he hadn't told me he was leaving.

Giving me no room to admonish him, my son said immediately: "Mom, you remember I told you I need a mentor? I need a man in my life who helps me and cares about me. Remember?"

I agreed.

"I found him today!" he announced, jubilantly. All this time, he had been at a neighbor's, only three doors away, getting to know the man he had determined was to be his mentor, a Ph.D. climate scientist who lived nearby with his wife and infant son. He frequently worked out of his home. Once found, my son started spending a lot of his time at their home.

I checked with my neighbor to make sure he was okay with being my son's mentor. He told me my son had asked him directly, and he'd agreed. He continued to mentor my son through his teen years, during vacations from college, and into his adulthood.

My son cured his own loneliness, filling his own deep need. Loneliness is about having more of our energy going out than coming back in. He realized he needed to take in a particular kind of energy, went in search of it, and found it, literally, in his own back yard. He used his brilliant brain to make the assessment, his people skills to approach and ask this man for a relationship, then participated in their family's life, deriving the special kind of energy he needed.

I had no ability to be angry with my son for disappearing. He disappeared from me in order to appear more fully for himself.

YOUR PERSONAL LABORATORY

Is there something you feel is missing in your life? Perhaps you have complained about it, hoping someday it would show up for you. If so, what is it?

Identify what's missing for you and write it down.

Using your imagination, think of the best possible way your "missing piece" could be found and brought into your life. Look at as many possibilities as possible.

Once you are clear on what you want, and how it might be found, ask for help. Say, "This is what I have identified I need/want. I ask that this be brought into my life, if it's right for me. I'm ready, now. Thank you for your help."

You've now set the law into motion that you want something new in your life. There is no guarantee that you will have it, or (if you do) when it will arrive. But you've set things into motion.

Next, your job is to keep your eyes open for possibilities, accept what shows up, and express gratitude for receiving what you need and asked for.

Write about your experience.

21

JEALOUSY

George and Anabelle were the parents of an adorable son, Jeremy, who at six years old was ready to enter elementary school. George and Annabelle wanted to send him to a private school in the community, one with a wonderful reputation for graduating top-notch students. They wanted Jeremy's high intelligence to be nurtured by an excellent educational experience, and were willing to pay the price, financially, to do that.

Unfortunately, gaining entrance into the school was highly competitive. Jeremy was not selected. His best friend, Sean, was selected. While they couldn't admit it right away, George and Anabelle were jealous, something they were able to discuss with each other, but only after moving through the emotion of grief (they could face fact more easily once they started allowing themselves to feel their real feelings).

"How can they tell at age six that one child will do better than another?"

"Did not being in a specific heritage group make a difference?"

"Was there something Jeremy did or said that turned them off to him?"

"Why is Sean seen as a better prospect than Jeremy?"

"What else, as parents, can we do to get him into this school?"

George and Annabelle questioned themselves in every direction, all the while watching daily as Sean came and went to his new school. For a time, both George and Anabelle were seething with jealousy. They comforted themselves with the knowledge they didn't want to feel jealous, yet how could they not feel it?

JEALOUSY'S CAUSE

Jealousy occurs when we mentally compute that someone else has something we can't have.

JEALOUSY'S MESSAGE

Sean's parents could have a son going to the preferred school, but George and Annabelle couldn't. The message is that someone can have something I dearly want. I can't have it. Most often, there doesn't even seem to be a reason why I can't have it. In most cases, the reason we can't have what is desired, is that we're standing in our own way to obtain it.

FINDING JEALOUSY'S LESSON

Have you ever heard the saying "the rich get richer, and the poor get poorer?" This is an important message about jealousy.

Behind the saying are the ancient, universal principles we've talked about before, for instance, whatever we pay attention to, we feed energy. The other one is: Whatever we feed energy to grows.

When we feel jealous, we're paying attention to the apparent good fortune of others. We're not giving attention and energy to ourselves. When we do this, we're helping others to have better experiences by feeding them our energy, while depriving ourselves of the energy we need to develop the life we want to have.

The lesson of jealousy is that instead of giving our energy away to others because we feel jealous for their good fortune, we need to use our energy to create our own good fortune. The lesson of jealousy, in short, is get creative and create what is right for ourselves.

George and Anabelle could get creative in a number of ways, for example:

- Go to the school, find out why Jeremy wasn't selected, and take steps to have him selected as a transfer student the following year.

- Look around to find another school with a similarly good reputation, make application, and do what it takes to get Jeremy into the school. (They might even transfer him out of this school to the first one, after a year or two, bringing him closer to home.)

- In a meeting with the school, discover areas of learning or behavior that Jeremy needs to develop, and either home-school him for a while to build in that learning, or enroll him in additional programs or with tutors.

- Accept that this school is not right for Jeremy and start looking at what type of education or school might suit him better.

These are just a few of the ways that are more creative, simultaneously moving Sean's parents and their son in the direction of having the support and opportunity the parents want for him. Instead of giving the attention—through jealousy—to Sean and his parents, George and Anabelle would give their attention to themselves, creating a life they really want for themselves and their son. It may not be the precise life or experience initially sought; but it could turn out to be better.

RELEASING THE ENERGY OF JEALOUSY

With jealousy, it's helpful to make a decision about whether our wish is to continue feeling jealous or to focus on getting creative. The minute we make the decision to learn the lesson (get creative), we're set free. Instead of feeling and focusing on jealousy, our attention will move toward addressing how to make as creative a solution as we possibly can.

That's when another important ancient, Universal Principle comes into effect: Pay attention, not to what we want to overcome, but to what we want to become. Doing this, again, has us working with creative energy instead of the energy of jealousy.

When we pay attention to what we want to become, we're giving our energy to our creative project, thus allowing it to grow. The energy of jealousy, which we're not paying attention to, will atrophy and fall away. We don't have to work at releasing the energy of jealousy, we just stop feeding it our energy through not giving it our attention.

Over time, as we learn to drop jealousy without giving it much of our time and attention, the amount of jealousy we feel, and the frequency with which we feel it, will drop. There will be no need for us to "do" jealousy. We'll be too busy creating the life we most want for ourselves.

My Personal Laboratory

For twelve years, I led a Woman's Group that met weekly in my office. One night one of the members told us how jealous she felt that her husband, a journalist, was receiving a trip to New York City to conduct some business. He was to be in New York for a week.

It was late November after Thanksgiving. I told her and the group some things about jealousy, then suggested that instead of being jealous and talking about that, she give herself permission to have the same kind of trip. "You're jealous because you think your husband is getting something you can't have," I said to her. "Stop now and imagine that you can have what he has. Give yourself permission to have what you want!"

She stopped, closed her eyes, and imagined. When she opened her eyes, she also wore a big grin. "I don't really want to go to New York City," she said, chuckling. After all, it's nearly winter. It's dark there too much of the time now. The weather is bad. I don't really want a trip to New York where he has gone. I want a trip to Hawaii.

We all laughed with her. She went home, made the arrangements, and missed our next group meeting because she was in Hawaii. She never again talked about being jealous.

YOUR PERSONAL LABORATORY

Do you feel jealous? Is there someone you feel jealous of right now? Put this person's name on your paper.

What are you jealous of? What is this person getting or having in life that you want for yourself?

Make a decision to keep your energy and not give it away to this person. If you want what the other person has, say aloud: "I give myself permission to create what I want in my life, without first giving my precious energy away to others through jealousy. Starting now, jealous feelings that arise will only stimulate me to get creative for myself!"

Stay open. Very often when you set things up like this, they start to come into your life, soon. Be aware of opportunities. If any opportunity arises that is related to what you want for yourself, follow it. Be certain not to stop yourself.

Write about what you experience emotionally through this exercise. Then write down what happens for you.

In my RV, the hot water heater stopped working. I wanted someone who would both fix it and show me how to fix it myself. As I drove through Canada, without a functioning water heater for nearly three weeks, I stayed confident that what I had asked for would appear. Finally, one night, I accepted the hospitality of a couple who were part of Boondockerswelcome.com, a group made up of people who offer a free spot to RV-ers to stay overnight. They came into my van to talk when I arrived and had set myself up, and all enjoyed the visit. The next day I mentioned wanting to find someone to help me fix my water heater.

"You do realize my husband is a retired plumber, don't you?" She insisted she would ask him to fix my errant water heater, which he did, teaching me as he worked. He was struggling with some emotions, so I traded with him—my knowledge and skills for his. My attention was placed on what I wanted. I identified it, then held the picture of getting the right help until it showed up in my life. This is what I want you to be successful in doing, too.

22

SHAME

WHAT IS SHAME DOING IN OUR LIFE?

Even with illness or disability with which a child may be born, there is never any reason for a newborn child to feel ashamed. Each of us is born with a loving energy, joy, and excitement for learning. Each of us is born with no cause for shame. (I realize there are religions that promote the concept of "original sin" and thus may believe that humans are born with reasons for shame. This discussion is not designed to include such an idea.)

For years as a psychotherapist, I've worked with people (including myself) who carried heavy loads of shame. I've never observed shame to bring positive benefit to anyone. Shame is the mental computation that something is wrong with me.

In working with people's self-concept and pain for almost 50 years, I've concluded that shame is learned or taken from others. In fact, I don't see shame as a real emotion even though it can certainly have real consequences. As noted earlier, real emotions have both a positive and a negative side.

If we feel shame, it's not present to do anything positive for us. It just affirms there is something wrong with us. We believe there's little we can do about it. And it's nearly impossible to get out from under shame in our life. I've never seen shame assist a person to make needed, positive changes that enable a happier

140

life. Shame is more like a heavy manhole cover placed over the person, something to carry while trying to live life. It's nearly impossible. I don't endorse or recommend shame.

For many years I walked Earth filled with shame. I didn't even know I was feeling shame. It was just how I'd always felt. I was afraid for years to look at people directly, eye-to-eye, because I believed the other person could see something wrong deep inside me that I couldn't see myself.

When we form the idea there is something wrong with us early in our life, it just becomes "the way things are." It doesn't identify itself as something we can do anything about, something that even has a name. We can find out if we're carrying shame just by asking ourselves: "Do I believe there is something wrong with me?"

If the answer comes back "Yes," even if it's a very small "Yes," then we're wrestling with shame. Answering this question has you Facing Fact. Just doing this is starting on a path to freedom from shame.

The next thing we need to do is to start identifying shame, how it behaves in our life, and thinking about what we'd like to have in our life in place of shame. When we identify all of this and make a decision to allow ourselves to live a shame-free life, it's possible to do so. What is also possible is pure personal empowerment, which living with shame denies us. Once we make the decision, then we can begin to feed ourselves the real information about who we are.

When I was in therapy, my therapist recommended I write the words: "There is nothing wrong with me" on 3 x 5 cards and spread these cards all over my home, on the refrigerator, bathroom mirror, inside the front door, wherever I cast my eyes on a regular basis. When I saw the card, I was to repeat the words out loud. When we repeat our truth like this, over and over, our subconscious mind accepts it as truth and our emotions and experiences change, too.

THE SIGNAL OF SHAME

Because shame is a man-made, synthetic emotion, it gives a signal that is not real. Its signal is to tell us there is something wrong with us. That's not true. What's true is that there is nothing wrong with us. If we have anything "wrong" with us, it's that we've accepted this message that there is something wrong with us.

Give it up. Now! Today! Immediately!

We feel shame, but largely because it was laid on us at an early age or passed on to us by a shame-filled parent. Any message that is repeated, over and over in actions and/or in words, creates a belief that stays in our brain. If we got the message there was something wrong with us during those first sensitive seven years of life, that message became a belief.

If I challenge a person's shame-filled belief, that person will tell me, "Yes, there is something wrong with me." And then start to share things that were done or have happened over the years that prove there is something wrong. Once we believe something, we collect evidence to support that belief, developing a self-fulfilling prophecy. Having evidence doesn't make the belief true, it only tells me there is a belief and lots of evidence was collected to support that belief.

A few years ago, I worked with someone in therapy who had a huge laundry list of proof that there was something wrong with him. At four, he pushed his brother out the door of a moving car. He knew the door was open, so he took advantage of it. At 13, he picked up a butcher knife and thought about killing his parents. He was expelled from college. His list went on and on. In therapy, we went through each of these pieces of supporting evidence. This man was convinced he was "the Devil's child," and there was something so wrong with him that it could never be fixed in his lifetime. At the time, this man was in his early seventies. That is a lot of shame.

Four year olds are working on personal power issues. At four, the boy wouldn't have an idea of the dire consequences falling from a moving car could have (although his brother was not seriously hurt because the car was moving slowly on a country road). He felt annoyed with his brother and experimented with his power, which four year old's do constantly. By pushing his brother out of the car, the annoyance was gone. There wasn't something wrong with this boy. The behavior was normal four-year-old-experimenting-with-power behavior. But without anyone helping him to correct the shame, he had been living with this heavy burden for more than six decades.

The next age for people to work on issues of personal power is 13. With anger that was held down through his efforts to follow the religious teachings of the family, this boy's anger grew to murderous proportions. Of course, he thought about taking power by getting rid of what felt to him like his oppressors. He thought of murdering his mother and father with a butcher knife from the kitchen. Together we noticed, however, that it was a thought, not an action. Though he picked up the knife, he never hurt anyone. There was nothing wrong with him for having these thoughts, or even for picking up the knife with murderous intent. They were the result of his juvenile self attempting to find a way to take power in a situation that had been upsetting for years. Love in his heart won out over anger, resulting in him not hurting anyone.

In college, this young man attempted to be good. He got upset through his work on the student Ethics Committee. He found others cheating, felt it wasn't right to report them, and instead took actions the school viewed as trouble-making. He was expelled. There was nothing wrong with him. He just didn't know how to deal with something he learned about that bothered him deeply. The consequences came down on him, and not the people who had cheated. Nevertheless, when the consequences fell, because he was filled with shame, he believed it proved him as "the Devil's child."

This man was a senior citizen by the time I worked with him on these issues. Shame was such a powerful part of his life that he didn't look other people, especially older women, directly in the eye. He preferred to stay in his retirement center room rather than interact with others, and watched himself critically every time he went out in the world. He worried others thought he was a child molester, even though he had never done anything to support this belief. His interpretation of the religion in which he was raised led him to believe he was the work of the Devil. It had set him up to carry shame his entire life.

As a result of our work together to show him he was going through normal life stages, and not exhibiting wrongness, this man was released to have a more normal life in his later years. He felt emotions again. He realized, slowly, that he was a good man. Everyone who knew him loved him and appreciated his goodness, but because of the shame he carried for decades, he hadn't seen goodness in himself. When at last he could see it, he was able to relax, relate more openly with others, and stop characterizing himself as the work of the Devil. As he moved through the latter part of his life, he began to see himself as a more normal person, was able to enjoy social interactions, and completed his burning need to get relief from his internal agony so he could stop feeling he had to be in therapy.

THE POWERFUL LESSON SHAME HAS FOR US

As noted, a child in 1491 learned from parents that the world was flat. The child was expected to share the belief and would have believed it. By the next year, word started coming back from intrepid sailors that the world was not flat. It was reported as round. Today, we know the world is somewhat elliptical. This information is not based on belief; it's measured and proven by scientists.

I bring up this point again to illustrate the lesson of shame: Some of the things we learn from others are wrong. Whatever we learn, especially about ourselves, that doesn't feel good to us, is likely incorrect. The message that there's something wrong with us, which is offered by shame, is incorrect. We no longer need to live under the shadow of shame. Our first step in learning when we experience shame is to forgive our self and the people who taught us to feel shame, then let go. Move on.

RELEASING THE ENERGY OF SHAME

The man whose story I shared in this chapter illustrates how to release the energy of shame. Our choice of actions is informed by many of the ancient, Universal Principles I've shared, such as choosing to focus on what we want to become, not overcome. Consider taking these actions to release the energy of shame:

- Accept the possibility that there is nothing wrong with you. Create and use 3 x 5 cards with the written affirmation and say it aloud as often as possible: "There is nothing wrong with me!" Over time, you will accept this as your new belief.

- Investigate what was normal and right about past behaviors used to justify keeping shame in your life. If this proves too difficult to do alone, work with a psychotherapist or coach.

- Begin the new behavior of stopping, every time you make a decision or take action, to ask and answer this question: "What is right about me in this?"

- Start looking for, and identifying, all the things you see yourself do right every day. Savor them. Tell yourself over and over again that you're a person who has a lot of things right with you. The subconscious mind (where our beliefs are stored) cannot resist repetition. Repeating this message will create belief in it. Pay attention to what you want to become: A person who has many things right with you. Then what you want to overcome will atrophy and fall away. You don't have to direct or send the energy of shame away. Just fill your life with what positive there is in you instead.

MY PERSONAL LABORATORY

In my mid-twenties, I was living in Seattle, working with the second of a succession of psychotherapists. I really liked my therapist, Mr. Lowe, and shared a lot about myself with him.

One day, I met him on the street. I was stunned. My eyes immediately went to the sidewalk. I couldn't look Mr. Lowe in the eye. He was warm and kind in his greeting, yet I couldn't look at him.

As we parted, I realized I thought something was wrong with me, hidden deep inside, that Mr. Lowe could see, but I could not identify. I had no clue how to find that. I didn't know that it could be corrected. I accepted that it was just "who I was" and would always be. I was too ashamed to even tell Mr. Lowe about my reaction in our future therapy sessions.

Years later, through helping others with similar issues, I learned that it was shame. Having been deserted, yanked away from my mother without explanation, lectured by the washerwoman in the basement of the boarding school at age three, punished for any number of transgressions when I had never learned there were rules, and molested by my older male relative, I had a large number of reasons to believe something was wrong with me.

The last psychotherapist in that succession of helpers told me: "Write these words, 'There is nothing wrong with me,' on 3 x 5 cards and put them everywhere in your house. Every time you see a card, read it out loud." Over time, shame disappeared.

YOUR PERSONAL LABORATORY

When you were young, did you decide there was something wrong with you, or have an adult important to you shame you? Do you still carry that shame?

Perhaps you apologize to others for a characteristic behavior of yours, refuse to take chances so people don't have the opportunity to see your flaws. These are signs that you are infected with shame.

Spend some time ferreting out any shame you may carry. Write down what you find. Notice how it makes you feel.

Make your own 3 x 5 cards that say, "There is nothing wrong with me." Place them around your home so you can see them frequently. For at least three weeks, but really for as long as it takes, read the words aloud whenever you see the cards. (If you live with others, tell them you're doing an experiment to make yourself feel better, and ask for their forbearance.) Keep track of what other emotions you feel.

The subconscious mind cannot resist repetition. The more often you tell yourself, "There is nothing wrong with me," the more your belief will grow. When it becomes a belief in your subconscious mind, shame will exit from your life. Good work!

Write about your experience.

23

REMORSE AND GUILT

Most people are very familiar with guilt, but don't think much about remorse. The differences between them haven't been made clear for most of us.

Remorse is a real emotion designed to help us deal with mistakes we make, so we can correct those mistakes and move on.

Guilt is a synthetic emotion used to keep ourselves stuck in the past, frozen, and less connected to others. Guilt is a hidden form of anger.

We're talking about remorse and guilt together because of the frequent confusion. It's important to know that remorse is designed to help us grow and evolve; and it can. Guilt is designed to keep us under control and frozen, our gaze directed to the past.

Remember that when we accept guilt, we violate the ancient, Universal Principle that says: The only time we have power is in the present; the only person over whom we have power is our self.

Guilt encourages us to give up our power in the present in favor of something that influences us from the past.

GUILT

The message of guilt may be different at different times, depending on the circumstances under which we learned guilt in the very early part of our life. If we inherited guilt from one or both of our parents, it may be difficult to understand where it comes from. Children are a bit like computers who download information, patterns, and emotional reactions from our parents between birth and 12 years of age. These patterns are more difficult to work with, because we believe they're ours, when they really aren't. "Why do I feel this way?" we ask ourselves, and can find no real reason in our own life that would create such feelings.

Overall, the message of guilt is: "Freeze! Stop! Don't Move! Whatever we do will be wrong and will hurt us or somebody else!"

Consider whether this is the way you want to live your life. Think about whether you can become empowered, loving, and spiritually evolved when you run your life by guilt. In nearly 50 years of helping others, I've never observed guilt as the agent that takes people to the lives they want to live.

WHAT CAUSES US TO FEEL GUILT?

Too many people believe guilt is a positive force in life. Guilt is seen as a form of conscience, helping us to make better decisions about what we do and how we treat others. As a psychotherapist, I've never found someone who runs their life on the basis of guilt get positive benefit. Guilt makes us feel bad. When we're feeling guilty, we withhold ourselves from others. We learn to use fear of feeling guilty to stop us from doing things that might summon guilty feelings. Guilt focuses us backwards on what we believe demonstrates what we've done wrong in our past. It keeps us from doing wrong things again by stopping us from taking action now.

There is little a person can do with guilt except drop it, but that's nearly impossible. Guilt sticks like resin or glue, hanging on us, leaving us hoping nobody can see the guilt we're experiencing.

Remember synthetic emotions have only a negative aspect, rather than the positive and negative aspects that real emotions have. In my experience, there is nothing positive about guilt. Without realizing it, humans tend to use it as a weapon against themselves and others.

"I'd feel too guilty, I can't do that!"

"You'd better not take that path, you'll feel guilty for what you've done!"

How did we get so sensitive to guilt when it's not a real emotion? We're taught guilt from a very early age. Parents admonish the child: "You hurt Janey's feelings. Don't you feel bad? Tell her you're sorry." The child usually does what the parents say to do, feeling guilty, but not necessarily sorry.

Politicians, coaches, religious leaders, teachers, doctors, and many others, participate in this mass effort to control us, and get us to control ourselves, with guilt. We're told we're inhumane, sinful, won't have friends, will kill ourselves physically, and a host of other things, setting us up to feel guilty if we don't do what we're told or expected to do.

Advertisers use guilt to encourage us to purchase products. Parents use guilt to get children to behave. At the Denver, Colorado, airport I noted the voice of the woman telling people to get on the train that ran between terminals implying guilt to get people on board. She said: "Move away from the doors! You are holding up the train!"

We learn guilt in every part of life. We believe others make us feel guilt, which is something nobody can do, because we get to choose what feelings we allow in ourselves. Since nobody tells us guilt is not a real emotion and we don't have to experience it, most of us believe everybody feels guilty. In fact, guilt is not at all necessary. In addition, it can suffocate us, so we feel powerless, victimized, and bad. To the extent we allow guilt to run our life, we're actually making ourselves powerless, victimized, and hindering our forward progress. This is neither necessary, nor does it accomplish any positive outcome.

Since it's nearly impossible to drop guilt, it's beneficial to know that it's a form of anger. Guilt is defined as: Anger we turn inward on ourselves, that we feel like we don't have a right to have.

I gave up guilt almost 30 years ago. I've never regretted it. I've lived an ethical and good life, and motivate myself to take action by following my heart. I've felt better and better about myself over the years, no longer allowing guilt to limit my choices and actions. Enjoying this type of freedom is entirely possible for you, too.

REMORSE

As a practicing psychotherapist nearly 25 years ago, I knew little about remorse. Nobody seemed to pay much attention to it. This was unfortunate, because remorse is a very important tool, designed to help us recognize and correct mistakes and missteps. We feel remorse when we've taken an action and don't feel good about what we've done. The not-feeling-good-about-it part is designed to get our attention. Once we're paying attention, we can take steps to remediate the situation.

WHAT CAUSES US TO FEEL REMORSE?

Remorse arises to draw our attention to something we've done that really doesn't fit who we are, that doesn't make us feel good. What we do in life is meant to help us feel good, even joyful. When we don't feel good, like when we're experiencing remorse, the message is: "Look at this, you did something and you're not feeling good about it. Check it out. You might want to make a change."

By paying attention to this call, we'll find ourselves:

- Wanting to forgive ourselves for our misstep,

- Considering how we got ourselves into the position we're in,

- Once forgiven, deciding what change we'd like to make (or new decision), and then

- Implementing the change or decision, checking once we've made the change to see if we're feeling better.

This is how remorse is supposed to work. Of course, we need to listen to that "not right" feeling and pay attention to its message for the system to work. That's what we call: "Partnering with the Emotion," which is working with the emotion to accomplish the goal of helping us better navigate our life, allowing us to live more happily.

HOW TO FIND THE LESSONS OF GUILT AND REMORSE

The basic lesson of guilt concerns whether we live better lives by driving ourselves with visions of negative consequences, or by providing plenty of loving support. Because of the thousands of successful therapy experiences I've had with people, I come down on the side of providing plenty of loving support. We take joy in learning and growing. We want to know how things work best, helping us to feel good about ourselves, to be close to others, and to share love. Guilt pulls us away from such a life. By contrast, loving support from ourselves draws love and support into us from others. The extra love and support we amass in this way spills over, spreading love and support outward, over those we encounter and those we love.

As I was writing this, the story of a father dealing with a middle-school boy who was bullying his son, attending the same school, arrived in my inbox. The father spent time with the bully to find out more about what was causing him to bully. What he found out drew him to take loving, compassionate action. The boy's family hit hard times and was homeless. The boy was himself bullied at school, because his clothes were dirty, tattered, and old. This father purchased new clothes for the boy, who also developed a friendship with the father's son. Everyone's life was improved and enriched because of the contribution of this father's loving actions. Think how things might have turned out if the father had shamed or passed guilt to the bullying boy instead.

THE LESSON OF REMORSE

The lesson found in remorse is about our decision-making process. It may be slightly different each time we feel remorse, but it usually has something to do with:

- Making the decision too quickly.

- Not listening to what is right for us.

- Compromising in some way like not being ethical or trying to take a shortcut that won't work.

- Manipulating or some other form of attempt to control others.

To find the lesson in remorse, ask yourself: "What is it about the decision I've made that doesn't feel good or right to me?"

Then listen.

Usually the first thing to come back to us is the lesson. When we find the lesson, make an intention to learn and finish it. Remember, the second we learn the lesson we're finished with it and free to move on.

For most of the past two years, I've roamed the United States and Canada in my 24-foot recreational vehicle (RV). As I move around, I stop to get fuel and groceries. Recently, I stopped in a store for the items I needed, which included two two-and-a-half gallon containers of spring water, which I like for my morning tea. Because my conversation with the checker and other patrons was stimulating and fun, I forgot to point out that the water was on the bottom of my cart and needed to be scanned. I didn't realize until I was nearly back to my RV that I hadn't paid for the water. What to do? I was tired and hot and had parked my RV at the far end of the parking lot. I didn't want to turn around to go pay for the water. I could put it in my van and leave, with nobody the wiser. Then I thought to myself: "But I'm a person who lives by principle. I'm the one who will be the wiser. I'll experience remorse if I don't pay!"

That's what it took for me to turn around and pay for the water. I went back to the same checker. A woman he was helping said to me, "How nice that you came in to pay!"

"It's not about nice," I responded. "I really didn't want to come back to pay! But I knew there would be hell to pay inside of myself if I didn't pay, because I live on the basis of principle. I chose to come back so I can live with myself!"

"I know what you mean," she said.

Once we understand the importance of living by principle and the power of remorse, it's easier to make decisions even ahead of feeling the remorse. I didn't need to feel guilty to make the right choice. The thought of the remorse that would sit on my shoulders was enough.

RELEASING THE ENERGY OF GUILT

As stated, releasing the energy of guilt is difficult, if not impossible. It's a bit like the brain tumor that entwines itself around everything else in the brain, making it impossible to remove without taking healthy tissue and brain cells with it. A neurosurgeon has to decide how much of the glioblastoma tumor to cut out, working hard to save important brain cells.

Fortunately, the energy of guilt isn't that difficult to release, because as stated, that energy is the emotion of anger. To release guilt use these steps:

- Identify the anger by asking ourselves: "What could I possibly feel angry about in this situation?"

- Name our should, for example, "I believe I should never cause another person difficulty; and if they have difficulty, it's my fault."

- Face Fact: What's the truth? If another person is having difficulty, and we didn't intend it, have we really done something to them, or is it the other person's issue they need to work out? Keep in mind in our Giant School each person has lessons to learn, and most of our lessons come through interaction with others. Perhaps the other person has a lesson to learn, and we've been the catalyst to bring it to their attention. It's vital not to deprive them of their learning opportunity.

- Make a decision about what we intend to do in the future, should such a situation or decision arise again.

- Forgive, both the other person for the reaction and our self for whatever our part was. Forgiveness is the process of letting go, so when we've done this forgiveness, the energy of the anger is released. Guilt will slide out the door on the wings of this forgiveness.

A FINAL NOTE ABOUT GUILT AND REMORSE

We do ourselves the favor of beginning to notice, when we feel bad inside, whether we're experiencing remorse or guilt. If it's guilt, process, and let go of the anger it hides, before going on. If it's remorse, welcome it and partner, so we learn more about our decision-making process and create changes, making working with remorse easier. Always keep in mind: remorse and guilt are not the same.

MY PERSONAL LABORATORY

My older sister, Keriac, taught dance and performance in San Francisco and Europe. She stayed in Europe up to six months at a time.

When her daughter, my niece, was about 19, Keriac called me from Europe and asked me to go see her daughter, who was having some relationship problems that Keriac thought were serious. This was in the days before cell phones. My niece was living in San Francisco. My own children were young, so I couldn't leave them for long periods of time. I decided to call my niece to offer my help.

She never returned my phone call, not the first one and not the subsequent six calls. In some of my messages I was explicit regarding the problem and the help I could give her. Still, she never called.

I gave up. I had no idea of what she did with her time, when she would be at the San Francisco apartment; and she wasn't returning any of my calls. I couldn't leave my children just to sit on the street until she came home, whenever that was.

I notified my sister that there was nothing I could do.

Keriac was angry and irritated with me. In fact, she stayed angry and irritated for many years. We talked soon after her return and I explained why I was unable to give the help she requested. She challenged me, saying when people are in trouble you have to make them see and talk with you. I told her I didn't agree with her. I suggested that if my niece wanted my help, she would have responded. I thought the issue had been completed between us.

Nearly seven years later, my sister came to my house for a visit. She was planning to spend time with her daughter after visiting with me. She brought up this issue again. I stood my ground, telling her I gave up because I got the message that her daughter didn't want my help.

"You needed to push through her non-responsiveness," she opined. "You're just telling me this because you still feel guilty that you didn't help her!"

"No, I don't feel guilty," I said to her. "I made my choice. Given the same circumstances, I'd make that same choice again."

"No, you feel guilty! Everyone feels guilty!"

"Now you know somebody who doesn't feel guilty," I told her. "I no longer 'do' guilt. I feel no guilt regarding the choices I made."

"I'll ask my daughter when I see her," she shot back, sounding like she believed her daughter would verify her way of seeing things.

A few days later, Keriac called. I loved that she was so dedicated to being truthful. "I talked with my daughter, and she agreed with you that she didn't want your help, and that's why she never called you back," she told me. "I'm sorry I didn't understand."

YOUR PERSONAL LABORATORY

Do you "do" guilt in your life? Are you sensitive to the way people talk, believing they try to make you feel guilty? Next time you notice this, check it out. Determine whether they're working to make you feel guilty, or you're reading into their statements, believing they want you to feel guilty. You may need to check things out with several people over a period of time to be able to discern what is true. When you do, write about what you find out.

Do you believe someone can "make you feel guilty?" What would you need to change in yourself so that no one can "make you feel guilty" again in your life? Will you do that? Write about it, please.

For one week, keep your focus totally in the present. Don't allow the past, and past events, to influence current experiences. If something needs to be worked out between you and another person, only talk about what can be changed from now on. What happens? Write down your experiences and your insights.

Imagine what your life will be like never experiencing guilt again. Once you can feel that, explore what you need to do in order to create that state in your life. Then do it.

Record the thoughts, experiences, and emotions you feel. Come back in a few weeks and revisit what you have written.

24
INTIMACY AND LOVE

Intimacy and love are states or emotions we want to experience and are somewhat intertwined with one another. Intimacy is not really an emotion, but because of this entwinement, it's important to include it in the discussion about the emotion of love.

Love is an amazing emotion, with possibilities and depths much greater than we can explore here. A great number of people recognize that the basis of all creation is Love. It's not merely an emotion; it's the driving force of all the particles and creatures of our universe. Most religions preach some version of "God is Love." When we choose love as the guiding principle of our life and live in the most loving way we can, our life has a flow, joy, and ease to it. A teacher I encountered offered this idea: Creation exists so love can become aware of itself, arguing that it's difficult to see outside of love when we are love. When we choose love as our personal guiding principle, we become a most willing part of exploring and experimenting with love that creation (something that is much larger than us) can better know what love is and is not, in a limitless permutation of possibilities.

In our everyday world, love is the emotion that brings us together with others. It's what we strive to give to our children and encourage them to give. It's what we share with our family members, friends, gurus, coaches, and what we experience when we do something we're good at that feels like it fulfills us or our purpose. Life works best for us when we give plenty of love to ourselves, too. Love is undefinable. It's a feeling we all hopefully experience that leaves us filled up, happy, and calm. When we experience a deficit of love, life doesn't go well.

Intimacy, on the other hand, is the act and feeling of sharing love. It requires us to be vulnerable. Intimacy involves trust, especially, trust of ourselves. If we open ourselves to someone and allow deep intimacy, we need to trust ourselves to be okay if things don't happen the way we expect. Usually we talk about not trusting the other person, but in intimacy, ultimately the issue is about trusting ourselves.

In our world, intimacy is often equated with sexuality. In this discussion, we aren't speaking of sexuality, but of the vulnerability and closeness we share with others when we allow ourselves to be open and close with them, having no secrets.

As we know, some people are afraid of intimacy. The level of vulnerability is more than some can manage, leaving them too open and feeling out of control. Such people seldom risk intimacy, thus depriving themselves of the deep pleasures and joys possible when we relate closely with others. When people do open up to intimacy, the heart and soul get fed in amazing, wonderful ways. It's key in intimacy to focus on the sharing of love and closeness, rather than believing we need to own the other person in order to stay safe. We attempt this owning through possessiveness, manipulative control, broadcasting guilt, and sometimes through marriage or insistence on long-term commitment. It's my learning that relationships are about growing, not about belonging, ownership or security. Intimacy shared between people who are dedicated to helping each other grow as much as possible is a beautiful, usually long-lasting thing.

WHAT CAUSES US TO FEEL INTIMACY OR LOVE?

Love: Because the energy of love lies under all of creation, we feel love just by staying open to it. Little babies do this naturally. The trick for most of us is not to lose the ability to stay open to love. We tend to close down when we feel bad about ourselves, guilty, shameful, or have painful experiences. We're taught to shut love down in ourselves, largely by being trained to make decisions and take actions that aren't right for us. We're often encouraged to take better loving care of the people around us than we take of ourselves, being admonished not to be "selfish." Unfortunately, this is backwards. When we love ourselves, first, we then have plenty of love inside of us to share with others. Then, like coffee in a cup that the server doesn't stop pouring, the love in us spills over and covers us and everyone around us.

We feel love when we allow ourselves to feel it, when our relationship with our self is a practice featuring love, and when we allow ourselves to draw closer to others as we do in intimacy. This may be easier or more difficult, depending on what we've learned about love and intimacy in those first seven years of life.

Growing up with the belief that I was unlovable, as an adult I had to figure out what love really is, what it feels like, and how to love myself. Until I did that, the so-called love relationships I had didn't work out, as evidenced by two divorces. It was difficult to figure out what love was when I couldn't really identify it, hadn't experienced it early in my life, and didn't think I was worthy to have it, yet was also hungry for it. If we believe we're unlovable, yet can feel love for a person or creature that is safe for us, such as a baby or a baby animal, we can use our imagination to feel love and transfer that love feeling to our selves. This is a powerful remedy for feeling unlovable. Doing this for a period of time can develop self-love in us.

Intimacy: Intimacy is not really an emotion, but often stimulates and interacts with love, so we consider it here as a feeling and action as intense and important as our emotions.

To feel intimacy, we must take a risk by allowing our self to get close to another person, to be revealed as we are, and not always just as we want others to perceive us. In my experience, it's difficult to do this if we're not honest and real with our self.

Can we acknowledge to ourselves when we're petty, mean, or self-centered? Can we accept and love our self even when we're being judgmental, doing something we believe is stupid to do or making mistakes? Can we acknowledge that we believe we're handsome or pretty? Being honest with ourselves is challenging.

The most difficult skill of love is respect. Respect is the ability to accept a person exactly as they are, without needing to change a hair on their head. To allow our self to feel intimacy, we need to offer our self that kind of respect. It's not about being right or perfect; it's about being and accepting our real self.

Love doesn't ask a beautiful sunflower to be a rose. It loves the sunflower as it is. Similarly, love isn't asking us to be someone we're not. Every single person on Earth is lovable. Being our self is the cause for love and the route for experiencing intimacy.

WHAT ARE THE SIGNALS OF LOVE AND INTIMACY?

Love: Love is a real emotion. The positive side of love is the one we all know and enjoy as feeling good, warm, open, supported, and connected. The negative side of love occurs when we attempt to love someone who doesn't want to be loved by us, or having someone we don't want to love us insist upon doing so.

A woman I knew complained about a man being mean to her. It turned out he was going places she would be, and leaving flowers and notes on the windshield of her car. The problem was this woman didn't want love from this particular man. It felt more like stalking, leaving a bad taste in her mouth, and a sinking feeling in her stomach, whenever she returned to her car and found a beautiful flower under the windshield wiper. This is the negative side of love. It's giving love when it's not wanted or invited.

When we feel love toward someone we want them to come closer. Love signals us to make contact. We want to know more about that person. We want to spend time with them and give to them. While we're in their company, and afterwards, we feel really good.

Love doesn't require us to open completely, though we usually feel fantastic when we do, as with intimacy. Love leads us to want to be in the vicinity, to interact with, to smile, and fill ourselves up with the other person. We want to give, and to see the happiness in the other person.

Intimacy: Intimacy on the other hand signals: "Open up, get as close as you can. Share yourself as completely as possible."

As suggested earlier, we're unable to experience the state of intimacy unless we're loving with ourselves, and respect ourselves enough to accept ourselves as we are. The good part about this stance is the more we can accomplish this in our life, the more the people we attract to us will reflect this, loving us more deeply and accepting us as we are, too.

HOW TO FIND THE LESSONS OF LOVE AND INTIMACY

Love: The experience of love strengthens and supports us. The lessons of love are to find that strength and support, and allow it to buoy us through our life. Love doesn't invite us to cling to it, but to let it in, adopt it, and do this so well we integrate it with who we are.

Things we can do to identify love and the ways we experience it, include:

- Allow yourself to feel love.

- Once noticed, ask yourself: "What's allowing me to feel so loved (or loving) right now? What am I doing? What is the other person doing?"

- When you recognize love coming from another, after drinking in their gift, ask yourself: "Is there a way I can give this to myself on an on-going basis?" If so, identify it and make the intention to include it in how you relate to yourself.

- Express the gratitude you feel for this love.

- If you want, though you may first want to savor it a while, share this love with others.

Intimacy: The best way to find intimacy's lessons is to identify what we push away from ourselves when deep intimacy is possible.

Do we come close, but only for a short time before pulling away? Do we fear intimacy and don't even let ourselves be alone with others? Do we stop ourselves through judgment, perhaps thinking we're not good enough or we're not worthy of love or closeness? These behaviors indicate the lesson for us is really about how frightening getting close to others is for us. To become all we can be in life, pay attention to this fear and make it a thing of your past. When we allow ourselves to be alone and close with someone and realize we are equal to others and worthy of love, fear of intimacy becomes a thing of our past. This fear invites us to step into it and take a risk in order to deal with it. Taking small steps toward being intimate with others, and continuing to take small steps, will help us learn the lessons intimacy has for us.

Becoming intimate with our self, first, means getting to know our self honestly and deeply and accepting who we are. This makes intimacy with others much easier.

But what if we're good at being intimate with others? We feel like we don't have any boundaries that keep us separate, we're trusting and open and ready to connect deeply? There may still be lessons for us. Ask your self if you're willing to be intimate with everyone who comes your way? Do we see other people in this world as the same as we are, as all One? Can we allow others to see our flaws? Do we accept full responsibility for our part in interactions with others? While being open to others, are we still loving to our self? Check these areas out. Since we're fallible humans, the chances are great there are still areas of work we can step into, which will lead us to even greater depths of intimacy.

RELEASING THE ENERGY OF LOVE AND INTIMACY

Love: Why would anyone want to turn loose of the energy of love or intimacy, allowing it to move away, to move on?

Energy, which emotion is, is designed to move. When we hold on to any emotion, we stop its movement. Then that emotion cannot do its job, convey its full message, or bring the intended lessons. This is true for love and intimacy, too. We need to keep Emotions in Motion!

When we release the energy of love, we allow love to circulate to others. Crucial to our ability to do this is to realize that when we let love go, we don't have less love for ourselves. Long ago, I read a story about a mother of three young boys who frequently vied with each other for her attention and love. During a storm, the electricity went off. Seizing the opportunity, this mother got out four candles, giving one to each son and keeping one for herself. After she lit her candle, she invited each boy to light his candle from the flame on hers. When they were done, she drew attention to the fact that all of them had a flame equal to the others. She noted that while they lit their candle from hers, she still had a strong flame. Nothing was subtracted from anyone, yet they all added light with their candle. This, she shared with them, is how love works. When you share it, everyone gets love, nothing gets subtracted from anyone, and everybody gets to feel good and a part of things.

Sharing love, as we do when we release it and allow it to move through and beyond us, is the very thing we need to do to keep on experiencing love and feeling loved. The best way to feel love is to share it, offer it, give it away, and bring it forward in ourselves, through even the most challenging situations. The energy of love goes out, circulates, and returns to us for another encounter.

Intimacy: Similarly, holding on to intimacy puts us into a constant state of being vulnerable, open, and intensely connected to others. A constant state like this could soon cause numbness. Just as love needs us practicing love, each in our own way so it can become aware of itself, we need to allow ourselves some time off from intimacy, in order to know intimacy better. We need to know both "intimacy" and "not-intimacy." We release intimacy by moving onto the next thing or person showing up in our life. We let other people go in order to move on with their lives, freeing all of us to connect intimately with even more people, including them.

Like this line from a prayer once given to me: "Hold, release. Hold, release. Thank you, God, I am at Peace." We feel more peaceful inside ourselves when we practice both holding and releasing love and intimacy.

My Personal Laboratory

You may think that if you've fallen in love and married, you're good at intimacy and love. That may be, but it was not true for me.

Even after a couple of years of marriage, when my sweet young husband would tell me, "I love you," I reacted by saying, "You're just saying that because you're my husband, and you have to." This had to discourage him.

The problem was that I couldn't allow myself to be vulnerable enough to accept his love. What if I accepted it, then got dumped? It happened in my childhood; so what was to keep it from happening now?

One thing I've learned through my years as a psychotherapist. We cannot accept ideas about ourselves, or compliments, unless there is a "home" for it inside of us. I have to know and accept something as real in order for me to let it in to myself.

In my young marriage, I had no "home" in me for love.

Eventually, I realized that a major way I used my husband was to counteract my belief that I was unlovable. Surely if he told me he loved me, and loved me enough to marry me, I had to be lovable. I had the evidence outside of me; but I still had no "home" for intimacy and love in me.

Michael Brown, who speaks about *The Radiance of Intimacy (Into-me-and-see)*, postulates that we have the opportunity to be intimate with other humans as practice for being intimate with God. When we share intimacy with each other, we can expand the "home" for intimacy inside of us. If intimacy and love are difficult for you, try experimenting with creating a home for them inside yourself.

YOUR PERSONAL LABORATORY

Take a look at your history with intimacy and love. If you grew up in a loving home, where you learned and felt both the art and skills of love, you're indeed fortunate. If that's what you find, take time to be grateful and write what you're grateful for.

If, like me, your childhood was such that you closed the door on vulnerability (one of the most challenging of the skills of intimacy), consider whether it's time for you to start allowing yourself to be vulnerable, to get closer to others. If so, start slowly. You can even be intimate with a dog or cat first. Just allow yourself to open your heart and let some other creature know you for who you are. Write about what occurs when you do this.

If you're in a loving relationship, identify some simple steps to allow yourself to be more vulnerable and intimate with that person. Perhaps it's your partner, or your children or grandchildren. Open up and let them in for a tender visit.

What was that like? Write about your experience(s).

In 1994, I made the decision to make love the guiding principle of my life, starting with loving myself first, and then others. My life changed forever. As a person who believed she was unlovable, cried herself to sleep in her 30s because she had no friends, and told her young husband he was just telling her he loved her because he had to, it's a miracle that my life has turned around 180 degrees. I feel great, far less vulnerable, and find almost everyone I meet becomes a loving friend.

If you want this for yourself, make the decision to dedicate yourself to living by the principle of love. As author Matt Kahn says, "Whatever happens, love that."

Make notes on your experience and progress.

25

FEAR, STRESS, AND ANXIETY

Everyone is familiar with fear. When we experience fear, we go into self-protective mode, following the often-cited "fight or flight" pattern. Either we run away from what we fear, or we turn and encounter it, and fight it off. This is what we're told is possible to do with fear. It's what humans have done about fear since the dawn of humanity.

WHAT CAUSES US TO FEEL FEAR

The mechanism of fear, according to theorists, was developed in our brains during the time humans were in danger of being attacked by saber-tooth tigers. The fear mechanism assisted humans in preserving life, supporting fighting the tiger, or getting away from it.

Saber-tooth tigers were a real danger to humans. This is a very worthy reason for our bodies to go into reaction, moving blood to our body core to protect us, and shooting our system full of adrenalin to give us what we need for fight or flight.

The problem with fear today is the lack of saber-tooth tigers. Without saber-tooth tigers, what is real for us to fear?

There are, of course, physical dangers. Attacks threatened by other humans, car and plane accidents, neighborhood dogs, and wild animals if we put ourselves in their territory. Other than these, most of the things we fear are the result of our imagination. For example, we imagine we'll be fired; and we're afraid. We imagine our lover is going to reject us, we're going to run out of money, we'll lose our home; and we're afraid. A majority of these fears, for most of us, don't materialize. The power of fear, paired with our brain, is such that we can imagine things to fear so well that our body goes into the preparation phase, ready to deal with the saber-tooth tiger that never materializes. When this occurs, we start to live in a state of chronic anxiety.

ANXIETY

Fear expands and anxiety occurs when we're unable to shut down the mechanism for dealing with things that menace us—fears based on reality—and our body and brain stay in a continuing state of flight-or-flight readiness, ready to confront a danger that never materializes. Most of the fear people experience today is a product of imagination, with ideas drawn from a variety of sources, such as parental teachings, frightening movies, unhealed childhood traumas, television reports and news, and things we see and hear about in our daily lives. Because the actual threat seldom shows up, our entire system stays at the ready, unable to fight or run away. A huge number of people are filled with anxiety, most of which never goes away or gets dealt with, because the threat isn't real and we're not making sure our fear mechanism gets turned off once in a while.

STRESS

And that brings us to something everyone talks about these days: Stress. Stress is our mental and physical reaction to being in a constant state of readiness to take flight or engage in a fight. We also experience stress when things are chaotic, which they are in these times of extraordinary change. With climate change, political change, constant updating of technology, financial changes, construction on roadways that slow travel, needs of our children changing, changes in health, our favorite restaurant closing down, and changes on social media platforms, modern human beings are experiencing an inordinate amount of stress. This stress is interwoven with fear and anxiety, causing many to have sleepless nights and chronically tense bodies.

Anxiety and stress flow from fear, making too many of us sick, tense, worried, and unhappy. We've also learned that continuing stress can disable or kill us.

The question becomes: "Is it necessary for us to have fear so uppermost in our daily lives?" My answer is "No." It is quite possible for us to engage in what I call: "Fear-less Living." Doing so requires us to make simple, but important changes.

THE SIGNAL OF FEAR

When we first become aware of feeling afraid, what kinds of things do we do? We may catch our breath, throw our hand up on our chest (fear's center in our body), crouch for protection, scream, or look for our escape route. We become intensely aware of our environment, our brain begins to run through what we need to do to keep ourselves safe.

In other words, fear is saying, "Watch out! Exercise caution! Something is ahead that requires us to stay aware and ready to take action!" Fear advises us that we need to use extra caution to handle something unexpected or unknown.

THE SIGNAL OF ANXIETY

Anxiety speaks the same as fear: "Watch out! Be Careful! Take heed!" We're given constant warnings: "Watch out! Be Careful! Take heed!" This message comes over and over, and over, and over, and over again, sometimes without ceasing. We may stop paying attention to this warning for a bit, giving ourselves a moment of relief. But when we're again alone or quiet, the warning sounds again: "Watch out! Be Careful! Take heed!"

There seems to be little way to shut this warning off. We can distract ourselves; but it returns. Sometimes the same anxiety can go on for days, months, weeks, and even years. As Dr. Fritz Perls told us decades ago, the mind doesn't rest until the Gestalt is completed. Unless something changes in our brains or our actions, anxiety can persist, continuing to wreak havoc in our lives.

THE SIGNAL OF STRESS

The simple message of stress is, "This is way too much for me. I need a break. I need to get off of this merry-go-round." Unfortunately, when we hear this message, we don't often heed it. Our concerns and sometimes our fears, such as fearing the loss of a job, keep us forging ahead, not listening to the clear message of stress, telling us we're overloaded. Sadly, accident or illness can result from prolonged anxiety and stress.

50 years ago, I stayed home from my job. I called in sick. After a few hours of lying in my bed, I realized I wasn't feeling sick. It seemed to me I just needed a break from my job. I realized I wasn't allowed, in our work culture, to call up my boss and say, "I need a break. I'm staying home today." Instead, I had to use the code words, "I'm sick." I really didn't like the system, but that's what it was.

I continued to ruminate, slowly getting the idea that when we don't listen to our body's messages about being near to overwhelm, and take some time to ourselves, that is when we tend to get sick. To live in my world, I felt like I kept up by going farther and farther away from myself, doing more and more. I didn't know how to say, "No." When I got far enough away from myself, I would get sick. Then, I could say, "No" because I had the excuse: "I'm sick. I can't do anything now because I'm sick!"

It seemed to me if I could develop the ability to cut back on my outside activities, whenever I noticed I was stretched too far, I might avoid getting sick. I set my intention to develop that ability. Over the years since then, as I cut back on stress by listening to when I was approaching overwhelm, I've led a healthier and healthier life. Consider this: We get sick because we don't listen to the messages coming from our mind and body that we're stretched too thin, we're stressed. When we listen to those messages and take care of ourselves before we get sick, we're able to avoid illness a lot of the time.

When we experience stress, the stress has a message for us. "Check where you can cut back. You need a break!" We might also think of this signal as one that says, "It's time to love yourself a whole lot more!"

FIND THE LESSON OF ANXIETY

Being on continual alert in our body and brain is taxing and tiring. When we're filled with anxiety, we don't realize what a toll anxiety is taking on us. Only after we've released the anxiety do we realize how tense our shoulders, how tight our belly, and how vigilant our brain have been.

The lesson of anxiety is about humility, about recognizing and living with the knowledge that we're not alone on Earth. We can ask for and get help.

Ask for help from the most emotionally neutral person you can find. We want someone (like a coach or therapist, but it could be a mentor or spiritual counselor), emotionally neutral because we don't want to be concerned about them getting upset and anxious, too. It's best if this person can give advice and backup without us feeling responsible for them, which we often do if we consult a relative or close friend.

Find out how this person has released anxiety in their life, or have them tell you about others they know who have done so. Find a role model.

We can also begin to work the anxiety out of our body by taking a hike, working out, swimming, practicing yoga, running or some other form of strenuous aerobic exercise (be sure your body is in good health first). If we do these things with a friend, we may pay attention to talking or being with our friend, and not allow thoughts that increase our feeling of anxiety to be forefront in our mind.

Perhaps it's easy to ask for help, but for some people it's not. With the principle, help that isn't asked for never works, it's vital to remember to ask for help. In the larger scheme of things, real help is not given unless we ask for it. I suggest experimenting. Try asking for help a few times and see what happens. The lesson of anxiety is we're attempting to carry the world on our shoulders alone. We need to learn that some of the other nearly eight billion people on Earth are here and can help us. And if we subscribe to a spiritual belief, those not on Earth are ready to help, too.

FIND THE LESSONS OF STRESS

We all experience stress. We all have things that operate as stress busters for us, such as exercise, eating, indulging in a favorite hobby, playing the piano, or lying in the sun.

Stress tells us we're out of balance, with no room for anything else. We find it very difficult to relax and focus on anything but the pressures we perceive in our lives. The message of stress is: Let go, let go, let go!

FIND THE LESSONS OF FEAR

Fear has many lessons for us. The first lesson is to step into life and engage it. The principle I discovered is that when we operate on the motive of fear, we're guaranteed to create what we fear. To deal with fear, face it. Stepping into whatever brings us fear shows us something surprising: Our fear is usually worse than the reality. We end up creating what we fear because fear causes us to focus on what we fear. Remember when we focus attention and energy on something it grows. Therefore, if we fear our spouse will stop loving us, and we focus on finding all the signs and symptoms that show our spouse prefers others or is not fully there for us, eventually, we will lose our spouse. I know because I did this in my first marriage.

Plug in any scenario to complete this story, and observe that living our life in such a way that we cater to a particular fear actually creates it as our reality. If we listen and take heed, fear teaches us: Step in and face whatever scares us. Don't think of it as an act of courage, but see it as what we need to do in order to be in charge of fear that arises, rather than allowing that fear to dictate our life.

The second lesson is we tend to talk about our need to have courage when we deal with fear. In my learning, courage is about feeling the fear, and doing it anyway. When a person doesn't understand how things work in this Giant School, courage may be what is required. But when we understand the way things are set up in life, fear is bringing us something to learn, and the lesson will repeat and repeat until we learn it. We can sidestep a lot of the fear by stepping into it, seeing this as less of an act of courage and more one of common sense.

Remember: "I will deal with this fear because I don't want it to keep coming up all the time. It might feel scary now, but think about what it will be like if I put it off and it grows in strength!"

Fear offers us the lesson that just because something is unknown or untested, or is new territory for us, doesn't mean we can ignore it. Fear is a part of life that we need to get to know and learn from. Keep putting one foot in front of the other. When we accept fear's invitation, what happens can be amazing and wonderful, more often than anyone expects.

Finally, fear offers us the lesson of humility, too. Most of the fear we experience results from feeling like whatever happens in my life, it is totally up to me. This stance is one that lacks humility. Humility, in the way we're talking about it here, is the constant remembrance that there is something larger than ourselves. There is nothing that I need to do totally on my own. There is always a person or a force nearby that wants to help. All we need to do is ask. We don't even have to know who it is or be able to see them. Just ask.

To get help we must ask. When we're engaged with fear, we tend to feel alone, helpless, and overwhelmed. Just try saying out loud, the next time you're feeling afraid, "Please, help me. I need help now. Please, help." Watch what happens.

The first time I tried asking for help this way, reluctantly, because I didn't think it would work, I felt immediate peace. Fear has a lesson for us: We're never alone. There are ways to work things out. Just ask for, and accept, help.

RELEASE THE ENERGY OF FEAR

Facing fear, asking for help, and focusing on what we want to become, instead of what we want to overcome, will release the energy of fear. We can use visualization to release fear. Here are two effective ways to do that. Read both examples through before choosing one to use.

First process: Sit quietly with eyes closed. Allow attention to move to the outside of the Earth, where we discover layers of human emotion, such as anger, hurt, fear, and other forms of energy that create limitation. Find the layer of fear. Enter it. In this layer are all our personal fears, as well as the fears of every other human. We may find things very chaotic. It might seem dark. Notice what it's like, and how you feel while visiting this layer of fear.

After visiting this layer of fear for a few minutes, move out of this layer of fear and search for another layer surrounding the Earth. This time find the layer that is Faith or Trust. We're not speaking of religious faith here, but the kind of faith it takes to put our head on our pillow at night and believe we will awaken and be alive the next morning. Find the layer of Faith or Trust and enter it. Here is where our personal faith and trust, as well as the faith and trust of everyone on the planet, is located. Take a look around and note what you see, feel, and experience. Notice what the light is like here.

After familiarizing yourself with this layer, make a decision about which of the two layers visited you choose. To release the energy of fear, decide to stay in the layer of Faith or Trust. Give yourself permission to stay in this layer and to be able to return easily to it if you should temporarily step out of the layer. Feel what it feels like when committing to remain in the layer of Faith and Trust. Drink in the feeling. Be grateful. Slowly open your eyes and return to everyday reality, knowing that you have committed to Faith and Trust.

The second process for releasing the energy of fear is to imagine in front of you a big, blue ball that is itself a semi-permeable membrane, meaning we can put things in or take them out easily. With eyes closed, set your intention to remove all fear energy from your body. Start with the toes and search out every bit of fear you can find in your body. Finding fear, pull it out and stuff it into the ball. Fill the ball with every bit of fear energy you can discover. When you have all the bits, take a minute to breathe, and to assess whether you've done all the searching for bits of fear that you need to do. Then imagine pushing or tossing the ball up into the sky, sending it away. Watch as it leaves, getting smaller and smaller as it rises up and away. When it is about 100 feet away, grab a nearby sunbeam and cut across the space between yourself and the ball, as if there is a string connecting you to the ball. Have the intention to cut and disconnect it, using your imagination to release the ball completely, so it doesn't boomerang back. Watch until the ball is out of sight, aware you are releasing fear harmlessly into the Universe. Sit for a few minutes experiencing freedom from fear energy. Allow joy in. Open your eyes. Be grateful.

MY PERSONAL LABORATORY

In 1973, I began a stress-busting practice. Each summer for a week I went backpacking with my dog in the Marble Mountain Wilderness Area in Northern California. My children stayed with their respective fathers and I had a total week of nobody needing attention from me. My dog responded to hand signals.

In those early years, I worked very hard finishing my master's degree, beginning my business, confronting the raging anger pouring out of me, and mothering a very powerful toddler girl on my own. My child was a powerful personality and needed more strength to deal with than I thought I had sometimes. I had no relatives closer than thousands of miles away and no time to recruit friends for help. With no Internet, there were also no MeetUps, Support Groups, or people I could contact on Social Media.

When I talked with friends, I was told, "Take care of yourself!" This made me laugh. How do I take care of myself when I'm building a new business, being a single parent, and taking care of a home and a third of an acre of orchards and garden, cats and dogs, and learning the very basics about an emotion like anger?

In the wilderness alone, I contemplated the question: "What does it mean to take care of myself?" It means to bring myself into balance. Was it possible, with all that was going on in my life, to get to a state of balance?

I had learned that to balance off regular behaviors in life, all we need to do is introduce the opposite of those activities, and for only three hours in a week.

I made a list. My week consisted of being indoors, paying attention to others (child and psychotherapy clients), sitting a lot, and staying by myself. Doing the opposite meant I needed to get outdoors, do something for myself, move my body, and spend time with others. I only needed to do these opposites for three hours each, in a week. In the mountains, I set my intention to build these things into my life.

After my return home, I started taking a weekly hike in the hills behind my home. Even though I carried my daughter in a back pack, I was in my body and being healed by the beautiful greenery of my surroundings. I joined an exercise class offered by a friend and determined to make a few friends in the class. This got me moving my body, interacting with others, and paying attention to what I needed, all in one package. I went to exercise three times a week. That's three hours!

Within a very short time, I could feel the tension leaving me, both in my brain and in my body. I made a few good friends in exercise class, though the leader of the class didn't always appreciate me talking during exercise time.

A lesson of stress is to pay attention to bringing balance back into our life. We bring balance by building in opposites, needing only to do those three hours during the week. The only person I had changed was me. My circumstances were the same. But I was far less stressed, because I had found the formula for neutralizing it.

YOUR PERSONAL LABORATORY

Take a look at your life to identify where you experience stress. Make a list of what you do regularly. Make a second list of the opposite to those things you do regularly. Create a plan for building the opposites into your life, three hours each and every week. Follow this plan for at least three weeks. Record your responses and your outcomes. If you like how this works out, continue with your plan for balancing for a longer time, tweaking as it feels right for you.

26

SECTION SUMMARY

L iving life becomes much easier when we realize that emotions are talking to us all the time, selflessly offering themselves to us so we can live better lives by navigating well enough not to keep having wrecks.

To help you appreciate this, we've offered this book section to give you the precise message of 12 different, everyday emotions and emotional states.

At one time or another, we all know these emotions. When we don't understand they are trying to help us, we try to hide that they've arisen in us, failing to lay claim to their wisdom. No longer.

You now have the information needed to partner with 12 basic emotions and emotional states when they arise inside, allowing them to offer their guidance and do their job. Congratulations to you and to those emotions.

There are things you've never heard about some of the emotions before, such as loneliness not being about being alone. You may resist what we've offered about some emotions, perhaps disqualifying what we've shared. That's okay. Each of us is different and we need to honor our differences and move at our own pace.

However, I ask you to experiment. I love experiments. I can try some new idea or behavior out for a time to determine for myself whether it's a fit for me. I encourage you to take this opportunity, too.

Remember that any behavior we repeat daily for three weeks becomes a new habit. If you don't like the results of your experiment, stop before you hit the three week mark.

People who live with us often resist when we make changes, so you may find people questioning you for experimenting in this way. Remember each person comes to the Earth to explore for him or herself. Something that may be strange, or even "wrong" for someone else, may not be so for you. My father said I was "overly sensitive." I discovered that was not true: I'm "just right sensitive" for myself. Make a decision about what is more important to you: experimenting and growing, or not being criticized and remaining the same? There is no right or wrong choice, only the one that fits for you.

Now that we have offered the message for these 12 emotions and emotional states, let's gather more tools for working with them, giving us maximum advantage to use the emotions we experience.

SECTION 4

EMOTIONAL PRINCIPLES AND TOOLS

27

ENERGY DRAIN STIMULATES POWERFUL EMOTIONAL REACTIONS

There are so many people in today's world who are manipulative that we need to talk about manipulation. Manipulation is also referred to as co-dependence and energy sapping; and the terms are interchangeable. We talk about manipulation not because manipulation is an emotion, but because so many emotions are brought up when manipulation occurs. Emotions are stirred when we're manipulated. When we're manipulated anger, in particular, arises, usually very quickly and far out of proportion to what is happening. This is because we believe that others should not attempt to take advantage of us, rob us of our energy or thrust guilt upon us that we don't believe we deserve.

Since 1972, I began my work to understand and work with manipulation, including how this common human behavior begins, how it works, how people drain the energy of others, how and why we manipulate ourselves, how to recognize a "Lifestyle Manipulator," and what we can do to end manipulation in our life. As I developed a system for understanding and eradicating manipulation, it became apparent to me that we're meant to grow out of manipulating, just as we grow out of bed wetting.

Manipulation is a thing of childhood and is designed to get set aside as we mature. We're far behind in achieving this reality as it seems most humans accept that manipulation is normal. My conclusion is that manipulation is common, but it's not normal.

MANIPULATION BEGINS

Everyone is born manipulative. At birth our little bodies and immature brains don't function well enough for independent living. We all need at least one outside agent to act on our behalf. Without it we can't survive. Our first outside agents are usually parents.

Manipulation is about using another person's energy for ourselves. Babies manipulate to survive in early life; and it's expected that babies need care from parents, the outside agents who can exchange energy with the world on their behalf. Babies scream, cry, and use other ways to attract attention, to make sure needs are met. If parents or other caretakers don't assist an infant to get food, have diapers changed, be touched, secure a safe place to sleep, etc., then the infant will die. A tiny infant needs parents to do what the baby can't do alone.

As our bodies grow up, people who continue to manipulate believe survival without an agent is not possible, thus supporting the deep-seated fear that if others don't help us exchange energy with our world, we will die. On-going manipulation results from this belief.

Is it normal for people to continue manipulating as adults? Most people I ask say, "Yes." Manipulation throughout life is seen as normal, but in fact it isn't.

It's normal not to have bladder or bowel control before age two or three, but not viewed as normal after the age of four or five. It's normal to be manipulative up to about age four, but not normal after age 20. People accept that "everybody manipulates." We don't understand that the design is for us to end manipulation during childhood.

A major job of childhood and adolescence is to become our own agents, exchanging the energy for surviving and thriving directly with our world, without sending it through another person first. We're meant to become responsible for our choices and their consequences. From infancy to full maturity, humans are designed to move from needing an agent for survival and to stay alive, to wanting to have the help of others, but knowing we will be all right if we don't get it. The design is for us to move past "need" and into "want." We're not intended to remain eternally dependent on others, physically or energetically.

What does manipulation look like in a grown-up?

Manipulators look like adults, but they don't behave like adults. A person who manipulates as a way of life, while looking like an adult, may blatantly lie, have temper tantrums, scream incoherently at someone who doesn't behave as they want, blame others, do something childish like sticking out their tongue, or otherwise make you ask: "How could a grown person behave like that?" We don't view these behaviors as mature, yet a manipulative adult can do such things, feeling justified in the infantile behavior, while the people around them attempt to relate to them as adults.

Manipulators employ many techniques, like spreading guilt, bestowing presents, heaping praise, or colluding with others to get someone to fill their needs.

A mature person doesn't behave this way. Mature people take responsibility for meeting their own needs. They ask others for involvement or help when they want it; but they don't need it. They don't employ behaviors designed to control the lives of others. The mature person knows there are three choices when others don't want to help fill needs:

- Decide to let the need/want go unfulfilled.

- Find a way to get the need/want filled in a different way.

- Fill the need on their own.

These options aren't available to the immature manipulative person. This person sees only that someone else must fill the need they feel inadequate to fill themselves. Because the need is perceived and felt as a matter of survival, it can't get released. This person believes survival is assured only when others behave in specific ways, so the manipulator's needs get met. The manipulative person doesn't take full responsibility for life, believing the only way to get needs met is through controlling others so they pass along energy to the manipulative person.

When things go wrong, the Lifestyle Manipulator blames others. Characteristically, when the manipulation is thwarted, the manipulator will say those others are bad, wrong, or crazy. Listen for it.

Manipulation is rampant in our culture. Since people are supposed to outgrow the need to manipulate by adulthood, parents need to help children make the shift away from requiring others to be their agent in order to function in life. A large proportion of parents haven't helped children make this transition, for three reasons:

1. Parents may not know children need help to make this transition.

2. Parents may feel it's too much to ask a young child to take this responsibility.

3. Most often, parents may not have outgrown manipulation themselves, which leads them to cling to their children, desperately needing agents and fearing being separate and alone.

ENDING MANIPULATION

Let's look at what it takes to move manipulation out of our lives. The First Rule of Manipulation is: It takes one to know one. This means that if people in our life manipulate, we're also manipulative.

It was a shock when I first discovered this rule. Like most, I thought I needed to keep others from manipulating me. Yet life is lived from the inside out. What we have inside of us is what we'll draw in from outside. Being manipulated tells me I manipulate.

Realizing this is bad news and good news.

BAD NEWS

It's bad news, because it means we have work to do to grow up. We need to learn how to spend satisfying time alone, to decide to take responsibility for every part of our life, and face our fears. Becoming non-manipulative requires that we grow up and be comfortable being separate from others and operating as our own agent. That's when we'll no longer be manipulative. That's when we can behave interdependently, rather than dependently.

Manipulation is a round-about way to live life, in which we're obliged to go through an outside agent, instead of going directly for what is right for us. In business, an agent always takes a cut of what we get, leaving us with less than our full earnings. When we manipulate, it's similar to having business agents. Those agents take a cut of what we get, and don't always do things our way. Going through an agent takes more time and can't be controlled enough to allow us to get all that we need. This means we're obliged to work with many agents just to get enough of what we believe we need. It's a lot of hard work for a not-totally-fulfilling result. In the end, being manipulative compromises our freedom and is a lot of hard work.

People who are manipulative also encounter a lot of problems. Because manipulative people don't get all the energy they need from one broker, they can never relax, constantly craving and seeking the next hit of energy The worst relationship problem resulting from manipulation is abuse. The underlying cause of abuse is manipulation, a pattern in which two people who are still emotionally very young attempt to get survival energy from each other. Though this pattern is repeated all over the world every day, it's an impossible algorithm, because neither person has enough of the needed energy to give to the other.

GOOD NEWS

The manipulation habit can be kicked. We humans are designed to thrive by taking responsibility for ourselves. As we take more responsibility, we become more in charge of our life. And because we make more of our own choices, and we're willing to take responsibility for the consequences of those choices (good and bad), we increase our personal freedom. Taking responsibility is one of the building blocks of self-esteem.

In maturity, we live life straightforwardly. We get to decide what's right for us, go after exactly what we want, and receive the full reward for our efforts. Once we taste life as a responsible mature person, we're not tempted to manipulate again, because life is so much more satisfying.

EMOTIONS INTERTWINED WITH MANIPULATION

All emotions can become entwined when manipulation occurs. However, two emotions, anger and guilt, are almost always involved, and several others are stimulated to a slightly lesser degree.

Anger: I've found few people who like being told what to do. Even when we tell ourselves we "have to do" something, we go into resistance to being told. Procrastination is an internal refusal to do something we tell ourselves we have to do. Try this out in your life; and watch yourself resist and procrastinate.

Manipulators are master "have to do" people, expecting others to do what they believe they need them to do. Since we don't like to do "have to" things when we know what they are, we certainly resist the manipulator's "have to" that hasn't been explained to us (and may never be).

Guilt is often used to whip recalcitrant potential agents into line. The manipulator, accusing that person of being "bad, wrong, or crazy," frequently uses guilt as a control mechanism. We are accused of hurting the manipulator's feelings, doing something wrong, or letting the manipulator down. The manipulator expects us to immediately apologize, make amends, or take other action that gives them energy. As we know, with manipulators this pattern repeats endlessly.

People who use manipulation as a primary way of relating to others I refer to as "Lifestyle Manipulators." What the Lifestyle Manipulator wants is to stay connected. If there is a bit of unfinished business between the parties, it's easier to stay connected, and it's proof to the manipulator that the connection still exists. If you're the one being manipulated, however, frustration and anger arise because it's impossible to get finished with issues. The nature of manipulation is that the manipulator doesn't really want to work things out and finish them, contrary to what might be verbalized. Hence, relating to a Lifestyle Manipulator can feel like an endless run on a gerbil wheel.

Manipulation brings anger up in people who are manipulated, because they feel they have to act or respond in certain ways to keep the Lifestyle Manipulator happy. In addition, the same issues arise repeatedly, without resolution. The Lifestyle Manipulator doesn't clarify what is wanted, accuses others of being bad, wrong or crazy, expects apology for transgressions they define, can't see the other person's point of view, and constantly expects others to fill needs, suggesting that the people they select are the only ones who can do the job.

You can manipulate yourself by giving yourself "have to's," insisting you behave in ways that don't feel good to you, and by telling yourself you're bad, wrong or crazy to want or do what you think is right for you.

Awareness of feeling anger as a result of manipulation (yours or someone else's), is a first and necessary step for ending manipulation in our life.

Guilt*:* When the anger is hidden, as it is with guilt, it is much, much harder to work with—or get finished with. Recognizing the inherent anger and dealing with it directly is the fastest and most effective way to start getting manipulation under our control.

The handmaiden of manipulation is guilt. Lifestyle manipulators believe others are responsible for not giving them what they believe they need. Lifestyle Manipulators don't see their part in situations, thus believing that if things aren't going right, someone else is causing it. Because hurt is often used in manipulation, Lifestyle Manipulators freely hold others responsible for hurt they feel. Many accuse others of hurt when they don't really feel it. They just know what will get the other person to fold and give them the energy they believe they desperately need.

Note: This doesn't mean a manipulative person is "bad" in any way—or even intends to hurt others by inducing guilt, stimulating anger, or threatening hurt. They're merely immature. Desperate, such a person is not meaning to cause a problem; they just need to focus on themselves and their energy cravings.

People who manipulate as a lifestyle have an uncanny ability to identify THE thing that's most sensitive or important to the person manipulated, and use that as their tool. If not hurting someone else is a priority, then the manipulator will accuse the target person of hurting them. If being known as a giving person is important, the manipulator will throw accusations of: "You're greedy." Or "You're unloving," or mean, non-compassionate, uncaring, ugly, stupid. Whatever the lifestyle manipulator reads as the soft spot is what gets focused upon.

A caring person will feel terrible when receiving reports of hurt they cause to someone. This person ends up giving the manipulator a lot of personal attention and energy, attempting to work a way out of the guilt of having hurt another. A manipulator doesn't care if the targeted person stops feeling guilty or not, but does care about continuing to stay connected with that person, and continuing to get attention and energy.

As long as we remain in the world of manipulation, we're likely to carry an unending burden of guilt and anger. If we wish to alleviate that burden, then identify the anger that underlies the guilt and process that. As long as we stay in relationship with a manipulative person, however, this will only offer temporary relief, because guilt is a powerful and often-used tool of those who manipulate; and the manipulative design is for that to never end.

OTHER EMOTIONS INVOLVED IN MANIPULATION

"Whatever Works" is the motto of the Lifestyle Manipulator. They want to continue receiving attention and energy, stay connected, and keep particular people as primary sources of their energy. It makes them feel safe.

Therefore, every emotion a human has turns out to be "fair game" in the world of manipulation. Hurt, fear, anger, guilt, worry, anxiety, loneliness, love, jealousy, and shame, are the most common emotions we experience when manipulated. Each of these emotions needs to be dealt with when stimulated.

Perhaps it's easier to step out of the world of manipulation, instead of having to always work with the many emotions that manipulative people poke and bring up in us.

THE SECRET TO THE WAY OUT

The secret for getting out of the manipulation trap is in the First Law of Energy Sapping: It takes one to know one.

If we find ourselves manipulated and are feeling angry, afraid, or guilty in relationships with others, and we're frightened to let people go believing we won't get what we need without them, this means we're still living by manipulation. Get off the merry-go-round. All we need to do is end our own manipulation.

Remember: "What you have inside of you, you tend to attract from outside of you." In this Giant School of Earth, manipulative people are reflecting our own lack of maturity—our continuing involvement in manipulation. If you want to eradicate manipulation (and all the emotions that are brought up with it) from your life, begin working to end your own manipulation.

We've been talking about "Lifestyle Manipulators." This is to help us see the patterns more clearly. Most of us have what I call pockets of manipulation, places where we're still not taking full responsibility for ourselves. Manipulation is not our total way of relating. Instead, we remain manipulative in certain parts of our lives, yet are mature in many other pockets.

The fact an adult may still manipulate doesn't mean there is anything wrong with that person. It means they haven't fully matured, thus don't take full responsibility for interacting directly with the world, asking for what they want, or dealing with the consequences of choices they make. Having pockets of manipulation when we are adults is not shameful; it's showing us where we're not mature, giving us an opportunity to take responsibility and grow all the way up.

Seeing manipulation in ourselves gives us a new choice: We can end our own manipulative stance and behaviors. When we do this, our entire life experience will also change—for the better.

The design is for this learning to be completed before full adulthood. Like anything we're designed to learn in childhood, but are blocked from learning, it's a more difficult task once we are living as adults. But it's worth the effort to end manipulation and begin to live a manipulation-free life, as soon as we're aware this issue needs to be completed.

Whenever we experience anger, guilt, or fear, it's important to determine if it's because we're getting manipulated. These emotions arise when manipulation occurs, in order to alert us to the manipulation. They push us to end our long-held belief that we need others to behave in certain ways or give us specific things, in order for us to survive.

My Personal Laboratory

At the age of 29, my marriage ended abruptly. My husband said he wasn't ready to be a father, even though he willingly and actively participated in creating our 10-month-old daughter, following two years of discussion.

In addition to being on my own, feeling abandoned and becoming the primary parent, I was angry, hurt, and felt betrayed. It didn't take long to think: "That man used me. I need to figure out how someone uses another person, so I never have to go through this again."

I thought back over the relationship. I listened more carefully when a client came into my office to talk about being manipulated. How did this happen between people? Why couldn't we see it coming? Why were so many of us falling victim to manipulation? Was it really necessary to accept manipulation as a normal part of living? The questions swirled in my head as I sought answers.

Six months into my intensive inquiry, I came up with the First Law of Manipulation: It takes one to know one. I realized I couldn't be manipulated unless I was, myself, manipulating. This was a shock. What was I manipulating him for?

I came to understand I held a belief: "I'm not lovable." This brave young man asked me to marry him eight years before. Having a man want to marry me proved I was lovable, didn't it? I realized I was using my husband to demonstrate I was lovable, despite what I believed about myself. That's how I was using him. I needed him to demonstrate he loved me by marrying me, and living as my husband. Otherwise I was clearly not a lovable person.

Important concept: Nobody can manipulate us unless we're in some way being manipulative ourselves.

I realized we're all born manipulative. There comes a time when we make effort to end manipulation, starting at age two, demanding: "Me do it myself." At two years old, we're not capable of surviving on our own, not even a little bit. The real changeover isn't possible until between the ages of three and four, when we can pull up our own covers, get our own glass of water, and ask for what we want.

We need help to start becoming our own "agent" for exchanging our energy with the world. If we don't get it, our bodies keep growing so we look like adults, but emotionally, we remain somewhere between three and four years of age. That's who we take into our so-called adulthood.

I identified specific characteristics of this "looks like an adult but is emotionally a child" individual that most of us become, a person I came to call a "Lifestyle Manipulator." I observed the many ploys people use to move others around, like pawns on a chess board, in order to get what they believe they need for survival.

I figured out specific things we can do to end manipulation in us—and in our lives. Once I figured it out, I went through the process myself. It felt long, lonely, and challenging, but well worth the effort. Once I was on the other side I never looked back.

One thing Lifestyle Manipulators don't like is being alone. I've gone far past my old manipulative days. Today I'm writing in my RV, camped in a "dispersed camping" site offering no water or electricity. Last night there was one other camper at this site; and I felt a bit crowded. I've come through to the other side, and gotten to the stage of "want, but not need," which is easy and often preferable. It has enabled me to sail through the 20 years of being a single parent, the death of my spouse, and the recent total change of lifestyle.

Afterword: Six years past our breakup, my former husband called to apologize for having left me and our daughter. As I started to accept his apology, he told me he still felt guilty. So guilty, in fact, he said he sometimes couldn't look our six-year-old daughter in the eye. I said: "I will forgive you with one proviso: Forgive yourself. Because if you don't forgive yourself, she won't have had you when she was little; and she won't have you now either." With a sigh of relief, he agreed. That was more than 40 years ago. When we allow the flow of emotions, we have room to forgive others and ourselves, which opens the door to genuine connection.

YOUR PERSONAL LABORATORY

Take a look at your life. Are you mature or manipulative? Do you take responsibility for yourself, your choices and actions? Do you ask people for what you want, yet remain okay if they're unable to do as you ask? Are you mature in some areas and manipulative in other areas? Write down your answers.

Look at your life to see if you're manipulated by others. What do you feel when you get manipulated? Write this down.

Make a decision: Are you ready to give up the manipulation in which you engage? Do you see the ways you manipulate, identify what you believe you need from others that you cannot do without, and believe you cannot do for yourself? What would it take for you to stop manipulative behaviors? What can you do for yourself? Be honest with yourself.

If you're not ready to give up your manipulation yet, say so. We do best when we make change because we're ready, not because we think we should. Give some thought to what it might feel like to give up manipulation. Consider selecting a date by which you'll do what it takes to end your own manipulation. Write all of this down.

If, however, you're ready now, begin by taking responsibility for your choices and actions. Spend most of your time alone, until being alone is no longer difficult for you. These things become easier as you keep doing them, though they may be agonizing at first. Stick with your choice. Get help if it's overwhelming to face alone. Record your path and experiences.

28

PARTNERING WITH THE EMOTIONS WE FEEL

I've taken care not to reference emotions as "your emotions" or "my emotions." We tend to think the emotions that come up in us belong to us. They don't. Emotions are friends and messengers. To make them belong to us is tantamount to choosing one of our friends and making them belong to us. A friend is present in our life to experience their own purposes and learning, appearing and disappearing in our life as both parties intend and need for growth together. The same is true with emotions. Consider referring to "the emotions that came up in me," or "the emotions I felt," or "the anger I experienced," instead of referring to the emotions felt as "mine."

Another vital message is: You don't belong to emotions either. Over the decades and decades of pushing emotions away, we've lost track of what emotions are for, how they operate, and how to have a right relationship with them. We've come to fear we'll lose control, or the emotion might make us do or say something we'll regret or for which we could be punished (by ourselves or others). These fears indicate our belief that emotions can own us, taking us to thoughts, decisions, and behaviors that aren't right for us. Only if we turn ourselves over to the emotions that arise in us can this happen. It's our choice.

We partner with friends to do things, find enjoyment, meet goals, exchange support, and fill up emotionally. Then we let them go back into their life for a bit, getting together another time to partner again. Think of emotions like friends. Aim to partner with emotions the way we partner with a friend.

We've already mentioned respect as one of the essential skills of love. Consider treating emotions with respect. This means to accept the emotion exactly as it is, without feeling the need to change it or hide from it. Let the emotion be its full self. It's easier to work with something when the entire issue is exposed and we can see all the parts. Love the emotions that arise in us, realize they're hard-working, never-abandoning friends dedicated to helping us have a good life.

THE PARTNERING PROCESS

Partnering requires interaction. We have an idea why we're there; but we also need to know why our partner is there. Hence, I recommend learning the common signal of each emotion that arises. Emotions come forward to deliver a signal and offer us an opportunity to learn and complete the gestalt of previous life experiences.

To help with this, here is our list of the 12 emotions and emotional states along with the signal.

Anger: Our idea of how things work in this world is incorrect. Update it. Take action.

Anxiety: Unknown ahead. Watch out. Be Careful. Take heed. Felt repeatedly. Decide where to place your attention; and close the door on the negative emotions arising.

Fear: Watch out. Exercise caution. Something unknown is ahead. Stay aware and ready to take action. Know that we're safe in this Universe. Move ahead.

Guilt: Feeling angry, but believe we don't have a right to the anger we're feeling. Accept and identify the anger and release it.

Hurt: Signals us to look at how trust was broken and decide what we need to restore it.

Intimacy: Opportunity to open and be vulnerable with others. Allow our self to connect deeply and fully with others. Embrace vulnerability; allow yourself to open up.

Jealousy: The mental computation that someone has something we can't have. Get creative by giving to ourselves what is right for us.

Loneliness: More energy is going out of us than is coming in. Take in energy now. It's time to pay attention to loving our self.

Love: Come closer. Allow our self to "feel the love" and connect with others.

Remorse: We did something and we're not feeling good about it. Check it out. Look at what you've done. Requires us to forgive ourselves and make a change.

Shame: A belief there is something wrong with us. Recognize that shame is not a real emotion; there is nothing wrong with us.

Stress: This is way too much for me. I need a break. I need to get off this merry-go-round. Heed this message and get off the merry-go-round.

Know the signal of a particular emotion, take time to be curious and investigate how it's operating in the particular circumstance in which it is arising. Feel free to ask pertinent questions:

- What is this emotion trying to tell me?

- What's the scope of the issue?

- Does this issue and emotion involve only me or others, too?

- When did I first experience this emotion? (Perhaps it's something from the past that hasn't been completed, stimulated by a similar situation in the present.)

- What do I need to do to complete this emotion now and release it?

- What is the bigger lesson of this experience involving this emotion?

- How can I best learn this lesson?

- What are the best ways to transform any so-called "negative emotion" into love?

- Where would I be focusing my attention, and what decisions would I be making, if I were complete with this emotion and had released it to move on?

As we practice this approach, the answers to our questions will come more quickly.

LISTEN

Ever had a friend ask for help or for an opinion only to find out they didn't listen to your response? The friend went forward without taking your advice into consideration. This happens to most of us. How did you feel?

Emotions aren't people, so we're not going to hurt feelings if we don't heed the message. However, why bother to partner with the emotions that arise, and then pay no heed to what we're told?

Listening to the message of emotions is vital. It reduces the amount of work necessary for us to learn and offers us a smoother path to the life we want. Think of emotions as a short-cut to apply to make our personal life work smoother and better. Listen.

LEARN

Until I realized Earth is a Giant School, little of what happened in life made sense to me. Random things just "happened to me," I thought.

Now, I realize everything that occurs in my life is something I can use for my learning and evolution. It's exciting. Emotions are the most dedicated, ever-present teachers. I embrace all emotions, search out the message and lesson, and look for the learning that I know is there, much like the boy who received a pile of manure for Christmas and was exited to find the pony he was sure was under the pile. I'm grateful to have emotions as my personalized, ever-present Mentor. Looking back over the years I see that every time I embrace and learn the lesson my life improves in some way. In addition, the entire learning process becomes much easier.

Once I understood how this "school" works, I decided to cooperate with it, rather than resist it. I invite you to do the same. Look for the lesson emotions bring. Embrace the learning. Rejoice. Move on.

THE POWER OF GRATITUDE

Many people talk about the importance of gratitude. If we're in school and a teacher works hard to help us understand a particular part of the course, most likely we feel grateful to the teacher for working extra-diligently to make sure we learn the material so we can move on. In this same way, we can allow ourselves to feel gratitude for emotions, notice and express that gratitude.

MY PERSONAL LABORATORY

When my daughter was in the sixth grade, she attended a demanding school about a mile and a half from our home. Our home was up on the side of a hill in one of the small towns near San Francisco, California. I lived there with my daughter, my son, and our ancient Labrador Retriever, Strider.

My daughter spent the weekend at her father's home. He returned her to school Monday morning, so I didn't expect to see her until the after-school pickup. Instead, she came in through our gate about 9:30 A.M. in a puddle of tears. "What are you doing here?" I asked.

"I was worried about Strider," she sobbed. "I thought he died." Strider was in the end days of his life. I took her into the room where our beloved dog was lying peacefully on his bed, staying to comfort her.

I noticed a knot in my stomach, a very uncomfortable feeling. "What emotion is causing this knot?" I queried myself. I realized I wasn't trusting what was happening. I followed the feeling of distrust and discovered I didn't believe my daughter's explanation. After a time, I said to her "I'm sure you were worried about Strider. But my stomach is in a knot. I know that when I have a knot in my stomach, it means there is manipulation going on. What is it you're not telling me about why you walked all the way home just now?"

My daughter broke into deeper sobs, telling me she had never gone into the school that morning, because she had a disagreement with her teacher on Friday. She was frightened to go back to the classroom. We talked about what had happened, before I returned her to school, and helped her straighten things out with the teacher.

Paying attention to what we feel emotionally (and emotions are always felt in our body, so include physical feelings, especially), can reveal hidden things. It's important to know, too, that emotions are always conveyed, even when we hope to hide them. In this instance, I didn't know what wasn't being said, but I knew that something was still hidden. When I investigated, the whole truth emerged. A lot of people miss recognizing what is going on with others, largely because we're not listening to ourselves and working with what we discover.

When becoming an Emotional Master, we'll be much more highly attuned. We'll be more aware of what is going on with others in our life, and can bring our compassion and love to use with ourselves and with the people we care about.

YOUR PERSONAL LABORATORY

Have you felt emotions telling you something, yet didn't listen? Take a moment to write about such an experience, including what happened when you didn't listen or take action based on the information you were receiving from those emotions.

Next, recall a time when your emotions were telling you something and you did listen and take action on the basis of the prompting or information you received from the emotions. What happened?

Before moving on, make a decision and declare it out loud. What is the intention for yourself the next time your emotions tell you what action to take? Write your decision down: "Next time, my intention is to _____ whenever the emotions that come up in me are offering me a message." Read your statement out loud.

29

PARTNERING WITH EMOTIONS: DEVELOP YOUR EMOTIONAL AND SPIRITUAL SELF

As a beginning therapist in 1971, I was afraid of most things spiritual. I'd been raised in the Christian tradition, but had turned against it when I found important people in my life espousing Christian ideals, yet behaving in despicable ways. Ideas of The Occult, having Past Lives, or asking Angels or Guides for help with my small little life—all of these were either frightening, overwhelming, or simply unbelievable to me. I often told people: "I have enough difficulty dealing with this life; I can't be bothered with dealing with other lives besides this one!"

Then in 1974, I found myself enrolling in a Spiritual Awareness class offered by the Spiritualist Church that met in the American Legion Log Cabin in a small town near me. In that class, they followed the Socratic Method. Students had the job of standing to ask questions that were important to them. It was extremely scary to me, but I stood and asked about things that felt important to me. The leader gave us answers. The answers were full of Principles. I had never been aware that such Principles existed; and they really spoke to me. Here are just a few of the Principles I started to learn.

- Each person on Earth is individually responsible for his or her life.

- Energy follows attention.

- Help that isn't asked for, never works.

- God is ever-equal to our understanding.

- Gratitude is the Law of Increase.

- The way something starts out, it tends to continue.

- What you put out into the world comes back to you.

- The only time we have power is in the present.

- The only person over whom we have power is our self.

- What you have inside of you, you tend to attract from outside of you.

- Creation exists, so that Love may become aware of itself.

I attended those classes and participated in the church for nearly three years. Each week I learned new Principles. I found this interesting and exciting and worked to put the Principles to work in my own life. As I did so, I discovered more principles, which were not taught in that class, such as:

- Pay attention, not to what you want to Overcome, but to what you want to Become.

- When you operate on the motive of fear, you're guaranteed to create that of which you are afraid

- Emotions held inside grow.

- Life is most effectively lived from the inside out.

These principles underlie what I'm sharing in this book. When used in your daily life, they are profoundly helpful in learning to work masterfully with emotions. They support the idea of our world as a Giant School, and when used with the messages of emotions, they guide us in all our lives. For example, humility—the constant remembrance that there is something or someone larger than us—is powerful in reducing stress. A lot of stress results from believing we must figure difficult things out for ourselves, by ourselves. Humility helps us to see that we can work in partnership with that something larger than ourselves, thus reducing our load. This, in turn, gives us a bit of distance from the challenge, allowing us to develop perspective and come up with solutions.

Initially, I worked to test these principles in my daily life. As I did so, I became impressed with their power and viability. Later, I took the risk of sharing a few of these principles with my clients and students. When they integrated these principles into their lives, the results were remarkable. As my psychotherapy work, guided by the principles and what I learned about emotions, started to work for my clients, my work became astoundingly effective and drew in more clients.

A REAL-LIFE OPPORTUNITY TO TEST THIS APPROACH

An area businessman was referred to me for therapy. When he arrived, he challenged me saying, "I've worked with 15 therapists with my problems, and none of them has done me any good! I'm going to give this a try with you, but I don't expect you to be able to do any better."

This man worked with me for several years, dealing with issues in business, family, and several instances of tragic loss. He made profound changes in how he lived his life, ran his business, and learned a lot about himself, too. Notably, he stopped having the "same old issues" repeat in his life, resolving most of them and becoming more of a creator of his own life. His personal power increased as he discovered how to end many years of living at the effect of circumstances and the behaviors and choices of others.

He was a student of ancient religions, devoted to studying the masters in those traditions. He and I didn't always see eye-to-eye regarding how the world worked, but we had enough agreement for him to use my approach to make major changes in the ways he lived. Principles pertain to life. Most of them are acknowledged in all religions.

The therapy I conducted, following the principles I'd learned, was incisive, to-the-point, and helped people change in lasting ways. A woman recommended by a friend promised me she would work with me for one visit. At the end of the hour, she said "I've been working with my therapist for five years. You have just covered more ground, and helped me more, in this one hour than she has done in the past five years!"

She resigned work with her previous therapist and continued working with me. The power of following the ancient, universal principles and listening to and partnering with emotions makes a huge impact on human lives. What had taken years could be accomplished much more quickly with this combination.

Most of us have difficulties in life because we slip out of harmony with these principles. They define the way things "are." When we work with the way things are designed, life unfolds miraculously. Just as Mother Nature follows principles, our lives follow principles. We can work with or against these principles. Working with them makes life easier. Adding our partnership with emotions to heeding these principles makes miraculous outcomes possible, and frequent.

Calling my work Transpersonal Therapy, it involved "helping people to bring their lives into harmony with ancient, universal, and spiritual principles." The therapy I did included the ideas that we're human and in physical bodies, along with the idea that we're spiritual, and much larger and more expanded than our human selves. This way of perceiving ourselves makes living life easier. Choosing to embrace learning through our experiences, to follow ancient spiritual principles, and to partner with the emotions that arise in us through our experiences leads to calm, peaceful, and powerful living every day.

SPIRITUAL PRINCIPLES AND EMOTIONS

I once listened to a disagreement between my father and older sister. She was an agnostic; and he was a pillar of his Methodist church. They were disagreeing about the existence of God. In desperation, my father delivered this statement: "I'm 63 years old. I have a degree in electronics and have nearly earned my master's degree in electrical engineering. Every day of my life I have learned something I didn't know the day before. This has brought me to one inescapable conclusion: There is someone out there who is one heck of a lot smarter than I am!"

Having that "something larger" is of benefit to us humans. A great illustration of the importance of combining the idea of being human and working with something or someone larger than ourselves is Alcoholics Anonymous. One thing that has stood out to me is that it's very hard to function well in a totally material world, where things are in flux and there is little overall principle with which to work. Recognizing something larger gives humans something onto which to hold, allowing people to relax their tight grip on making decisions and attempting to control, without every single thing being up to them.

You don't have to hold a particular belief to take advantage of the concept of having "something larger" available to you and your life. You can choose for that "something larger" to be your larger mind, your Higher Self, God, or, as some say, "The Great Whoever." You can even think of it as a deep part of yourself. Just having something larger than our own human selves, and realizing that larger something works on the basis of principle, improves life and makes things easier.

Nowhere is this more evident than in working with emotions. Some deep part of ourselves orchestrates things in our Giant School. In this school, we have repeated experiences that are designed to alert us to what we need to learn. A deep part of our selves brings up memories and emotions at the precise moments we're ready to complete the learning being offered.

Without this understanding, it seems like issues come from "out of the blue." They don't. The fact is we have experiences in our present so they connect with similar issues in our past, so we can heal both the past and the present issues, which are related or intertwined with each other.

Emotions come with experiences. When we partner with them, know their message, and make choices based on what they're telling us, we can pass smoothly through any experience, while also learning the message of that experience, so we don't have to keep encountering the same issue. In this way, emotions are an integral part of life and learning.

When issues from the past arise, we have the choice of healing them by going back in our imagination and taking back our power (and we can take a helper there, too). We can also take action to restore our personal power in our present. Healing the situation changes the trajectory of our life. This works best when we work in harmony with the spiritually-derived ancient, universal principles and the emotional messengers accompanying our experience.

Keep in mind that I'm sharing one way of working with emotions and life issues, one that has worked miraculously well for me and for hundreds of people to whom I've taught this system. There are many paths. This approach has three really important benefits:

1) It follows the way things are set up in this world, which results in us going with the natural path of evolution.

2) It combines the larger, spiritual way of perceiving things with the smaller, human way, allowing life to be more understandable and for us to feel more secure.

3) With more than 45 years of clinical testing, this approach has been demonstrated to be lasting. It's not necessary for us to go over and over and over the same issue, type of experience, or emotion. Instead, those are dealt with; and we move on, immediately.

My Personal Laboratory

More than 30 years ago, James (not his real name), learned in his work with me to take advantage of working with both the ancient, spiritual principles and his emotions, with an astounding outcome.

James drove a long distance to see me, and came to me in a panic, wanting to begin psychotherapy immediately. An accountant with an independent business, he had recently received a letter from the IRS saying they believed he had falsified documents on the income tax report he filed on the behalf of a client. James told me the accusation was accurate. He was panicked that he would lose everything because of his misstep. His wife threatened to commit suicide if the matter was made public. He was fearful of losing his wife and worried about losing his reputation and source of family income.

Because of the process followed by the IRS, James told me his attorney believed the matter would take more than three years to resolve. As the IRS investigation deepened, James could expect a series of letters. If they continued to think he was guilty, each letter would bring him closer to legal charges and a legal hearing, as well as public cancellation of his license to practice as an accountant. He needed to know what he could do.

First, I told him, we were fortunate he had some time to work on the situation, because he needed to change laws he'd set in motion throughout his life (called "laws," they're patterns he had been following that were acting like principles and creating unwanted outcomes). That would not happen quickly. I advised him: "Focus as little attention as you possibly can on the situation." The Principle we were following was: Whatever you pay attention to, you feed energy; and it grows. By not focusing attention on the worst possible outcome (especially highly emotionally-charged attention that came from panic), he wouldn't feed the issue much energy, and it would be less likely to grow. Together, we created other things on which to focus attention.

I told James he needed to move away from being panicked. Since each experience in life is an opportunity to learn, if James focused on the learning, it was possible to alter the outcome for which he was currently on a trajectory. I could not promise things would turn out well, but it was his strongest chance to successfully move through and beyond the current situation. I asked James to make a commitment to learn every lesson we could find, because that was most likely to result in a more positive outcome. He was asked to work with the energy of the situation, not the facts as he knew them. This was hard for James the accountant, whose life was dictated by working with exact facts; but he made the commitment.

Next we talked about what could possibly have made him decide to falsify documents for someone, when he knew it was illegal and might get him into trouble. We discovered James had developed a lifelong habit of capitulating to his older male cousin, starting at a very young age. Out of fear his cousin would reject or leave him James had developed the habit of going along with this older male.

The man whose papers he had falsified was very likeable, and older than James. James "transferred" his behavior with the cousin over to his client, and just "went along" with the man's request for the falsification. Notice that the cast of characters was different, but the pattern was the same. This is what happens when we have lessons to learn. An old behavior pattern arises, with emotions attached. When we follow the old pattern in the new situation, the outcome is usually harsher. This is a primary way emotions bring learning to our attention.

Fortunately for our project, James' wife also met with me a few times. It was important that she also stop sending the energy of fear, anger, and terror in the direction of the IRS. I gave her tools for releasing these emotions and working with them.

James and his wife both started imagining him receiving a letter saying "no further investigation" and stamped "case closed." They envisioned a file with his name on it, covered with cobwebs and marked "closed." They were both now following this

Principle: Pay attention, not to what you want to overcome, but to what you want to become.

Following ancient, spiritual principles, and employing the tools for partnering with the emotions that arose, James and his wife stepped back from the issue. They started seeing it as a learning opportunity, and began to place attention and energy on where they wanted things to go, rather than on the dire outcome they first imagined. They began to use the emotional energy of strong desire for a better future for themselves, to invoke and feel the possibility of that future. This is the pattern for manifestation (creating what you want in life by pairing your thought and emotion, holding them together until you can feel the way you'll feel when you receive what you want).

A vital lesson was part of this situation. James and I focused on identifying it for him to learn and complete. We determined the lesson was about his pattern of giving himself and his own executive away, essentially giving the power over his life to someone else. Instead of deferring responsibility and power to others, James focused on learning to be in charge of his own life (ending manipulation).

James was asked to assume personal responsibility for his life. He needed to decide he would never do something that was not right for him in his business, no matter what. All actions he took had to originate with him, not with his clients. He agreed, to the best of his ability, he wouldn't compromise his ethics or his choice of action. He would end the practice of "going along"—with anyone.

He severed ties with several clients, those who had already asked James to behave unethically. This was scary, because it meant cutting out a significant amount of James' income. I assured him that at the end of this process, he would make this money back and more. He'd have to trust me on this, and he did. He took 72 hours to make this decision, because he also decided to begin following The 72 Hour Rule.

James followed these principles:

1) Each person is individually responsible for his or her own life. (He assumed responsibility for his own life and allowed his clients to take responsibility for theirs.)

2) Unethical behavior, and requests for unethical behavior by James, was no longer a part of his life. Clients could be unethical, but they were no longer his clients. No judgment, just clear action.

3) James allowed himself to be the good person he liked being.

4) All decisions are made following the 72 Hour Rule.

5) James lived his life on the basis of principle, not personality. He followed his rules about how his business was done, and didn't base decisions on his unique relationship with any of his clients. James refused to fill any request for one client that he wasn't willing to fulfill for all clients.

6) James learned and listened to the messages of the emotions arising in him.

James began to feel remorse. He was allowing emotions to tell him his best choices, living by principle, and was incorporating both of these into his business and daily life, prodded by the rise of remorse. Though the IRS kept continuing its investigation and mailing James its letters, he placed less and less attention on the outcome.

Each time I met with James, we worked to keep him moving the emotions that came up in him. He would become angry with himself for putting himself, his business, and his wife into the difficulty they were in. Clearly, he believed he "should not have done" what he did. James learned that he had done the best he could with the tools and information he had, particularly with the lifelong pattern of capitulating to his older cousin. The task before James was to curtail self-judgment and forgive himself. He couldn't undo what was done. The best he could do was forgive himself (and his cousin), and learn from the experience. When he started living by new patterns, the lesson(s) would be learned and the consequences would change. That's how the Giant School works.

Each time he received another letter from the IRS, kicking his case to the next higher level of investigation, he felt afraid. James learned to step into the fear and face it. He looked at "the worst possible thing" he could imagine happening, asking himself if he could survive that. Increasingly, he decided he could; and the fear he felt began to take more of a back seat in his life.

Anxiety and stress were powerful, almost daily, adversaries. James and his wife, together, began to take long walks in the countryside near their home, swim, and do things that were fun and enjoyable, giving their bodies and brains a chance to rest.

James and his wife envisioned that final letter, the one that said "case dismissed" and was stamped "case closed." During the ensuing three years, James cleaned up his practice to be an ethical accounting business. He worked to strengthen himself through partnering with emotions, learning his lessons, and changing his life. He and his wife developed their life together, making sure to also have fun.

Remember in this Giant School when you learn your lesson(s), you're immediately finished, free to move on. What do you think happened with James' case and the IRS?

After nearly three years, James received a letter saying the IRS decided to close his case, having been unable to find sufficient evidence to prosecute. The bottom of the letter bore a stamp: "Case Closed."

But what about the other man, the one for whom James had falsified the document? The IRS continued its case against him, prosecuted him, and found him guilty. James had done his spiritually guided emotional work; the other man had not. It was truly a stunning outcome.

We were amazed, delighted, and joyful together. Not only had James proved the system of how this Giant School works, but he changed a future, possibly horribly negative outcome.

He did this by focusing on learning the lessons inherent in the experience. This included listening to emotions and following their suggestions, and learning to live by the ancient, spiritual principles. He chose to focus his energy and attention on feeling, learning, growing, and where he wanted to go. His life, and that of his wife, was saved.

Living in our Giant School doesn't require us to be punished for every mistake we make. The system is designed to teach us. Thus, when we use our error to focus on what we need to learn, and we learn it, punishment is not there. Punishment has been shown to drive behavior underground. Punishment leads people to hide, not to change. Just as parents forgive a child, especially when behavior changes following a mistake, that something larger (or is it our own deep self?) forgives us when we learn and change after making mistakes.

Within the next three years, James reported to me that his income doubled. He and his wife began to live a very nice life together, happily adding the children they both wanted.

James' story is one of the clearest I've personally encountered that demonstrates how combining work with emotions and the incorporation of ancient, spiritual principle into your life and decisions can take you places you might never imagine possible.

I believe the best outcome whenever anyone makes a mistake is that the person learns, makes amends, and changes his ways. The Universe seeks this outcome, something I have observed countless times when I've helped someone to work through a mistake or problem like I helped James. Without exception, when someone learned and changed the basis underlying an error, they experienced a miraculous release.

The important thing in this world is that we learn and grow. It's what our Giant School is set up for us to do. When we cooperate with this learning, the course of one's life changes immediately, positively, and painful consequences that have been raining down actually cease. This is an important thing for us all to ponder.

YOUR PERSONAL LABORATORY

How alone do you feel in your life, and in resolving the problems and challenges that arise in it? Do you remember that you have a built-in Mentor and allow yourself to partner with emotions?

Recall a time in your life when you made a mistake. Think about how you treated yourself: Were you judgmental and harsh with yourself or were you understanding and forgiving? Where did you focus your attention: On your mistake or on what outcome you wanted? Look at this situation and write about it.

If you were going to use your mistake to heal your life, the way James did, what would you do differently? Do you deserve to be punished, only, or do you deserve to have heavy consequences lifted due to you taking responsibility, learning, and making change? What principles would you begin to follow? Have you forgiven yourself yet? If not, forgive yourself now.

30

CHARACTERISTICS OF EMOTIONAL MASTERS

A big part of my quest to develop the ability to Master Emotions is driven by the desire not to keep working on the same issues over and over without ceasing.

To date, most people teaching about emotions are content to offer Emotional Management. Mastery and Management are very different. "Management" gets people through a particular emotional experience, but doesn't get at the root cause that brought the emotion to our attention. This approach is not lasting. Students of Emotional Management are encouraged to go back frequently to check on specific emotions, re-do the exercises, and make sure some sort of emotional leakage doesn't occur. This is tedious. It makes working with emotions seem complicated and leaves us believing we may never move on to other aspects of life. Emotions keep threatening to go out of control; and we call on ourselves to patrol and control against this happening.

"Mastery," the approach I'm offering, arms us with skills that handle emotions as they come up, dealing with them rapidly and in ways that last. If an emotional issue is not complete, that deeper part of ourselves repeatedly brings it to our attention. When the work with the emotion is complete, however, that emotion takes a seat further back on the bus, calling far less attention to itself. Eventually, the emotion can make just a momentary appearance, quickly subsiding when we identify its message and complete the lesson it has brought.

My intent is to offer a simple, straightforward way of working with emotions that provides long-lasting solutions, relying on our in-built Mentor to do its job of mentoring us through what we need to look at and what we need to do. Keep this in mind: It's possible to get finished with emotional issues and move on to other emotions, to other issues, and to other things in life.

BECOME AN "EMOTIONS WHISPERER"

To understand this idea better, look at the different approaches of horse training. Suppose I led you to a field where a herd of wild horses was grazing, and asked you to break a horse so it's rideable. At that moment, there are two ways to approach the task.

Way #1: Do exactly as I ask. Break the horse until it's manageable to ride. The approach is to work with the horse enough for it to pay attention to the requests of future riders, with the aim of getting the horse under control to the extent the horse behaves as requested. The horse learns to obey. This is managing the horse.

Will this training hold as different riders ask different behaviors from the horse? After carrying a number of riders will the training break, requiring the management person to re-train, going over the previous lessons, to help the horse be fully rideable again? This is highly likely.

Way #2: Extend the task by becoming a "Horse Whisperer." Now the approach is to instill in the horse the desire to work with riders as a result of choices made by the horse. By making the horse a partner and inviting the horse to use its own resources to help accomplish tasks together, the horse develops a process of working with the rider, regardless of who the rider is. At all stages, the horse is given the opportunity to make choices to cooperate and is rewarded for that cooperation. When a succession of riders comes along, the horse matches behavior choices to that rider and doesn't have any learning dismantled. No retraining is required, no matter how many riders are involved.

This approach involves helping the horse cooperate in self-mastering, which also means reaching mastery with it. Once the horse has the idea of cooperating there's no need to go back and retrain or revisit old lessons, because rather than learning a series of tasks, the horse has learned the process of how to partner and cooperate with any and all riders.

How Gentling Emotions is "Whispering"

We can apply this concept to working with emotions. I can ask someone to learn the signals, identify the lessons, and know what to do to get in charge of emotions every time one rears its head, and give some things to do to "get through" emotional experiences. This we call: "Emotional Management."

Or I can ask a person to learn the signals, identify the emotions, and apply this information in a way that works for that person and with the emotions. It's not about remembering techniques and approaches for quelling outbursts or ferreting out meaning. Instead, work with emotions deals with what the emotion is attempting to communicate, resolving the underlying learning so fewer and fewer similar emotional issues arise. When we do this, we have effective tools to deal with the emotion as part of an easy, efficient, and long-lasting process that, once mastered, does not have to be repeated *ad nauseum*. No matter what the emotional situation, we will know how to work with it successfully, because we know how to work with and complete that emotion's mission, following a process that is effective with all emotions. This is called: "Emotional Mastery."

Characteristic Behaviors of Emotional Masters

It's my desire to inspire everyone who encounters this approach for working with emotions to aspire to become an Emotional

Master, a "Whisperer" with emotions. Here are some elements of what an Emotional Master is like.

Balanced, Calm, and Peaceful: When we understand how emotions work, what the message is, and where they fit in the scheme of life, we're prepared to deal with whatever arises. This allows some equanimity. No need to get upset, feel afraid, or get angry because an emotional event occurred. Instead, recognize it as a lesson, work with the parts, learn the lesson, be grateful, and move on. The calm peacefulness felt when attaining mastery over emotions stays with us, and is our first response to the emotional event. The calm centeredness doesn't disappear, and cannot get taken away. Think about having a life without big ups and downs, just tiny blips. That's Emotional Mastery.

Observer: Once we understand the World-as-a-Giant-School idea, we're able to stand back and watch what unfolds, rather than feel like we have to jump into the raging waters of emotionalism. Here's how that can go: "Oh, I've lost my purse. I wonder what I'm trying to teach myself by misplacing my purse? What works best for me to get it back? Where did I last have it? Who can I ask for help?" Emotional Master's attain a level of detachment. There is still the experience, but it's just another life challenge that isn't a catastrophe or even an upsetting event. Instead of reacting, we identify the learning and look for the way through.

Embrace New Learning with Ease: When we know we're in school, the sooner we learn the lessons given, the sooner we can go out to recess. We step up and embrace the lessons, doing our part with ease and enjoyment. This helps us remain flexible. It's one of the secrets to having life flow more smoothly. Instead of spending time and energy in resistance, reacting emotionally, feeling victimized, or refusing to look, we get curious and seek out the lesson. Once found, we learn it in the most efficient way possible. We can see this with Emotional Masters who exhibit ease, flexibility, and the joy of forward movement.

Actor Rather than Re-actor: We've seen people go into strong and immediate reaction when emotions rise up: Slamming things on a table, throwing something, uttering loud curses, and offering hand gestures. These people react to emotions, allowing emotions to be in charge. While there is nothing wrong with such outbursts (and sometimes they just feel good), we can choose, instead, to develop the ability to act and use our energy more effectively.

Here's an example: When my daughter was a freshman in college, someone craftily reached through a first-floor window and stole her laptop, taking with it all her school work. She called, in full emotional reaction and tears, to tell us about the theft. After we discussed her need to report the theft to the campus police, I reminded her that she could remain upset, or could use her energy to bring the computer back to her. She and I had worked on this before, so she knew what to do. She chose the latter. Immediately after she reported the theft to campus police, she began to repeat these words: "It's my computer and it's coming back to me." She took the time to remember what she felt like when she worked with her computer, mentally opening it up to look at her work. She spent some time focusing her mind on the resolution, rather than the problem, using her emotional energy to focus on what she wanted. She stopped her panic and focused on what she wanted to become: A student with her own computer and all her school work. Within five hours, the police recovered the computer and returned it to her, homework intact. We can't always guarantee the return of lost or stolen items, but since she became an actor, rather than an emotional re-actor, she used this approach in creating many successes, and enjoying the outcomes she wanted.

Creative: Did you ever experience sitting down to take a test and having a strong emotional reaction (perhaps fear) that made it impossible to think, focus on the questions, and therefore made it impossible to take the test? When a person is flooded with emotion, or has a powerful emotional reaction to current events, there is little room for anything else. But when we're calm and balanced, and ready to embrace learning, we open the door to creativity and to the ability to put things together, including putting them together in new ways. Emotional Masters are amazingly creative. Being emotionally masterful swings the door of creativity wide open, making new and workable solutions to problems immediately available. We also open ourselves to synchronicity, in which people can show up, or events occur, that are exactly what we need when we need them—even when we didn't know we needed them.

Optimistic: Once we're an actor instead of a re-actor, things start flowing more easily for our life. It leads to more optimism. Instead of saying "this will never work!" we may say, "I don't know how, but it will all work out. I'm confident things will settle out in a good way." When we have a choice of where to focus our energy, we're less likely to focus on fear, anxiety, worry, or anger. Instead, since we have a choice, why not focus on happiness, enjoyment, success, and other great feelings?

Grateful: Emotional Masters are aware of the good fortune enjoyed when their life no longer features big highs and lows. They appreciate how many situations work out favorably, and how getting finished with emotional work leaves time for activities that are more interesting and fun. Even though we take a deliberate part in the changes and learning taking place, we're aware of how wonderful it is that we've learned to have life work more easily and smoothly. The phrase I was taught is: "Gratitude is the Law of Increase." When we're grateful for what we're receiving, we tend to get more.

LIVING OUR PURPOSE

Most people want to identify and live with purpose. A part of our purpose, that we share with all the people here on Earth, is our involvement in the Giant School. Whatever comes up in life is something to learn. Whatever we learn propels us in new directions. New directions are adventure, flexibility, and amazement. We seldom can imagine what's in store for our lives—all the great and amazing things—unless we step up, embrace life and its issues, and learn the lessons. Imagine what our world will be like when we partner with rising emotions, practice emotional mastery, and embrace our individual and group learning. You're part of creating this here on Earth, now.

MY PERSONAL LABORATORY

In 2003, I spent a lot of time learning how to manifest what I wanted in life, rather than work hard, as I was taught. One Saturday morning my daughter and I went shopping in Berkeley, California. Then I walked her down the block to the BART station and went on to my office, where I discovered I didn't have my wallet. I used it shopping, but it was not in my backpack where I knew I had returned it. After calling the store and doing some thinking, I surmised someone had removed it from my backpack while we waited at the corner for the light to change.

It was an opportunity to learn something. Because of my recent investigation, I placed my focus on discovering if I could manifest the wallet. I began to remember the wallet, how it felt in my hands, how good I felt when I had all my family pictures, identification, credit cards, money, and driver's license immediately available. Repeatedly, I added: "It's my wallet and it's coming back to me." I did this for two days before thinking to report the theft to the credit card companies, which I then did.

My daughter returned from her weekend away. I caught her staring at me, casting quizzical looks in my direction. Then she said, "Why aren't you upset?"

"Go look at the license plate on my car," I responded. "It says EMOT BAL, for Emotional Balance. I don't wish to be emotionally out of balance."

She was not satisfied. "But most people would be angry. They'd be upset. They'd be crying even. Why aren't you?"

"You know anger is energy. You know if I got angry I'd be reacting as if something had happened that isn't supposed to happen. But theft does happen, so there is little point in reacting with anger. Besides, whoever stole the wallet already has my wallet. Having my wallet is enough, why would I want to give them my energy, too? Getting angry gives my energy to them.

Instead, I choose to face fact and accept what has occurred and work with it. I know I'm going to learn something here. I don't want to waste my energy in emotional reaction when that is ineffective. I'd rather focus on learning."

Now my daughter was satisfied, yet a trifle amazed. That was Monday. I continued my work on manifesting my wallet for the next two days.

On Thursday, I went to my office in a neighboring county. On my office's telephone voice mail there was a message for me. It was left by a person who worked for CalTrans, the agency of California state government that tends the roads. The man told me he had my wallet and wanted to return it to me. It was found by the road crews 30 miles from where I was when it was taken from me.

I returned the call to arrange for a reward and to get my wallet back. I learned that the caller lived only a mile from my home. He told me he would bring it to me, so we arranged a meeting. At the meeting, I offered a reward or a donation to the crew's coffee fund. He accepted neither, as it was against the rules.

On Saturday morning my wallet was stolen from my backpack. During the week, I practiced working with the emotions that arose, choosing how I wished to relate to them, and focused on the learning I could do. By Thursday evening, the wallet was returned to me without a scratch on it. The credit cards, driver's license, and money were gone. I would have to replace those. But my library cards, my medical cards, and my family pictures were still there. Even one of my business cards was in the wallet, which allowed the CalTrans worker to contact me. I used that wallet for nearly 10 more years.

I took this incident as a test of sorts, a very big test of all I was learning, working with, and doing. It was a lot like a test given at the end of graduate school. And I passed. As I examined my wallet and the remaining contents, I realized the proof was in my hands. Achieving a level of emotional mastery had eased my week, kept me calm during the experience, allowed me to experiment with recovering my possessions and worked to restore my wallet to my possession. I was elated.

YOUR PERSONAL LABORATORY

Think of a way a stranger has violated you. Remember what they did, how you reacted, and how things turned out. Write about that. If you like the way things turned out, that's enough. Put your pen down and walk away.

If you didn't like the outcome, take some time to think about how you would like to do your part differently next time. You can't change what has happened, but you can use your experience to determine a different intention for next time, which is focusing on what you want to become. To help you, consider these questions:

- Did you fully face fact and accept what had happened?

- Do you intend to allow yourself to suffer the insult of the experience and also allow yourself to be emotionally upset?

- If you were to focus on "what you want to become," instead of on "what you want to overcome (what has happened)," what do you envision?

- How do you think you will feel if things turn out as you want them to?

- If you were grateful for things turning out in a way that feels good for you, where will you experience that feeling in your body?

Write down your answers. Whenever such a stranger violation occurs in the future, come back and check out your progress.

31

FINDING AND LEARNING EMOTION'S LESSONS

The stories I've shared point out how important it is to learn the lessons that are brought to us. These lessons can heal trauma from the past, correct current mistakes, and strengthen us, helping us unfold a better life.

How did we find these lessons?

In short, we asked for them. The question to ask is: "What could I possibly be trying to teach myself by creating this experience in my life?"

By asking this question, we're taking responsibility for our life. Responsibility is one of the building blocks of self-esteem, so asking this question each time will lead us to feel better about ourselves, too. What follows is a nine-step process for helping to find these lessons.

NINE-STEP PROCESS FOR FINDING THE LESSONS EMOTIONS OFFER

Take out a sheet of paper, open a notebook, or open a file on the computer to make a written record of what you discover about yourself and your emotions. Follow these steps:

1. **Look for an emotion that is coming up in your life or has come up recently**. If the emotion is powerful or explosive, it indicates the emotion is connected with something from the past. The emotion has been sitting inside of you, growing, and has become explosive. Make note of the emotion in your written record. Write a short description of the current situation involving the emotion, being as comprehensive as possible. For example, imagine you're the father of an 8-year-old boy. Here is the kind of statement you might make: "I was sitting on the sofa when my son ran up behind me and tackled me around the neck. I became furious, angered by someone impacting my body without my permission. I yelled at him and sent him to his room."

2. **Note the cause of the emotion you find.** In this case, anger indicates: "Something happened that I believe should not happen: I was physically attacked."

3. **Take a look at the reality: *Face Fact.*** Eight-year-old boys often jump on others, particularly brothers and fathers. Your son was exuberant and wanted to share with you, his father. This is normal for an 8-year-old, but wouldn't be expected under other circumstance. You got angry, thinking such a thing shouldn't happen. Therefore, your idea about the world is incorrect. Can you change it?

4. **Ask yourself: "Can I forgive**?" Your response may turn into: "I know my son doesn't have the capacity to think through all the consequences of his actions. Can I forgive him for jumping on me without warning? Can I forgive myself for my reaction, which is understandable, but didn't take into account who he is?" Decide to forgive.

5. **Forgive. Forgiveness means "to let go."** Let your son's choice and behavior go, to the extent that he is free to start over again, as if this experience never happened. Allow yourself to forgive yourself for rigid expectations,

for feeling angry toward your son, and for not being the kind of dad you wanted to be at that moment. If it's part of your belief system, ask God (or the "Something Larger" you recognize) for forgiveness, too. Allow the forgiving energy to flow to your son and into yourself. Savor it.

6. *Look for the lesson*. "What could I possibly be trying to teach myself here?" Write down whatever comes up. If nothing "clicks" or feels like you're on the right track, add this question: "Have I ever in my memory had an experience like this before where I was attacked physically without my permission?" Write down whatever answers you get. Usually one will stand out, creating an "A-ha" moment. Look for what you still need to learn from this old experience.

7. **Think about the earlier experience and decide how you want to work with it.** Remember who was with you, what happened, and how you felt. Usually when an incident from the past comes up, we remember experiencing feelings of helplessness, hopelessness, overwhelm, and powerlessness. Traditionally, when children have bad experiences, the problem is they can neither speak up nor get out. Decide to heal this experience. Decide whether you want to do it immediately, in your imagination, or whether it will be better for you to take power in the present situation. When you go to reclaim your power, make sure you allow yourself to either speak up or leave, or both.

8A. **Take that power. Go back in your imagination with the aim of completing your emotions and closing the Gestalt.** (In your imagination, take a strong ally, if you wish). Perhaps when you thought about it, you remembered your older brother or a friend, just a year or two older than you, who tackled you mercilessly when you were playing. Your parents gave no support. In your mind, tell that person what they did, how they hurt you, and what pain it has caused you since then. Then, take power. Tell the perpetrator you won't allow him/her to treat you that way. State an action you will take if they even try, for example, I'll walk away, I'll bring a powerful friend back, I'll refuse to listen. Make sure your imagined experience puts you in the position of power, and that you're firm in setting unapproachable limits for that perpetrator. Be sure to talk in the same way with the parent(s) who didn't protect you. When you have said all you need to say, and are feeling empowered, return to the present. Celebrate restoring your power. Take time to imagine using this power in the present should a similar situation arise.

8B. **Or take that power in real time. Make an appointment with the perpetrator of your current emotional pain and claim your power directly.** In this example, your perpetrator is your 8-year-old son. Set boundaries and ask him to alter how he relates to you. It's helpful to explain the original trauma to your son, telling him that you're in the process of healing it. Thank him for his part in bringing that up, while firmly establishing a boundary about being pounced on. Work out another way he can express his exuberance. Let him know he has done nothing wrong; just something that doesn't work for you. Emphasize your clear and firm boundaries around the issue of "pouncing."

9. **After a period of looking at your life and making sure you can see all the places needing these boundaries, let yourself enjoy the healing**. Then go on with your life. Make note, as time passes, that "pouncing" or "tackling" become things of the past. When you've learned the lesson about taking power and protecting your body, you're free to go on to other things. You may be surprised at how little "pouncing" you now experience, even though your

son may be only a few weeks older than when the incident stimulated such an angry reaction.

If this proves too difficult, or the pain from the past is so strong you're reluctant to face it on your own, secure the assistance of a counselor, psychotherapist, or coach. Likely, you're healing your own little kid self. Since little kids usually cannot speak up, and/or they cannot leave, you might need help doing these, even in your imagination. Young children deserve helpers. You're now grown up enough to recruit your own.

EIGHT STEPS FOR FINDING AND LEARNING THE LESSON IN CURRENT MISTAKES

The emotion of remorse will help you identify when you've made a mistake in the present. You'll start wishing you hadn't said something, done something, or had paid better attention. You'll wish you better understood what the other person was talking about, or thought things over before making your decision, speaking, or taking action.

Pay attention to this remorse. It's saying to you, "What you did (or decided) doesn't fit you, it doesn't work well for you. You need to repair and set a new course."

Here is the sequence to follow for utilizing remorse to find lessons and heal yourself:

1. **Acknowledge you made an error.** Usually, you won't feel good about what took place, which is remorse. Take a look at what you did or decided. Consider why you don't feel good about it. Remind yourself that everyone makes mistakes and making a mistake is an opportunity to learn. Then decide if you'd like to learn and change.

2. **To make changes start imagining what you wish you had done.** Pay attention, not to what you want to overcome, but to what you want to become. Allow yourself to play

229

with this concept in your imagination. Where would different choices or actions take you? Which one of those different choices gives you the best feeling when you imagine it? Determine to choose the one that leaves you feeling the best: "Next time."

3. **Change the decision or make a plan for a different action choice "next time."**

4. **Implement the decision or new plan**. Make amends to others as necessary.

5. **Ask yourself, "What could I possibly be trying to teach myself by making the decision that didn't feel good to me?" Listen to the answer(s) you get.** Write it down. Select the one that speaks most clearly to you regarding the situation.

6. **Decide whether you're ready to learn the lesson. If you are, set your intention to do the learning, and ask for help.** I like the phrase: "Please show me what I need to do to learn this lesson. I'm ready for any consequence that accompanies this learning. I'm fully ready to learn the lesson. Please show me what I need to do, think, or change in order to completely learn this lesson." Say this out loud (the spoken word has power).

7. **When your answer(s) comes, implement it**. Insert into your life your new way of being, deciding, or acting. Work with it. Practice will cement your new modus operandi into your life.

8. **Savor learning of the lesson. Express gratitude** for the wisdom you now have and the courage it took to seek it out and make change. Congratulate yourself on your progress and evolution.

Regardless of the issue or emotion, follow this general process to learn the inherent lessons. You'll be delighted and amazed at how good you start to feel.

When you find the lesson(s) in each experience, and complete the lessons inherent in any mistakes, you are fully under way as a person living a responsible life, making admirable progress in our Giant School as a developing Emotional Master!

MY PERSONAL LABORATORY

For 20 years, I was a single parent to children born seven years apart. My older child, a daughter, finished college and moved on. The younger, a son, was still at home and attending high school. He complained for quite a while that he wasn't happy in high school. We began to look for alternatives for him.

When we found the right alternative for him, we had barely three months to prepare him to leave home for college a full continent away. I faced a curious problem. Because of the chaotic challenges of my early life, I was plagued with an inability to make decisions whenever change arose in my life. Realizing the huge change I was facing at age 52--that my parenting days were coming to a close in the brief period of three months and two years ahead of schedule, I froze. I started having difficulty scheduling my therapy clients for the coming week. Small decisions were overwhelming to me. After more than 50 years of suffering this problem of freezing when I was experiencing change, I finally decided to see if I could complete it and move on.

Every time I noticed the issue arising, I said (aloud, if I could): "Please, show me what I need to learn to end this pattern of freezing. I'm ready to deal with whatever learning and consequences are involved. Please, help me learn what I need to learn, so I no longer experience the issue of being unable to make decisions when I go through change."

As often as I thought of it, or as often as the issue arose, I asked for help this way. Four days and nothing happened. However, on the fifth day, I awoke at 4:30 A.M. with some words going through my mind, clearly and insistently. ***Love the changes.*** I was curious about what this meant.

Thinking on it, I realized every time change started to come into my life, I feared, dreaded and attempted to avoid those changes. Instead of "loving the changes," I was "fearing the changes." My emotional reaction of "freezing" was drawing attention to a major change I needed to make.

"What does 'Love the changes' mean?"

The question led me to think about small children. If they're playing in a room, and a family member passes through the room, announcing, "I'm going out to the yard" or "I'm going to the store" what does the child say? "Can I come? Can I come?" The child is ready to make a change and do something new. "Love the changes," I realized, was being child-like, so when changes presented themselves I embraced them, ready to explore something new. I realized that due to things that had occurred in my early life, I started fearing change around the age of two, when my father came and took me from my birth mother's home. I needed to go back and recapture the essence of the little child who stopped "loving the changes" on the day I was removed from the only home I'd ever known, and was never allowed to see my birth mother again.

I focused on finding a way to love and embrace whatever change was coming, especially the one currently taking my son from our home. I looked at the possibility of what things could come into my life that I might not imagine. I thought about having time every day to do whatever I wanted to do. I felt the upcoming freedom and began to get excited that my life could be different than it had been for more than 30 years, since my early marriage at age 19. "Love the changes," I began to think, over and over.

Within a few months of my son's leaving, I was offered and filled my first book-writing contract. Within six months, I met the man who became my husband. "Loving the changes" brought me things I wanted to have in my life. Having a partner had eluded me for 20 years, yet as I learned to embrace change, that marriage partner materialized.

Once again, my experience offered me difficulties, emotions, and messages. When I looked into those, and asked for help in resolving them, the help I received took me all the way to an incomplete gestalt dating back 50 years. By partnering with the difficulty and the emotions involving freezing, not only did the problem itself resolve, but I was rewarded in some big and powerful ways. I received an invitation to publish several small books; and I met my husband-to-be.

Such is the power of working with our emotions and developing Emotional Mastery.

YOUR PERSONAL LABORATORY

Do you have a pattern of inaction? Do you procrastinate about exercising your body, speaking up, asking for what you want, or engaging in activities you enjoy? Pick one of these. Feel the emotions that come up when thinking about the issue. Ask yourself what you need to learn in order to change the pattern of inaction. Once you identify the issue and receive information about needed learning, process by following the eight steps from this chapter. Write the experience down, both to cement it in your mind, and to have it for future reference.

1. Acknowledge, particularly to yourself, what the issue is and where it originated.

2. Imagine what you wish to do differently.

3. Make a plan for a different action.

4. Implement the decision or new plan.

5. Ask yourself, "What could I be trying to teach myself and what's the best or easiest way to learn it? Listen to the answer(s) you get.

6. Decide whether you're ready to learn the lesson identified. If you are, develop intention for the learning, and ask for help, if you wish.

7. Implement your plan. Do the learning.

8. Savor learning the lesson. Express gratitude.

32

VITAL TOOLS FOR WORKING WITH EMOTIONS

An **important note:** If at any point when doing the exercises offered here, you feel overwhelmed, become frightened, or think you have taken on too much by yourself, please make an appointment to see a counselor, psychotherapist, coach, or spiritual counselor. Emotions held onto for a time can become powerful. Having someone who knows a bit of how emotions work, and can see what is happening from an outside perspective, allows you to feel safer, and to go all the way through the process. If you'd like, you can take these exercises to that individual and ask for their help from the beginning.

Here are six approaches that can be used when working with one or more emotions. Be sure to give yourself privacy and time when using these techniques. Allow yourself to experience whatever arises.

TECHNIQUE 1: RELEASE THE EMOTION: "I'M ANGRY" (SAD, HURT, AFRAID)

As we go about living busy lives, too often we don't take time to allow ourselves to notice and feel emotions. Perhaps we think we'll have to do something with them, if we let ourselves know they're peeping out. To help in taking time, remember that we have the power of choice. We can decide whether or not we want to do more with the emotions discovered.

Emotions are energy, so taking time to face the fact of what energy is present has a somewhat magical effect. It releases some energy, leaving us feeling calmer and more peaceful. Even if we're unaware of experiencing any emotion, by doing this exercise we find what is present and release its energy. Then—or later—we can do the work of processing the energy and learning its lesson.

This tool is very effective when we feel like we're bursting with a particular emotion. Again, it's the release of the emotion's energy that's important.

Note from the title that we can use this tool with all emotions. Just ask which one is experienced, then plug the arising emotion in to the statement, and release it. Here's how it works.

Sit in a place without distractions or disturbance. Take a minute to notice how and what you're feeling. Where are you experiencing the emotion or feeling in your body? Then, in a cadence, begin to repeat aloud the words: "I'm angry, I'm angry, I'm angry." (You can substitute whatever emotion that's showing up for you.) Continue the cadence. Repeat and repeat the same phrase.

Whenever there's an association or thought, take time to say it out loud, too. For example, "I'm angry that I can't tell people how much I care about them." Once stated, return to the phrase and the repeated cadence.

Do this for a minimum of 10 minutes. Keep repeating the phrase (and the thoughts or ideas it elicits) without ceasing. Likely, by the end of the time, you'll feel run down and ready to stop. Check to see how and what you're feeling, especially in your body. Usually, you will feel calmer and better.

However, you might also feel angrier (more afraid, sadder, etc.) than when you started. If this happens, it indicates you've been storing this emotion, allowing it to grow in power. Before the 10 minutes is complete, you'll feel the emotion coming in waves, you'll have powerful thoughts, perhaps you'll raise your voice or you might cry. Whatever occurs, allow it to happen. There is nothing wrong. There is nothing wrong with you. If there's a strong reaction doing this exercise, just know it's an emotion you've been hanging onto for a long time, and it's ready to burst out of you. Allow this. You're addressing this deliberately; and you're in a safe situation for experiencing these feelings.

Years ago a group of people in Seattle, Washington, believing that ordinary people could help one another emotionally without having to hire a therapist, began the Peer Counseling Movement. Many people were helped by participating in this group, and processes that all of us can do were developed to assist. One piece of information that stuck with me is the Four Signs of Healing. These are the things that people do when they are healing emotionally: 1) sweat, 2) shake, 3) cry, or 4) laugh.

Crying as a result of doing this exercise is healing past pain associated with the emotions being explored. Though it's work and takes time to go through the release, feel reassured in knowing what you're doing is healing.

Shaking or shivering, laughing uncontrollably, or sweating are signs of healing. Allow these to happen.

Whether you get a small amount of relief, or go through a bigger emotional release from facing the fact of the emotion(s) arising in you, be sure to give some time to integrate and sit with what you've experienced. Emotional work is the hardest work there is. Take a break. You've earned it.

TECHNIQUE 2: FREE WRITING

Check in with yourself prior to starting this exercise to note how you feel. Then, sit down and write, as fast as you can, for 20 minutes, addressing a difficult experience or how you're feeling emotionally. Write to put words on the paper. Write by hand. Don't pause to think. When time is up, stop, and allow yourself to check what you're feeling again, noting any changes you observe.

The University of Texas' Dr. James Pennebaker has worked for years to develop the technique of free writing to release long-held trauma. Don't underestimate the power of this simple exercise. The power of the written word is great. Take advantage of it whenever you encounter emotional challenges or difficulties. When we write, we tend to face fact, which is a way to free ourselves of built-up emotional energy. We don't have to show what we write to anyone, which allows us to say what we want to say, without fear of judgment by others.

TECHNIQUE 3: WRITING LETTERS

Writing letters is a powerful way to complete emotional business, especially if you say what you want to in the letter, and allow yourself to feel whatever emotions come up during the letter-writing process. Old emotional wounds may involve people who are no longer in our lives, or parents and others who have died. How do you finish with people who aren't in your life? Write them a letter.

Do not plan to send or deliver the letter (whether the addressee is alive or dead). This letter is for you, to help you say and release all you need to without holding back. If you think you'll send it, you're more apt to hold back, be nicer than you feel, or in some way compromise your real feelings because you will anticipate the other person's reactions from reading the letter.

In dealing with emotions it's a good thing to set your mind, before beginning, to let everything come out. I recommend writing as fast as possible for this one, too. This will help you write more powerfully, and give less time to edit. Don't worry if what you say isn't entirely true. You want to put down how things feel, without being concerned about absolute truth. Don't concern yourself with spelling or punctuation. Just write:

- What happened.

- How you felt about what happened.

- How you feel toward the person.

- What you haven't yet told them and what you want them to do differently.

- What you will do if they will not make this change (something that benefits you).

- Offer forgiveness for yourself and the other person, if it feels right for you.

- Make a declaration that this ends the matter and they'll never be allowed to hurt or upset you again.

Once you complete the letter, hide it away (in a book, bottom of a drawer, or wrap it in a piece of black silk). The next day, take it out, read it out loud, and make any additions or corrections you'd like. Hide it away again overnight. On the third day, take it out and read it aloud, append it if needed, then destroy the letter, ripping it into tiny pieces (that are taken to an outside refuse container) or burning it. If you've been writing on a computer, put the file in your trash folder, then dump the trash.)

The exercise is designed to recapitulate how our brains work. Whenever we tell someone how we feel, we tuck things away, then pull the thoughts back out the next day and go over them again. We humans like to go over emotional situations. The step of destroying the letter or file in this exercise takes us one step further, taking the entire situation and ending it by destroying or getting rid of it.

This exercise allows us to be honest regarding felt emotions, to confront someone without enduring their reaction or creating any additional problems, to say everything needed without moving to censor or hold back, and to recapitulate your brain's normal process, bringing the matter to a close by destroying the letter. Very Zen. Create something important, then destroy it, as if it had never been there. The good news is your emotional self will know the letter was there, and you have reaped all the benefits of facing fact and releasing the emotion(s). You're completing and ending this emotional chain.

TECHNIQUE 4: THE CLOSED DOOR EXERCISE

The Closed Door Exercise is a simple, yet powerful, process to keep yourself from being drawn in emotionally by others. I was taught this exercise at the end of my second marriage. My ex-husband would write letters or leave phone messages; and when he did I would get upset or feel enraged. My ex was not following the orders of the court, had left me with a huge debt, was not supporting our child, whose full care was left to me, and would not set up a regular visitation with our child. All of it stimulated me to anger and rage, and was taking up a lot of my time, every time he attempted contact.

My wise friend pointed out the importance of no longer getting upset with him, because I was giving him my energy and allowing him to get me twice. She taught me The Closed Door Exercise. I did the exercise regularly for a month. No one but me and my friend knew I was doing it. After more than two years of ignoring the rules, my ex began following what was laid down by the court and started spending time with our child, who had missed his father. By working with the energy of emotion, a resolution was achieved, even when I was miles away from my ex-husband, and he knew nothing of what I was doing. Let me take you through the process of this powerful tool which now will be part of your arsenal.

Close your eyes throughout the exercise. Call up the viewing screen in your brain, on which images appear for you.

Think of someone who angered you this week. Remember the exact incident and what you felt. Take time to notice how you're breathing, and what you're feeling as you think about this person and the behavior.

Let this image fade. On your screen, visualize a closed door—a nice, solid closed door with solid walls around it. Look at it and study it. What is it made of? What is its color and texture? Does it have hardware on it? Look at the hinges. Once again, notice how you're breathing and what you're feeling.

Let the image of the door go. Instead, call the image of the person who angered you back again. What words were used? Or was it the silent treatment? What was the person doing or saying that shouldn't have been done or said, or what were they not doing or not saying that should've been done or said? Again, notice your breathing, and what you're feeling. Afterwards, let the image go.

Bring the door image back and concentrate on it. Look at the texture, color, solidity, solid walls, the fixtures. This is a concentration exercise. Place your full focus on the door. After a time, again notice how you're breathing and what you're feeling.

Let the image of the door go for the last time. Recall how angry you were feeling, and how awful the other person was being. What was the absolute worst part of the behavior? Perhaps you felt this person was unreasonable, punishing, selfish, or uncaring. Become aware of the hurt you feel about what this person did that led you to feel angry and upset.

Now, close the door immediately and firmly on this person and know they will not be hurt by your actions. Close the door, and become aware that what you're doing is closing the door on your emotional reaction to this individual. Concentrate on the door. The solid door with solid walls around it. Do this concentration activity for a minute or two.

Open your eyes when you're ready.

What did you experience? Most people experience short, frequent breaths and upset when they envision the person toward whom they feel angry. Then, when the door is closed, breathing slows down, they become less tense, and feel calmer, sometimes lighter. If this is what happened, then the exercise is working. If it didn't work for you this time, do it again when you can take time and concentrate fully.

When experiencing emotional upset with others, it is important to close our emotional response to them. Energy is passed from one person to another, often without our awareness, even when people are miles and miles apart. That energy will keep the person coming back to you because it feeds their energy needs.

The Closed Door exercise is an immediate and powerful way to close off this unwanted energy exchange. Whenever you find yourself upset with someone or their actions, use the Closed Door Exercise. Close the door on any energy exchange by quelling your emotional reaction. It is more powerful than it may at first seem.

Caution. Do this exercise when you're removed from the person toward whom you feel angry. It's almost impossible to do when they're around or you're on the phone with them.

A reminder. Just as when my wallet was stolen, you don't have to give double energy to someone who hurt or violated you. Double energy happens when you experience the insult, and then spend time thinking about the person and being upset. When this occurs, the only person who is diminished is you. The Closed Door exercise allows you to close the door on your emotional reaction, so you don't allow release of double energy.

Work with the Closed Door Exercise. Keep track of what happens in a journal.

MY PERSONAL LABORATORY

When I learned The Closed Door Exercise, I practiced it every time I had contact with my ex-husband. After a while, I went through the Closed Door Exercise every time I thought of him. He lived an hour's drive away from me and had no idea I was doing this exercise. I told no one.

After only one month, I had the experience of seeing my ex-husband change his behaviors. He began to follow the rules given by the court, made efforts to set up visitations with our son, and even fed our son and did his laundry before returning him.

I started this technique when our child was 12. In the next six years, I spoke with my ex-husband a dozen times--on the phone--and saw him three times. That's an average of less than three times a year. Considering that he began to see our son at least twice a month, this was a big reduction in contact. Our child met his father at a local restaurant, where he was often taken by a friend instead of me. Visitation was set up by mail, so I stopped getting phone messages (there were no personal cell phones in the 1980s). My life became a lot calmer and a lot less fraught with anger. In addition, my son had more contact with his father, which is good for children, who love both parents. Our home life was calmer, too.

YOUR PERSONAL LABORATORY

If you have an individual who is an irritant, utilize the Closed Door Exercise. You don't have to begin practicing with a person who is overwhelmingly annoying. What's important is to begin closing the door on your emotional reaction to people who take up your thinking time or emotional space, when you don't really want them to. Determine who you want to experiment with, then go through the visualization sequence. Do this without fail. Avoid "double energy" by spending none of your time experiencing upset over this individual. Remember, it's the energy of the emotions you want to get in charge of. Make no exception. If you notice you're obsessing or thinking a lot about the person or situation, switch to The Closed Door Exercise. The more you do this, the easier it will be to stay focused in the present and on your own life.

33

TOOLS WE NEVER WERE TAUGHT FOR WORKING WITH EMOTIONS

Combining spiritual energy work with emotions is a powerful, creative, efficient, and simple way of dealing with life. I have gathered additional tools in this chapter, which are more spiritually based. They're known to very few people and are amazingly effective. The following is the explanation for how each works, when to use it, and the benefits that accrue when making it a part of your life.

TECHNIQUE 5: PERSONALITY VERSUS PRINCIPLE

We've already talked about this tool. Here we'll go into a bit more detail. The way most of us lead our lives, we offer special things to some people. Especially if someone is related, is kind to us, appears to be beneficial in our life, or is someone with prestige, we will do for them what we really don't wish to do for everyone. When we lend our car "because you're my sister-in-law," or invite a known and active substance abuser into our home "because life is tough on him" – and we wouldn't lend our car or take in another addict if requested—we're living in Personality. The format is, "Because you are who you are/are related/are special, I will do for you something I wouldn't do for others."

Think for a minute of the stories you know, where someone got into difficulties, helping out someone because they had a special relationship. We all know how the car gets wrecked by the sister or brother-in-law (who, of course, doesn't carry insurance), and family heirlooms get ripped off and sold by the addict living in our home. It's sad. Attempting to do the "right thing," can lead to something very painful. We wonder why the difficulty, when all we were trying to do was help someone in need.

If you take a walk in nature and stop under a beautiful tree, and it's the day on which that tree is dropping a limb, the tree doesn't gasp and say, "Oh, it's you! I can't drop my limb today because you're special to me!" Instead, if you're standing there when the limb drops, it will get dropped on you. The tree will do for you exactly what it would do for anyone standing there at that moment. This is operating in Principle. Mother Nature operates in Principle.

The more we can live as Mother Nature does (in Principle), the more smoothly our lives go. When I learned this, it made me want to operate more like Mother Nature. It's not always easy to do; but it has made a difference in the smooth operation of my life. It can do that for you, too.

When someone asks you for a favor or to do something for them, ask yourself: "If I do this for you, am I willing to do it for everyone?" If the answer is "No," decline the request. If the answer is "Yes," go ahead and do what they ask.

You can experiment with operating in Personality and see what happens in a particular situation. Let me tell you about a woman I knew who, due to fear, was unwilling to operate on Principle.

Dr. Jones supplemented her medical income, in the later years of her practice, consulting with attorneys as they worked with medical malpractice cases. The attorneys needed a doctor to tell them whether the treating physician in a medical situation that had soured was following the "standard of care," meaning what is usually expected as treatment in a particular medical situation. Medical practitioners who didn't follow standard of care were judged as having committed malpractice, and were subject to losing their case in court.

Dr. Jones began this work some 15 years earlier, when a nurse she knew asked her to work one case. The nurse started an agency that supplied expert witnesses for attorneys. Dr. Jones liked and trusted the nurse, Amy. For all the years of their association, they had worked without a written contract. Dr. Jones also charged Amy's clients a lower fee, enabling Amy to inflate the price a small amount, thus making a larger profit for herself.

In the ensuing years, Dr. Jones began to work with other attorneys and agencies. As her reputation grew and spread, Dr. Jones developed her own contract, had a set fee schedule, and worked with attorneys only after half her fee was paid up front. The contract specified the second half of the fee was due within two weeks of completing her work. Every attorney or agency with whom Dr. Jones worked signed and followed this contract. Interestingly, Dr. Jones didn't use this contract or fee schedule with Amy.

After a few years, Dr. Jones decided to raise her rates. She sent out a letter to all the attorneys and the referral agencies that employed her, including Amy, specifying the new rates. Everyone who received the letter accepted the new rate and started paying it, except for Amy, even though she was still charged a discounted price.

Instead, Amy called Dr. Jones at home on a Sunday, berating her for raising the rates. Amy told Dr. Jones she was "not worth it," would not get the new fee, would destroy Amy's business, and was behaving without conscience. (Remember "bad, wrong and crazy?") Dr. Jones was furious at having her integrity questioned, at being challenged about giving herself a much-deserved pay raise, and for Amy holding Dr. Jones responsible for her business success. Dr. Jones knew Amy worked with many other experts and her success was not solely up to Dr. Jones. Angry and insulted, Dr. Jones got off the phone as fast as she could, and appeared the next day in my office.

When I heard the story, it was clear what the problem was. Dr. Jones had different policies and procedures for working with Amy than she did for all the other people with whom she worked. She charged Amy less, had no written agreement, and did special favors for Amy. Dr. Jones was operating in Personality with Amy, not Principle. I explained the concept to Dr. Jones, suggesting she update the way she worked with Amy. She needed to get into Principle with all the people she served as an Expert Witness, I advised. Dr. Jones expressed her fear that if she took an action that drastic, Amy would get so angry she would no longer send Dr. Jones any business. Dr. Jones got a lot of business through Amy. I suggested Dr. Jones keep in mind that she had to do more cases with Amy to make the same amount of money she could make with fewer cases working with any of her other legal employers. My telling her she might experience a dip in income, but then could make the same amount (or more) with less effort, didn't help Dr. Jones, at that moment, to make the shift she needed to make.

For the next year, Dr. Jones called me periodically, paying for my time to listen to her frustration about Amy, who Dr. Jones reported, was becoming more and more demanding. "I'm sad to hear this," I said to Dr. Jones. "You know the problem is that you are in Personality with Amy instead of Principle. As long as you treat her differently than your other legal case sources, you will have this problem."

I helped Dr. Jones with many ways to address the fear she encountered when she thought about bringing Amy into Principle. For a year, she could not bring herself to face that fear. Then, Amy asked Dr. Jones to do a rush case. When it came time to pay for the hard work Dr. Jones had done, Amy refused to give her the premium charge Dr. Jones had always billed for the rushed delivery of her opinion. Amy told Dr. Jones that it was such a simple case that she shouldn't charge a premium. It hadn't taken that much from Dr. Jones to examine the materials quickly, Amy told her, so she didn't deserve any extra for her efforts.

That did it. It was the magic line in Dr. Jones' head that allowed her to face the fear that was holding her back. Anger pushed Dr. Jones to take action. Angry with Amy for presuming to tell her what her time was worth and what she deserved, Dr. Jones felt very disrespected, and used that anger to take a stand. Just as she suspected might happen, Amy immediately stopped employing Dr. Jones, who suddenly lost about a third of the income on which she counted for her medical legal work.

"I told you so!" she said in one of our visits.

"Patience," I counseled her. "How many additional cases at your new rate do you need to do each month to make up for what you lost from Amy?"

Dr. Jones realized just three more cases could more than make up for the lost income of seven cases she worked on with Amy. Setting her goals, Dr. Jones contacted her other medical legal employers, saying she would like to pick up a few more cases. Within a month, her income had surpassed what it was before Amy dismissed her. In addition, Dr. Jones was careful to work in Principle with everyone, following her own policies and not offering special favors or rates to anyone. Dr. Jones was happily busy with a lot of work.

WHAT YOU CAN DO NOW

Are there people you're treating differently than you treat others? If there are, I'll guess that these are the individuals with whom you have the most difficulties. They likely ask for much more than you want to give, don't look to offer you much in return for what you give, or do things like ask you to do special favors for their friends as well. If these kinds of experience are part of your current life, then like Dr. Jones, you're operating in Personality. Once you see how it works, the choice to live by Principle makes compelling sense.

Decide now whether you wish to continue to live by Personality, or you are ready to shift into living by Principle. If you're not ready to make the switch now, check if you can see yourself making it in the future? If "Yes," when? If your answer is "Now," make this statement, out loud: "I hereby choose to live my life by Principle, starting on _____(date)."

The spoken and written word have energetic power, so making the statement out loud helps achieve those goals. Writing it down is even more supportive of intentions.

Now, or when the date you have selected arrives, make the changes in your life, contracts, and policies, bringing yourself into alignment with Principle. Use the 72-Hour Rule (see the next tool) to help make better decisions and keep yourself from being manipulated.

Be prepared because people you've related to through Personality will not be happy with this change, and will likely fall back on the "bad, wrong and crazy" routine.

You may need to be prepared, as Dr. Jones was, to no longer have certain individuals in your life. This can be challenging when the individual is a relative or close friend. Stay aware of the possibilities when you make this shift. Keep in mind that if you "operate on the motive of fear" and don't get into Principle with someone because you're afraid of losing them, they're likely to become a real thorn in your side and cause more pain as time goes on. That's because of the principle: "When we operate on the motive of fear, we're guaranteed to create that which we fear."

You're likely to have that particular person withdraw from you in your life in painful ways, even after you have opted to keep things the same between you due to your fear of losing them.

You can offer an explanation for what you're planning to do ahead of time, if you want, stressing it is nothing about the other person that is causing you to make the change. You're making a change you have learned will be beneficial for yourself and your future life. Once you make the decision and take action to begin living by Principle, it's vital that you not compromise or return to your old ways. If you do, you'll have to start all over again—and you'll need to work longer and harder to bring about the change you seek. It's the way this Giant School works. Once you share your plan don't stay and discuss it. If the other individual is manipulative, they will likely use this characteristic of manipulation: "All extraneous bits of information will be used against you."

The longer you engage in conversation, the more your resolve can be eroded, with every explanation you've shared shoved back at you, causing frustration.

TECHNIQUE 6: THE 72-HOUR RULE

It takes about three days (72 hours) for decisions, new information, and risks to move through us humans. If you've made a large purchase, such as a house or a car, you may have noticed a clause that allows you to change your mind about the purchase within 72 hours. When I learned about the 72-Hour Rule, it changed my life forever. It may change yours, too.

Here's how it works. Because it takes 72 hours for decisions, new information, and risks to move through us, it's best not to talk with anyone about your experience for three days. You can write things down or talk to yourself, even out loud. But don't talk with anyone else.

Why? Because things haven't settled around your decision, new information, or risk, which won't happen for 72 hours. During this time sorting occurs, as you mull things over, think about mistakes made, and decide whether you're okay with what occurred. Because we're open to the ideas, opinions, and energy of others, if you talk with someone else, your sorting experience gets compromised. The energy of their ideas, opinions, and desires can get mixed with yours. You'll end up confused, still not sure you're doing what is right for you. Many people describe what happens as feeling as though someone has punctured their balloon with a pin.

If, on the other hand, you wait the full 72 hours without talking with anyone else, your sorting will be complete. When the 72 hours is over, you can talk with anyone about these things, and will not lose your way. You'll be secure in what is right for you. You can listen to other opinions, hear criticism, or learn another way of doing things, without negatively impacting or altering the knowledge you have about what is right for you.

What Makes Us Vulnerable During Those 72 Hours?

During the 72 hours something called The Negative Reaction hits. That's when you begin to question yourself:

"Did I make a huge mistake?"

"I forgot to take this other thing into consideration when I made that choice—it's wrong."

"I can't believe I said that to him."

"I was so crass and non-compassionate in what I decided!"

"I can't live with myself. I'm not really the person I was when I took that risk!"

In our head, we're pelted with challenges and questions about the decisions we've made, the risks we've taken, or new information we accepted. The only thing we want to do is go back, change things, rectify the situation. But making any change during the Negative Reaction portion of the 72 Hours is not advised! Wait the full time. If you still want to make changes, make them after the 72 hours have passed.

The first time I followed this rule, I found myself gripping the arms of my chair until my knuckles were white, which is what it took for me not to talk with someone else. Remember, during the 72 hours, you're not talking with anyone about the situation. It is most helpful to go back and feel how you felt at the time you made the decision, got the information, or took the risk. Most people find they felt good. In fact, it is most likely the way you will feel again at the end of the 72 hours! Like a surfer riding a big wave on the ocean's edge, stay with it. Ride the wave all the way to the end of 72 hours.

As the 72 hours passes, you might forget the entire issue. If that happens, when the time is up, you may have no interest in talking about it, even though not talking about it during the 72-hour time was driving you crazy. The work of the 72

Hour time is over, its goal attained. You kept your own counsel, allowed yourself to sort and examine every part of the experience (consciously and unconsciously), so what you're left with really belongs to you.

Keep in mind: Some people find it impossible to wait out the 72 hours. Please don't judge yourself for this. It just indicates some learning might still need to get done.

In my experience, people who live their lives calling on others to help them fill their needs are the ones who have most difficulty with the waiting time. In the mental health field, this way of living is called Co-dependence. If you're used to living co-dependently, this task may feel impossible, even frightening. In this case, give yourself permission to start with 24 hours and work your way up to 72 hours during two to three months. Doing this may have surprising results, because you'll learn how much you've depended on others to make you feel okay, instead of taking responsibility for doing that yourself. At the same time, you're lengthening the time you're alone with your thoughts, doing your own mental and emotional sorting, developing your ability to assume responsibility. You'll learn to both interact with others and rely on yourself, and still feel good. This is empowering.

WHY I RECOMMEND GOING THROUGH THIS PROCESS

One of the hidden principles here on Earth that we all follow, but usually don't realize is in effect, is this: In order to get beyond something on this Earth, we must go through it.

I've already given a perfectly good reason why this is a principle: Earth is a Giant School. If we don't have the experience of something, we have learned absolutely nothing. We must go through experiences, with the purpose of learning, growing, and evolving.

This is an issue with "managing" emotions, with tapping or meditating them away: We don't go through the emotions and experience them. It's important that we have experiences, because that is the way we learn. Earth is designed as an "experience arena." In the long run, sidestepping the learning experience doesn't make things easier, it just makes things take longer.

Whenever offered something to go through and experience, jump in with your whole being. Going through the 72-hour period offers profound and lasting learning and many benefits.

BENEFITS OF ADOPTING THE 72-HOUR RULE

The most satisfying benefit for making the 72-Hour Rule a regular part of your life is personal empowerment. You'll be amazed at how strong, self-nurturing, and connected you'll feel, once the 72-Hour Rule is a part of your repertoire for living.

Also, you'll begin to realize that doing mental and emotional sorting this way provides a life nobody can take away from you. Take the time to make it yours; and it remains yours.

You'll make fewer mistakes by thinking things over and making sure they're right for you, before taking additional steps.

You'll start to feel like you have more room to be who you are, and not need to explain or make excuses.

You'll find yourself in the enviable position of only doing what you want to do, because of the certainty in marching to your own internal drummer.

You might even begin to feel wiser.

WHAT TO SAY TO OTHERS AS YOU ADOPT THE 72-HOUR RULE

Friends and family often like us the way we are, having grown accustomed to our ways of behaving; and they don't like change. When we start to live by the 72-Hour Rule, they may think we're crazy. They may criticize. They may make fun of us, or implore us to give it up. It's important we talk about how to deal with this situation.

1. Adopt your intention to follow the 72-Hour Rule. Be steadfast.

2. Tell others you're trying the 72-Hour Rule as an "experiment" for feeling better about the decisions you make in life. You don't have to cite an end-time for the experiment. Just say, "I'm trying this for a while." This helps with the problem related to, "all extraneous bits of information will be used against you."

3. Ask for help in supporting your efforts. When you say you're thinking something over for 72-Hours before talking about it, ask them to accept this and be patient with you. We don't need pressure from others for us to give up our experiment. Even if they don't fully support you, be sure to support yourself.

4. Tell them after the 72 hours you'll talk with them about what you've done or experienced. Be careful to set things up for them to ask you, rather than volunteering to tell them. People are curious for a time, and then forget the curiosity. Don't enslave yourself to their curiosity by agreeing to take the responsibility of revealing your experience, especially when they might not remember to ask.

5. If they do want to talk, give them a brief explanation of what you're doing, why you're doing it, and what you learned. Because we all see things differently, they may suggest you're wasting your time. Remember, you're experimenting with the 72-Hour Rule for your growth, not theirs.

When I first used this rule with my husband, Bob, he was angry. In his life as a doctor, he was accustomed to asking people about themselves and having them give immediate answers. He was concerned I was keeping secrets or making judgments about him. When he understood the process, the first thing he did was refuse to talk with me about something, citing his use of the 72-Hour Rule. The first time he followed the 72-Hour Rule, he felt morally superior and didn't hesitate to tell me so. (I found this aspect of his behavior delightfully funny.) Eventually, we both used the process, without upset for either of us. But be prepared. People don't like change, including change we choose to make for ourselves.

6.   Enjoy new-found confidence, good feeling, competent decision-making and empowerment. Be grateful.

MY PERSONAL LABORATORY

In the mid 1990's, I began dating my husband, Bob. One of his daughters had a very severe medical problem. She had seen a doctor a few years earlier who prescribed some medication. Nothing was done since, and the problem persisted, even though she could get a small amount of relief using the medication. I learned the medication was becoming less and less effective.

Investigating to find out why more wasn't being done, I discovered she had some issues about who she allowed to poke around her body. She preferred a woman doctor. To date, none had been found. Women doctors were rare in the specialty she needed. Through friends, I found a woman doctor in the specialty. My intended husband and I took his daughter to the appointments together. It was decided she needed a surgical procedure to correct the problem. The surgery date was set at a very big medical center in San Francisco. I began my preparation, not only to be at the hospital and take care of Bob's youngest child for the day, but to be there in whatever way Bob's daughter needed me.

Close to the day of surgery, Bob's other children showed up and started to get involved in the process. They were adults and we didn't yet know each other. I was told very little about Bob's relationship with them. They appeared to think I was an intruder and asked Bob to make sure I left the hospital at a certain point, so his daughter's step-mother (Bob's nearly divorced second wife) could comfortably enter the hospital and assist the daughter with her healing. Even though I was three corridors away from that room, I was informed I needed to leave the hospital, because my presence was too upsetting for the estranged wife.

Not informed ahead of time, I was stunned, hurt, angry, and felt pushed around when I sat in the hospital and was told I had to leave. The daughter wouldn't be getting this treatment she needed, had I not found the doctor, attended the appointments, and consulted with the family. Yet it was acceptable to exclude me.

I decided to refuse that request. Because the basis for my refusal was not conveyed to them as requested, things didn't end well, with the other offspring stepping in, whisking the youngest away for the day, and isolating Bob and me in a small hospital waiting room.

The daughter's healing was more important than the emotions I felt at that time, so I healed them on my own, without working them through with his older children. I forgave them and me for not connecting and working together earlier in the process. I also looked for what I might be trying to teach myself by participating in this painful event. From my point of view, even though I was just dating Bob at that time, I'd been working to alleviate pain and suffering for his daughter, and was neither appreciated nor wanted for my efforts. It was clear many family members didn't want me present during this family event. This was a hard pill to swallow.

At the time, I was unable to find a deeper lesson than that I needed to reach out and communicate with all parts of the family, especially when powerful emotional and medical issues were at stake. We went on with our lives. I became better acquainted with all Bob's children; and we began getting along well.

Four-and-a-half years later, a second medical crisis occurred.

This time, my former husband's 25 year old son suffered a traumatic brain injury when he was hit from behind while training on a local road on his bicycle. My daughter, the child of my former husband and me, called to ask my husband, Bob, the neurosurgeon, to come give a second opinion on treatment.

On the appointed day for the consultation, I arose early, made platters of vegetables and fruits to take to the hospital, and prepared to accompany Bob when he offered his diagnosis. Shortly before we left, my daughter called and told me: "Your son (not biologically related to the injured man) can come in and see my brother. Your husband can of course see him. You must sit out in the hall. The family doesn't want you around their injured son."

Stunned, I acquiesced, because what happened to their son was more important than where I could and couldn't be allowed to sit. As we drove to the hospital, I worked with the emotions, identified the hurt, realized I was angry because I thought nobody should be treated the way I was being treated, and stunned because I didn't expect this. Once I received the messages and worked with the emotions, I began again to hunt for what I might be trying to teach myself.

After all, this was twice. Same scenario. I was invited to come into someone else's family, allowed to get involved and to help, then smacked with prohibitions. I was told even though I was part of the family, I wasn't really part of the family, and was excluded. I wrestled with finding this lesson for several days, asking to be shown whatever I needed to see or learn in order to complete the lesson.

Then, one day, the whole scenario opened up for me. Remember, in my early childhood (up to about three years old) my sister and I roamed the neighborhood near our home, hungry, and partially clothed. Many kindly neighbors took us in, dressed us in warm clothes, and fed us. I'm sure I felt safe and happy when that happened. Then, just as it must have seemed I belonged there, my sister and I got this reminder: "You're not really part of this family. You live somewhere else. It's time for you to go back to your family. You can't stay here!"

These two situations, happening nearly five years apart in my adult life, were almost identical in emotional content to those early experiences with the neighbors.

Here's how: I was invited to come into Bob's family, and the family of my ex-husband. I could take part. I could help (or someone who was close to me could help). But there came a time when I was reminded: "You're not really a part of this family. This is our family. You must go now, or sit in the hall while our family is together." I was part of someone else's family, yet I was not really, and was not welcome to stay.

The lesson of these two very painful experiences was that I needed to heal my idea of "belonging," to heal the emotional wounding (close the *gestalt)* that occurred in me from when I was younger. I had a long-held belief (a collection of oft-repeated messages that coalesce into a belief and are held in the subconscious mind) that I wanted to change.

The belief was that I was part of people's family, but I didn't really belong. At some point, they had the right to toss me out, to send me away. No matter what role I assumed—even a primary role of getting needed medical help—the emotional message and learning were stronger.

We all lead our lives on the basis of what we believe. I didn't want an experience like this again. I needed to change this belief. I knew the needed change was for me.

An easy way to change a belief is to replace it with a repeated message. Remember, the subconscious mind cannot resist repetition. Having a message repeated and repeated leaves the subconscious mind no choice but to believe the message is real. I believed I was not a legitimate part of those families and that I would be asked to leave. It began as truth in my young life and became the truth of my adult life.

In both these medical experiences, I had recapitulated that early-life "I belong; I don't really belong" experience, because that's what I still believed. I created a new belief, which I repeated, sang, chanted, and sing-songed to myself for more than three weeks:

"I'm a member of everyone's human family. I am welcome to stay as long as I wish, until or unless I decide to leave."

Three and a half weeks later, just after I completed hours of nearly-constant repetition of my new belief, my ex-husband's wife called to tell me she was unaware I was told I couldn't see their son. She told me I was welcome to come see him any time I wanted.

In the 16 years since this event, I haven't had a similar experience. Instead, I find myself welcomed into the homes and families of people who are happy for me to stay until I say, "I need to leave."

This is the power of emotional healing.

YOUR PERSONAL LABORATORY

Do you have a situation that is either long-standing (and painful) or repeats (and is painful)? Have you ever had a similar experience? Find a situation that comes closest to this issue and work with it now.

First, write out what happened, as thoroughly, yet briefly, as you can. If emotions arise in you, allow them, feel them, and take your time to know what they are and where they fit for you.

Second, identify the emotions that came up in this experience.

Third, ask yourself whether you have had this (or a very similar) emotional experience before. If so, check to determine the connection between the past and the present experiences.

Fourth, determine the belief you must be holding in order to have this experience. Ask yourself: "What would I have to believe in order to create this experience?"

Fifth, create the belief you'd like to have in your subconscious mind instead. (Suggestions: Brief, present tense, positive, for yourself, without rancor or judgment.)

Sixth, repeat your new belief, ad nauseum for at least three weeks. Every opportunity you have, say it, chant it, sing it, write it, shout it. Repeat it in many ways.

Make note of what changes as you go forward, once you stop repeating your new belief. How is your life different? Record all of this.

Be grateful to yourself, to whoever brought the issue to your attention, to those who helped you in making the change, and to your own self for your courageous work.

34

THE IMPORTANCE OF SAVORING AND APPRECIATING OUR SELF

More than 30 years ago, I was invited to give a talk for the group in California promoting self-esteem. When I arrived at the conference, I realized this movement believed in removing all requirements that children face difficulties and inequities in life. Instead, every child received a certificate or award just for participating. There was a huge emphasis on giving compliments to children, and focusing on making them feel good, regardless of the depth of participation in something, or the strength of their efforts. The intention to help children feel good about themselves was positive and genuine.

It was disappointing to me, though, because of the principle: What we have inside of us, we tend to attract from outside of us. This group was promoting self-esteem by emphasizing that people outside of the child hand the child something to put inside. I knew this wouldn't work. What we have inside of us we need to participate in placing there. For anything to come into us, we must have a home for it. Our self needs to recognize and value it; and that happens only when we are participants in what we put inside of us.

About that time, I realized when someone gave me a compliment, I had a difficult time accepting it. I usually didn't agree with what was said about me, so I didn't want to accept what they were saying. It felt to me like I was agreeing to a lie about myself. That's when I developed the notion that people have a difficult time taking things in from others when they don't have a "home" for it inside of themselves. I held no home for compliments.

To offer a compliment when the object of that compliment has a negative self-image or very low self-esteem, goes nowhere. There's no home for what is offered. There is no receiving station, no cubby hole where it can stay, no room for it to be so. Someone could tell me great things about myself, all day long, but if there is no place for those things to land inside of me, the compliments will do nothing for me.

Life is lived from the inside out. What matters is not what you say about me and my efforts. What matters is what I say about me, to myself!

As my parent or coach, I may feel good when you praise me. But the good feeling is temporary. It's quite possible I don't even believe it when it's offered. To have any purchase in my life, it will need to be repeated, many times.

Ah, but when I genuinely appreciate myself, that appreciation and message stands a good chance of going in easily and staying with me forever. I see who I am at that moment. I'm here on this Earth to grow and evolve. There is a deep, inner place in me that knows whether I really am growing and evolving. Nobody else can tell me that I'm growing and evolving as powerfully as I can tell myself. When I recognize and appreciate myself, it sticks, because I have opened the door to its home.

Therefore, when doing emotional work, and helping yourself grow and evolve, it's vital to take time to savor what was done or accomplished, and to appreciate yourself for the effort. It's important to realize you're moving forward in the work you came to the planet to do. Taking a few minutes to appreciate and savor grows awarenes that movement is occurring. Furthermore, once you see it and offer this energy, it cannot be taken away. In seeing what you've done and valuing it for yourself, it has a "home" inside of you. Getting this type of support is extremely important to each of us.

In fact, the very best way to build self-esteem is to help people live their lives based on the seven characteristics people with high self-esteem exhibit. For example, each time a child takes responsibility, refrains from deliberately hurting others, and is honest about his or her own motives and actions, self-esteem rises.

After a period of practicing these behaviors, self-esteem rises and remains high, with very little additional effort needed. The important thing is that the child realizes the benefits of thoughts, choices, and behaviors, then recognizes them for themselves.

When we have an experience that comes with a strong emotion, and moves us toward greater Emotional Mastery, we grow exponentially by giving ourselves appreciation for figuring out the message, partnering with the emotion to follow the message, determining and learning the overall lesson, and then releasing the emotion so we can go on to other things. This is a big job. It's a very important part of life that we're in the process of mastering. We deserve credit, appreciation, and a big pat on the back.

The most impactful person from whom to receive this is our own self.

MY PERSONAL LABORATORY

When my daughter was about three years old, she was interested in learning to print letters. I showed her repeatedly how to make a capital A. She wrote one under the A I put on the paper. Then, she stopped. "Your A's are better than mine!" she wailed. "I can't do good A's!"

My brain started working overtime as I asked myself the best reply to give her so that she was encouraged to keep trying, but didn't develop a negative picture of herself.

"Of course, my A's are better than yours," I responded. "Do you know why?"

She was curious. "It's because I've practiced, and practiced, and practiced making A's my whole life! We all need to practice to make good A's. When you've practiced a lot, your A's will be as good as mine, maybe even better!"

Telling the truth—to ourselves and each other—is a good way to live. My little daughter now had the truth with which she could work, a goal to go after, and a way to get there. These things didn't come from me soft-pedaling and trying to make her feel better. They came from the truth. A three-year-old's A's aren't good A's. It takes practice to develop good penmanship. My respect for her led me to tell her the truth. She then had choice about how she would use that information in her life.

We all have things to learn, from the beginning and for our entire lives. Emotions help us with this learning. When we tell ourselves the truth, encourage ourselves, and go through whatever we need to go through in order to get beyond it, we advance.

Each of us is on the Earth to learn. It's important that we engage this learning, and do it for ourselves.

YOUR PERSONAL LABORATORY

Make a decision to start noticing and savoring what you do, especially what you do that you like. Start keeping a list. Be sure to list what you've done, and what you like about it.

Check with yourself whether an adult in your life gave you feedback about what they thought you did that was good. Did you agree with them at the time they gave their feedback? Do you agree with them now? If not, what do you believe about your actions? Write this down.

Think of a time when you did something you were happy about, that no adult observed or said anything about. Did you take time to think to yourself that you were happy with what you did or said? How do you feel about that thing now?

Which has had more impact for you, looking back: Things adults in your life complimented you on or appreciated you for, or the things you complimented yourself on or appreciated yourself for?

Take a week to appreciate yourself at least once a day for things you're pleased were part of your life for that day. Write them down. Come back a month later and read them over. See how you feel. Write that down, too.

35

SUMMARY AND CONCLUSION: OPEN YOUR HEART WIDE!

This book is an invitation to completely update our emotional landscape and relationship with emotions. This means, everyone is invited to Open Your Heart Wide.

Until we accomplish this update, we live in the past, even though believing we're living in the present. Because we construct our ideas, assumptions, and beliefs based on our experiences, we're constantly leaning on the past to navigate our present. And, as I have stated: The only time we have power is in the present. If we continue living in the past by not updating our emotional landscape, we have no hope of a fully-empowered life.

We're forgiven for not updating ourselves previously, because we were not given a full enough picture, and not enough tools, to accomplish this updating. However, we're living in a powerful time of growth, advancement, and transformation that is giving us the information and tools needed to get more in step with All That Is, with how things are designed to work. This book is one piece of the puzzle toward completing this update. Here's a review of the key points covered.

OPEN UP TO YOUR PERSONALIZED MENTOR-COACH

Every person is born with a built-in Personalized Mentor/Coach designed to help us navigate life. This mentoring system is called "emotions." They are included as part of our experiences; every experience we have is paired with emotion, bits of energy, designed to help us move successfully through the experience, resulting in healing and growth. While emotions participate in our lives intimately, emotions are neither ours, nor are we theirs. When we fail to learn the lesson of experience that is inevitably present, we become mired and stuck like an old-fashioned phonograph record stuck in a single groove, which goes over and over and over the same note without ceasing. When we do learn the lessons offered by experience, we complete, advance, close, release, and move on. Learning the lessons of our experience sets us free.

Just as in physics, the energy of emotion obeys laws. In life, we refer to these as ancient, universal principles. Learning and working in harmony with these principles makes life flow easier, despite the challenges we encounter. By knowing and working with the principles, we move with what is happening, just like a master surfer moving across giant waves in the ocean.

Combining knowledge of how to Master Emotions with Universal Principles accelerates growth by helping us make sense of life and learn the lessons we present to ourselves.

OPEN YOUR MIND TO THE EARTH AS GIANT SCHOOL

It makes sense that we are all in school. The Earth is an ideal school, offering a pleasant environment, immediate feedback, and circumstances (such as long-term relationships) that push us to stay conscious of our environment and the people in it. We have explored how this school works, why it was created, how experiments are set up and conducted, and how the constant presence of emotion serves to push us to complete our learning. I've also given lots of ideas for setting up and conducting experiments, using messages from the emotions that arise in us.

OPEN TO YOUR CURIOSITY ABOUT EMOTIONS

There is a lot we know about emotions and a lot we don't know. We defined what emotions are and why we have them, and explored the still-not-completely-settled question of where emotions come from. This led to the realization we don't have to know everything about emotions to know they're important to us, and to develop powerful and best ways of working with emotions, engaging them to fulfill their purpose.

In addition, we discovered emotions don't come in negative and positive versions, even though we can experience them in these terms. Emotions become negative when held onto as we resist their presence and message, which leads them to compress. Like yeasted dough in the bowl, the longer emotion rests inside of us, the larger the emotion grows. That's when emotion becomes truly negative. Negative emotions are held-onto emotions, which lock us into the past and suck away our personal power.

A new concept is that some emotions are synthetic, not real. Real emotions have both positive and negative aspects; synthetic emotions have only negative aspects. This is a difficult concept, because with an emotion such as guilt, humans have rationalized to ourselves that feeling guilty helps us behave ethically, when in fact, all guilt does is shut us down and keep us frozen in the past. When we allow ourselves to accept guilt, we live in the past, struggle to connect with others, and rob ourselves of power.

Our emotional landscape is set up between birth and age seven, with most of us acting as if that landscape is fixed once we reach adulthood. Emotional landscapes really are plastic, and can get re-molded and changed throughout life. If this is not done, we repeat our first seven years—emotionally speaking—for all the years we live. When we examine, update, and change this emotional landscape, we can recapture our power, bring ourselves forward into the present, and travel with emotions through the landscape of life, as if we were skating on a smoothly frozen surface.

OPEN THE DOOR TO YOUR PERSONAL LABORATORY

I shared my personal journey, which tells you what drew me into the study of emotions, and where that study has taken me. In the 1970s, I spoke about my work with emotions to a group of young doctors who were in the process of becoming psychiatrists. I said that I'm not different from my psychotherapy clients because we're all here learning, and going through similar loopholes and challenges. I continue to hold this belief. The young psychiatrists, however, were horrified. They assured me that even though they had done a lot of personal emotional work, they didn't consider the work they had done had anything to do with the work they were able to do with clients. I left them with the thought that we're all walking down the same street. Some people are a few blocks ahead, some a few blocks behind. Yet, it's the same street. No judgment for where we find ourselves. All of us put our pants on one leg at a time.

I've offered "My Personal Laboratory." Since our Earth is a Giant School, and we're all helping Love to become aware of itself, then each of us is given opportunities to learn. What one learns is helpful to all of us. Each life is a "personal laboratory," where we conduct "experiments" to find out what works best. These experiments are guided by emotions, if we allow that. Something bigger and deeper brings the lessons and accompanying emotions to us, through what we feel and experience. We, in turn, develop good (or not-so-good) feelings inside ourselves based on how—and whether—we accomplish the learning.

You're invited to share the lessons from your Personal Laboratory. I have given you specific directions on how to look and what to look for. It's my hope you'll dedicate yourself to this process, starting now, having learned through your experience in following these directions as you were reading this book.

Embracing the lessons leads us to greater understanding, helps us to work closely and profitably with the emotions that arise, and enables deeper and more powerful learning and evolution in life. I invite you to continue working in Your Personal Laboratory.

OPEN YOURSELF TO THE JOURNEY YOU SHARE WITH ALL OTHERS

When you think about it, humans come to the Earth and don't appear to remember where we came from (or if we did come from some other place). We're dropped into the stream of events occurring on Earth and allowed to stay for a time. When we come to the Earth, we take part in a process that is a journey. It's important to focus on the journey, rather than the different parts of our lives. Like a Zen sand garden, our job is to create as much beauty and perfection in this life as we can while we're here. The joy of the experience can be intense, but is fleeting.

Looking at life as the experience of participating in a Giant School can bestow more sense to this entire process and give our journey meaning. We're given an opportunity to come to a beautiful, vital place in order to study and grow. It becomes clearer how vital it is for us to embrace the experience, learn joyfully, share with others, and have the fullest experience possible. When we add the notion that all of us are One—that we're connected—we begin to see our journey is a benefit not only to ourselves, but to all others. We bear a responsibility (to ourselves and to those others) to make our personal journey as powerful and meaningful as we can. This is our legacy.

Emotions help with this task. Giving constant feedback to us, offering us guidance, and pointing us where and when we need to shore things up or change directions, emotions are on the job helping us with the journey. When we partner with emotions and take their advice, our journey makes more sense, has more meaning and effect, and offers more to us and to everyone. Open yourself to this journey. Have a great trip.

Open Your Mind to the Messages and Influence of 12 Emotions

There are 12 emotions and emotional states. Knowing what the emotions are attempting to communicate is key to becoming masterful with emotions. For easy reference, here is a review of the 12 emotions and their signals.

Anger: Our idea of how things work in this world is incorrect. Update it. Take action.

Anxiety: Unknown ahead. Watch out. Be Careful. Take heed. Felt repeatedly. Decide where to place your attention; and close the door on the negative emotions arising.

Fear: Watch out. Exercise caution. Something unknown is ahead. Stay aware and ready to take action. Know that we're safe in this Universe. Move ahead.

Guilt: Feeling angry, but believe we don't have a right to the anger we're feeling. Accept and identify the anger and release it.

Hurt: Signals us to look at how trust was broken and decide what we need to restore it.

Intimacy: Opportunity to open and be vulnerable with others. Allow our self to connect deeply and fully with others. Embrace vulnerability; allow yourself to open up.

Jealousy: The mental computation that someone has something we can't have. Get creative by giving to ourselves what is right for us.

Loneliness: More energy is going out of us than is coming in. Take in energy now. It's time to pay attention to loving our self.

Love: Come closer. Allow our self to "feel the love" and connect with others.

Remorse: We did something and we're not feeling good about it. Check it out. Look at what you've done. Requires us to forgive ourselves and make a change.

Shame: A belief there is something wrong with us. Recognize that shame is not a real emotion; there is nothing wrong with us.

Stress: This is way too much for me. I need a break. I need to get off this merry-go-round. Heed this message and get off the merry-go-round.

OPEN YOUR SELF TO PARTNERING WITH EMOTIONS

We don't own the emotions we feel, nor do emotions own us. Emotions are given to us as tools, our most constant companions through our entire lifetime. Because we haven't been taught to partner with emotions, I've included discussions and examples of how "The Partnering Process" is done. Use this process with any emotion that arises, deriving maximum advantage from the emotions and making our journey through life as smooth as driving on a 10-lane freeway! Listen and learn with emotions. By noticing and expressing gratitude for the presence of those emotions, we stimulate emotions to serve us better.

OPEN TO EMBRACING EMOTIONAL MASTERY

Become an "Emotions Whisperer," making the influence of working with emotions similar to a Horse Whisperer's influence with horses. This is entirely possible for all of us. When one of us develops to the "Whisperer" Mastery level, it raises the capabilities of us all. We'll find ourselves easily giving up the repetitive and only-moderately-effective tools of "Emotional Management," which require us to do too much work for far too long. Learn the lessons that accompany each experience and its paired emotion. When we learn the lesson, we're free to move on to other things. This is certainly a powerful incentive for reaching for Mastery. Life is more fun when we don't keep moving over the same emotional issues, with little to anticipate except a painful repeat at a not-too-distant date.

Using the principle, the steps to getting there are the qualities of being there, can speed us to Emotional Mastery by cultivating these characteristics and engaging in these behaviors in our daily life. Give yourself a leg up on Emotional Mastery by learning to behave in the ways Emotional Masters behave.

We all seek to live our purpose. Listening to and partnering with the emotions that arise in us is one of the fastest ways to identify and begin living our purpose. We're equipped with the ability to identify what we want and what we don't want. Getting to know our "wants" and "don't wants" is how we get ourselves into lives we enjoy, and into understanding and living our purpose.

OPEN YOUR AWARENESS TO HOW OTHERS DRAIN YOUR ENERGY

Discovering a deeper understanding of Manipulation (also known as Co-Dependence or Energy-Sapping) is one of the most life-changing experiences of my entire existence. Like most people, I grew up believing everyone manipulates, and it's something we must all endure.

I also hated it. I noted in the women of the 50's (my parents' generation), women weren't empowered and could only accomplish goals by manipulating others. I recoiled when I observed that manipulation. In my teens, I swore I would never manipulate.

Imagine my horror when I discovered the First Law of Manipulation: It takes one to know one. I, too, had grown up to manipulate. The manipulation I did was much less obvious, buried deep, and not consciously recognized by me. Realizing this was enough to spur me to dig down and find out just what manipulation is all about. I sought answers to questions like:

- Where does manipulation come from?

- Why do we do it?

- What are the ways people manipulate?

- Is manipulation normal?

- Is it possible to stop manipulating; and if so, how?

- Do men and women manipulate the same ways?

- How can you recognize manipulations while it is being attempted?

- Can you stop others from manipulating you? If so, how?

- How else can you get your needs met if you don't manipulate?

- What is a person like if they don't manipulate?

A major point of developing ourselves as Emotional Masters is to live as the amazing, empowered souls that we are. As we've seen, manipulation is itself "a thing of childhood," designed to be put away as we become adults. In the chapter on manipulation we looked at how manipulation and emotions go together.

Manipulation stirs emotions and leads us to sacrifice our power and integrity to those stirred-up emotions, rather than living the powerful and purposeful lives to which we're entitled. We all need to join the crusade to become manipulation-free. A huge portion of painful emotions will disappear when we become manipulation-free.

OPEN YOURSELF TO THE LESSONS THAT CAN SET YOU FREE

Now you know that recognizing and learning the lessons brought to you through experiences and the emotions that come along with them is a primary way for moving forward through life, smoothly and engaged with power. You also know that if you ignore or refuse the learning, you have the same experience over and over, perhaps changing the circumstances and cast of characters, but experiencing steadily increasing pain that feels like you're living in an endless *Groundhog Day.*

One of the sayings I've coined is: "You can't see tomorrow through today's eyes." Too few people have learned that life operates like a Giant School, that we're all busy learning from the experiences and emotions we go through. So, it's difficult to imagine how incredibly great you'll feel embracing the fact that you're in school. Get curious about what lessons and learning the experiences and emotions you feel are bringing you, and set about learning them. You will not believe how much calmer you'll feel, the drop in your stress level, the ease with which you traverse though calamity and challenges, and the improvement in sleep, health, and relationships that occur when you face fact and take responsibility for yourself as a learner.

I hope to encourage you to adopt this way of seeing what happens in life, and to work with the emotions and experiences that make up your life. It makes it an amazing journey. It also allows you to have a sense of humor, even in the darkest moments.

OPEN TO TOOLS THAT HONOR THE WAY YOU AND MOTHER NATURE WORK

Emotions have to do with all of life. It is vital, therefore, to know more about how life actually works. We talked about the importance of operating in terms of Principle (doing for all people what you're willing to do for one) instead of Personality (doing for one person something you wouldn't do for all who ask, because you perceive them as "special" in some way). Since Mother Nature operates by Principle, adopting this approach means living harmoniously with the way that all of life operates. This helps us experience life, daily, as a well-oiled, reliable machine.

Another way to keep from stepping into deep doo-doo (especially emotionally) is to teach yourself to operate according to the 72-Hour Rule. This honors the way humans function best, giving ourselves some sorting and settling time any time we make decisions, take risks or learn new information. We've learned to push ourselves to live by making immediate decisions and commitments. No doubt you've experienced the pain and confusion created when we rush ourselves, especially when working with emotions. The 72-Hour Rule was included to help you discover how to give yourself some breathing room.

Along with that is the pesky thing called the "Negative Reaction," which is an almost reflexive desire to fix things that aren't necessarily broken. When we're still inside the 72-hour period, not enough sorting and cataloging has occurred for us to see things as clearly as we need to. The most painful part of not recognizing that we're in the "Negative Reaction" is that we can so easily confuse ourselves and the people with whom we are interacting, and leave all of us feeling bad. Most people find themselves engaged in circular behaviors with others that don't feel at all good. Just having patience with our process for 72 hours can change things profoundly.

Working with the 72-Hour Rule and recognizing and honoring The Negative Reaction saves people confusion, pain, time, upset, and develops inner peace.

I've provided tools to set you free from some of the most vexing issues humans have with emotions. Facing Fact frees us from confusion and helps us see what the issue is and what might work best for particular situations. Facing Fact requires us to step into feelings of fear and look squarely at what's going on. Just the act of doing that opens us and makes things better. We're encouraged to incorporate Facing Fact into our life, for the rest of our life.

The Closed Door Exercise is a gem. Emotions are so volatile, especially when we're having problems with other people. It's priceless to have a way to keep ourselves calm and at ease through our most challenging interactions with people, without an overabundance of emotional reaction. The Closed Door Exercise works directly with the energy of emotions. As we bring this tool into our daily living, we'll see the amazing effects of working with the energy of emotion, the power of Emotions in Motion. It doesn't matter what emotions are involved, the Closed Door Exercise will keep them within bounds for us and others.

Remember we also said spoken and written words have power. So, when we write what we're feeling, how we're frustrated, and how we'd like things to work out, we empower ourselves while simultaneously setting an intention for what could happen in our future. This is an advanced way of working with emotions. In this Giant School called Earth, when we set goals, determine intentions, and communicate those in energetic (emotional) terms, we work with the way things are set up for us. It may seem like a miracle when what we envision comes to be, but it's not. It's the way almost everything can work when we work with the energies of emotion, framed by the understanding of living in our Giant School.

OPEN YOURSELF WIDE TO THE UNIVERSE: EMOTIONS AND SPIRIT

We've spent quite a bit of time talking about principles. Just as math is part of all creation, and laws are part of physics, principles hold up the world of human experience and life.

For a long time, people have focused on survival or on materialism. Now, it's necessary for us to focus on spirit. We are spirit having a material experience. There is more to us than the body, emotions and challenges on which we usually focus. It is paramount for us to look beyond these things and realize we're a part of All That Is. Realizing that we have a major part in creating the lives we lead demonstrates that we're co-creators of life, co-creators of our life. A very encouraging part of this recognition is to realize that in any difficulty or challenge, paying attention to making change with only one person—our self—is all we need to do. We're much more powerful in life than we've probably ever imagined.

When we work in cooperation with that which is bigger than ourselves our life on Earth takes on a much wider, deeper meaning. In addition to giving us perspective, it offers us something dependable onto which to hold. We also can more easily see that we're equipped with tools—such as emotions—to assist us with the task of having a life on Earth that we keep setting up for ourselves, in cooperation with that which is much larger.

OPEN YOURSELF TO THE FULLEST EXPERIENCE OF LIFE YOU CAN HAVE

Emotions are the Language of the Universe. You now have what you need to know to be conversant in that language, communicating with your body, with other people, and with your own heart and spirit, without blockage or impediment. In this Giant School, we have each come to explore and discover. Emotions are a primary tool for this exploration and discovery.

You've been shown how it is that we have the most amazing systems of help imaginable: a built-in, birth-to-death, 24/7 Personalized Mentor, which we recognize as Emotions. By learning the message of emotions, using that message to navigate our life, embracing the learning that accompanies emotions, and using the tools we have provided in these pages, you now have reconnected with your constantly-available (and free) Personalized Mentor!

This Mentor is available to assist us in having the most complete, satisfying, balanced, successful, and joyous experience in living our life that we can possibly imagine. It is our birthright. And now we know what we need to know to reclaim it for ourselves, use it to create what we want and what is best for us, and live by, every single day.

Enjoy your time in this Giant School. I'm happy to welcome you into the realm of Emotional Mastery.

Be sure to check out Emotional Mastery for Life on Facebook
For announcements of free releases of writings,
recordings and videos
Enjoy our Blog

ABOUT ILENE DILLON,
MSW, LCSW, MFT

Ilene Dillon has lived according to the information and wisdom found in this book, applying it as a single parent, while blending a distressed family, dealing with loss, death and grief, becoming a "Recovered Angry Person," and in many other challenging life situations that are a lot like what you may have experienced. In the past 50 years, Ilene has also used the same information and wisdom to help thousands of people develop personal and emotional mastery.

Ilene has dedicated her life to helping herself and others to live full, fulfilling, and masterful lives, regardless of what has happened in those lives.

For nearly 50 years she had a private social work practice in Northern California. Ilene was creator and host of *Full Power Living* (internet radio) from 2004 to 2017. She is author of more than 20 books, workbooks, CDs, and video courses related to Emotional Mastery and Parenting Consciously.

As a Professional Speaker, Ilene has spoken in Australia, Ireland, China and in many places in California and throughout the U.S. She's been a professional member of the National Speakers Association for more than 20 years, including two terms on the Board of Directors for the San Francisco, California, chapter.

Ilene is a parent to six now-adult children—two birth, one adopted, three step-children—and grandparent to five amazing grandchildren. Her husband, neurosurgeon Dr. Robert Fink, died in early 2016. Since then, Ilene, along with her 8 pound Maltipoo dog, Pi, has become a full-time RV-er, living and working in her Recreational Vehicle as she travels throughout the U.S. and Canada, writing out her wisdom in the *Emotions in Motion* book series, giving speeches, webinars, and on-line coaching en route.

As Ilene travels, she's delighted to offer workshops, interviews, and speeches with people on her route. She plans this route by following her heart, so you'll have to contact her.

To book Ilene Dillon for your event or area, as well as for online Webinars contact her at: ilene@emotionalmasteryforlife.com

or through her website:

EmotionalMasteryforLife.com

Ilene's upcoming radio and video appearances are listed on EmotionalMasteryforLife.com

Ilene has 4 books currently available on Kindle:

The ABCs of Anger

The ABCs of Love

The ABCs of Loneliness

When Fledglings Return

You may also connect with Ilene Dillon
on social media:

https://www.facebook.com/EmotionalMasteryExpert/

https://twitter.com/EmotionExpert

https://www.linkedin.com/in/ilenedillon/

https://plus.google.com/u/0/+IleneDillon11524

https://www.youtube.com/channel/
UCWM7bnuyWcexDohDiEOTlRQ

ABOUT ARLENE GALE

Arlene Gale, The Book Writing Business Coach, is a multi-international & national award-winning author and multiple No. 1 Best Seller in multiple genres. Arlene has helped hundreds of clients, in a variety of industries, earn millions of dollars in business as a result of writing & publishing well-planned, executed, and marketed books.

Arlene helps her clients duplicate these results from start to finish, because the goal is not just to write and publish any old book, but to write and publish a powerful and profitable business-building book no matter if it's a professional or personal story.

Arlene's services range from writing coach, co-author, or ghost writer and includes writing book proposals earning main stream publishing contracts with cash advances. She is well versed in advising clients in a wide range of publishing options.

Arlene has a proven track record as a professional speaker to both international and national audiences at business and writing conferences in a variety of marketing, writers, and other business topics.

Arlene also speaks at personal development conferences about, "What is your story?" The subject matter ranges from: "How does your story hold you back or motivate your actions?" "Whose labels do you wear?" "Dreams are illusions, create a plan to live." and "The power of choices." These topics also offer value for entrepreneurs to solopreneurs, from middle managers to CEOs, and every day people wanting more from life.

Arlene's clients range from those who are in business a long time and have a lot of content but have never written a book, those who have written books but weren't happy with the results, and those who are new to their own business and need business marketing and branding. Arlene not only helps clients with book writing success from start to finish, but she helps develop online course content, signature speeches, presentation material, and video marketing content plans.

Arlene offers self-paced online courses, hands-on online group coaching, in-person workshops, and one-on-one coaching.

***

Listen, subscribe, and comment on the *"Mindset Meets Mastery with Arlene Gale"* podcast on her website: ArleneGale.com/podcast as well as all podcast outlets. You're also invited to join the FREE and private Facebook group called "Mindset Meets Mastery" where we discuss myths, mindsets, and misunderstandings to support each other and work together toward success. It's all about being better together!

To learn more about Arlene Gale, to work with her
as a writing coach,

or hire her for a conference,

please go to her website at:

https://BookWritingBusiness.com

Please connect with Arlene on social media:

Facebook – BookWritingBusiness

LinkedIn – Arlene Gale

Twitter and Instagram – Arlene Gale

Subscribe to her YouTube Channel, too –
"Arlene Gale Book Writing Business"

***

Arlene's Main Books:

Face Forward Move Forward:
*The Journey to Discard a Painful Past and Determine a New
Legacy of Peace and Possibilities*

Book Business Blueprint:
*Build Credibility, Stand Out From the Competition, and
Skyrocket Sales By Writing Your Book*

WHAT'S NEXT FROM ILENE DILLON, THE EMOTIONAL PRO

After years of living a "have to" life, Ilene is following her heart and intuition. Following is a statement of what she sees potentially unfolding, but reminds us all that, "We can't see tomorrow with today's eyes." Announcements will be made on both Facebook and Ilene's Website.

Books Currently in Process:

I Didn't Come Here to Have Friends	An autobiographical book
Emotions in Motion: Ending Co-Dependence	A complete book on Manipulation
Born to Learn	An approach for Parenting Consciously

Books Planned for Publication:

Emotions in Motion: Anger Into Enthusiasm	An in-depth book about Anger
Emotions in Motion: Fear-Less Living	An in-depth book about Fear

Emotions in Motion: Guilt and Remorse	In-depth book about Guilt & Remorse
Places I've Lived	Stories from an amazing life

Emotions in Motion: In-depth books on the remaining emotions talked about in this book

Video Lessons: Short videos about emotions, aspects of emotions

Ilene is on the road. She'd be delighted to meet you as you focus on evolving. Write!